The Benefits of Belief

The
Benefits
of Belief

How Faith in God Impacts Your Life

Julián Melgosa

Pacific Press®
Publishing Association

Nampa, Idaho | Oshawa, Ontario, Canada
www.pacificpress.com

Cover design by Steve Lanto
Cover resources from iStockphoto.com
Inside design by Kristin Hansen-Mellish

The author assumes full responsibility for the accuracy of all facts and quotations as cited in this book.

Unless otherwise noted, all Scripture quotations are from The New King James Version, copyright © 1979, 1980, 1982, Thomas Nelson, Inc., Publishers.

Scripture quotations marked KJV are from the King James Version.

Scripture quotations marked NIV are from THE HOLY BIBLE, NEW INTERNATIONAL VERSION®, NIV®. Copyright © 1973, 1978, 1984, 2011 by Biblica, Inc.™ Used by permission. All rights reserved worldwide.

Scripture quotations marked ESV are from The Holy Bible, English Standard Version® (ESV®), copyright © 2001 by Crossway, a publishing ministry of Good News Publishers. Used by permission. All rights reserved.

You can obtain additional copies of this book by calling toll-free 1-800-765-6955 or by visiting http://www.adventistbookcenter.com.

ISBN 13: 978-0-8163-4513-7
ISBN 10: 0-8163-4513-9

13 14 15 16 17 • 5 4 3 2 1

Contents

Foreword   7

Introduction   11

Chapter 1   The Benefits of Prayer   15

Chapter 2   The Benefits of Scripture Reading and Meditation   33

Chapter 3   The Benefits of Forgiveness   52

Chapter 4   The Benefits of Commitment   70

Chapter 5   The Benefits of Service   88

Chapter 6   The Benefits of Churchgoing   105

Chapter 7   The Benefits of Joy and Gratitude   122

Chapter 8   The Benefits of Interpersonal Relationships   141

Chapter 9   The Benefits of Religious Coping   162

Chapter 10   Physical and Mental Health Wholeness   183

Foreword

R eligion has always played a role in the lives of humanity. A historical analysis of every past civilization will reveal a strong religious component intimately related to the lives of men and women. In fact, much of the architectural and artistic treasures of ancient cultures contain many signs of faith. More specifically, religious processes have played a central role in health and healing throughout history.

It is also true that the spectacular advances in science over the last centuries have eroded the credibility that faith and religion had in the past. Promoters of naturalistic worldviews feel uncomfortable with religious phenomena such as faith because these are so difficult to assess scientifically. Yet, there is evidence that when adversity strikes, people turn to God and religion to cope with the distress that these events cause. A survey in the late 1990s asked hospitalized patients, "To what extent do you use religion to cope?" Twenty-three percent said to a moderate or large extent, 27 percent indicated a large extent or more, and 40 percent considered it the most important factor that kept them going.[1]

During the last twenty-five years, we have witnessed a tremendous growth in scholarly research on the role of religious involvement in preventing, controlling, and treating both mental and physical illness. The second edition of the *Handbook of Religion and Health*[2] reviewed more than thirty-seven hundred quantitative studies published in academic journals in the area of religion and/or spirituality and some aspect of health or clinical practice. When we compared the number of such publications between the two editions, we found that the research literature had nearly tripled in the past ten years. This growth is also reflected in practice. Beginning in the year 2015, the Medical College Admission Test will include a new section on psychological, social, and biological foundations of behavior in order to ensure that physicians in training understand psychological processes and are better prepared to face medical school curricula that are being transformed to incorporate psychological, social, and cultural and/or religious aspects of the person. Practicing physicians are also being offered seminars and workshops to better understand the religious experiences of patients so that they can support patients' use of prayer, worship, devotional practices, service to those in need, and other practices that may positively affect their recovery.

The Benefits of Belief fits within this trend. The book outlines recent research in the area of religion and health—both mental and physical. Dr. Melgosa relates religious experience to research in order to answer questions, such as, Is prayer an effective way to help people remain calm and peaceful and to prevent depression? Does the reading of the Bible or sacred writings bring about health and well-being? Can forgiveness be a tool for emotional, physical, and mental healing? Can forgiveness help improve specific conditions such as chronic fatigue, fibromyalgia, or cardiac conditions? Is it possible to enhance the quality of marital relationships and perceived well-being by remaining committed to a community of faith? Will service to others for religious reasons provide health and happiness and prevent depressive symptoms? Is regular church attendance positively related to better physical and mental health, and does it help to prevent mental and physical problems among children and adolescents? How do religion and faith affect one's ability to be happy? Does religion tend to promote a more joyful life? Do religion and spirituality promote good interpersonal relationships? How is religious coping used to deal with illness and misfortune? Do people experience an increase in fortitude and solace when using religion to cope? Does religious coping help believers to face trauma and be transformed into better people during the process?

In addition to answering these and other questions, Dr. Melgosa uses Bible passages and characters to illustrate the research-based benefits of being religious. This is done in ways that are accessible to both lay and professional readers. In order to illustrate his points, the author also relates personal illustrations and experiences from a diversity of countries and cultures across Europe, Asia, and America, where he has lived.

Based on research, this book shows that faith and religion, far from being uncomfortable life obligations participated in out of fear, are positive ways of living life to the fullest. Although the religious life does not guarantee the absence of pain and suffering, it does offer ways to connect with God and remain open to God's providence in order to experience the best possible results in the midst of imperfect circumstances. In sum, *The Benefits of Belief* promotes the concept that living a religious life so that it influences one's principles, beliefs, and behaviors pays many dividends in terms of better emotional and better physical health.

Harold G. Koenig, MD
Professor of Psychiatry and Behavioral Sciences
Associate Professor of Medicine
Director, Center for Spirituality, Theology and Health
Duke University Medical Center, Durham, North Carolina
Distinguished Adjunct Professor
King Abdulaziz University (KAU), Jeddah, Saudi Arabia

1. Harold G. Koenig et al., *2012 Summer Research Workshops on Spirituality and Health* (Durham, NC: Duke Center for Spirituality, Theology and Health, 2012), 61.

2. Harold G. Koenig et al., *Handbook of Religion and Health,* 2nd ed. (New York: Oxford University Press, 2012).

Introduction

"He heals the brokenhearted and binds up their wounds." —Psalm 147:3

*A*round the turn of the twentieth century, a young graduate from Yale, after the death of his brother, suffered his first episode of manic depression (now known as bipolar disorder). The disorder led him to attempt suicide. Seriously injured, he was taken to various hospitals, both private and public, throughout Connecticut for three long years. As with any mental patient of the day, he was submitted to inhumane treatment and witnessed horrific abuse from caretakers and other patients. After three years of institutionalization, he was released and decided to expose the maltreatment at mental-care facilities. His name was Clifford W. Beers, and his book, *A Mind That Found Itself,* opened the eyes of the American people and caused an important health reform movement. In 1909, Beers founded Mental Health America (MHA), the largest nonprofit organization in the United States today that promotes mental health and helps prevent mental illness and addictions. It pushes the "Ten Tools to Live Your Life Well"[1]—simple advice based on extensive scientific evidence emphatically recommended for those who want to enjoy mental and physical health:

1. Connect with others
2. Stay positive
3. Get physically active
4. Help others
5. Get enough sleep
6. Create joy and satisfaction
7. Eat well
8. Take care of your spirit
9. Deal better with hard times
10. Get professional help if you need it

The MHA's Ten Tools are not just compatible with Christian living but are at the core of biblical principles and are markedly central to the lifestyle promoted by Seventh-day Adventists. For many decades, Adventists have been promoting the principles of a healthy diet, exercise, positive interaction with others, optimism, hopeful outlook, spiritual nourishment, and openness to divine intervention in good and bad times.[2] Today, scientific evidence is mounting in favor of these pillars of health.

Psychological and medical research during the past two decades have been showing that many elements of religion, such as prayer, Scripture reading, forgiveness, hope, and service to others are intimately connected to health and happiness. A recent publication about longevity by Howard Friedman, from the University of California, and Leslie Martin, from La Sierra University, tracked the life of about fifteen hundred Americans who were children in 1921.[3] In addition to personality, school performance, health habits, marriage, career, and social life, Friedman and Martin found that religious practice contributed significantly to longevity. Women were particular beneficiaries: long-living women were found to be deeply religious; those who reported having little or no religion had less quality of life and lived fewer years than their counterparts. The role of religion in the length of life was not via a mysterious process; rather, religion produced outcomes that are known factors in longevity: community involvement, family interaction, having children, fellowship, trust, and so on. Howard Friedman wrote, "While we cannot provide empirical confirmation about whether being pious is important to gaining eternal life, *The Longevity Project* did uncover good evidence that at least some aspects of congregational participation can be relevant to the length of one's mortal life. It was the social involvement and service to others that went along with being religious that explained why these people, especially the religious women, lived longer."[4]

This book is about the gains everyone can obtain from following the Lord's ways. Jesus promised His followers that they would receive "a hundredfold now" (Mark 10:30) or "many times more" (Luke 18:29). It is reasonable to think that these blessings are not necessarily material but are related to the exercise of wisdom, resilience, endurance, and to the many virtues promoted by religion that translate into good health, happiness, and well-being.

How does religion help? Religion provides answers to existential questions: What is the origin of the universe? What is the purpose of my existence? What is the afterlife? How should I relate to my fellow humans?

A person of faith who accepts God's revelation will have the best available answers to those fundamental questions and will be able to walk through life with much less anxiety, fear, and uncertainty than will the faithless person. Religion provides not only explanations, but it also offers guidelines that define what is appropriate and inappropriate. Far from curtailing freedom, these guidelines set up reasonable limits that can bring health, safety, calm, and security to the believer.

Religion does not inoculate people against affliction, but it helps them to build faith and to remain strong and content despite adversity. This is due to the understanding that "all things work together for good to those who love God" (Romans 8:28). Accepting God's will helps many to accept the realities of life but with the peace that comes from God. Religion can provide simple but profound maps of meaning and goals that facilitate structured solutions to life's complexity, which is why religious people are more likely to find a sense of direction that their secular counterparts lack. Lastly, God's revelation provides knowledge and information of His plans so that His children may be aware and prepared to face the future without anxiety and with trust in the Father's power (Amos 3:7).

Over the next pages, the reader will have the opportunity to review the many benefits that secular research is finding today in favor of a Christian lifestyle. Far from being the "opium of the people," religion offers a multitude of advantages to those who choose to trust God and follow His direction.

> Trust in the LORD with all your heart
>   and lean not on your own understanding;
> in all your ways submit to him,
>   and he will make your paths straight.
> Do not be wise in your own eyes;
>   fear the LORD and shun evil.
> This will bring health to your body
>   and nourishment to your bones (Proverbs 3:5–8, NIV).

May this book help you to enhance your understanding of the beneficial effects of religious faith upon your life so that you may find satisfaction now and, most importantly, may those practices lead you to closeness to God and to eternal life.

---

1. "Live Your Life Well: You Can Live Your Life Well," Mental Health America, accessed May 21, 2013, http://www.liveyourlifewell.org.

2. Although isolated believers were practicing some of the health principles later adopted, the Adventist health message began on June 6, 1863, when Ellen White was given the health vision in Otsego, Michigan.

3. Howard S. Friedman and Leslie R. Martin, *The Longevity Project* (New York: Hudson Street Press, 2011).

4. Howard S. Friedman, "How Prayer Leads to Better Health and Longer Life," *Huffington Post*, accessed May 13, 2013, http://www.huffingtonpost.com/howard-s-friedman-phd/where-exactly-is-the-heal_b_838603.html.

Chapter 1

The Benefits of Prayer

"Hear my prayer, LORD, listen to my cry for help." —Psalm 39:12

T he night before our hike, my wife and I reviewed the list: Weather forecast? Check. Study the route? Check. Gear? Check. Food and water? Check. We agreed to get up at 5:00 A.M. and leave at 6:00 A.M., in order to take full advantage of the day's light. As we were tired enough, we went to bed early to enjoy a good night's sleep.

The next morning, I got up, took my shower, and woke Annette up with a gentle touch, announcing that it was five-fifteen. She said that she was getting up. I proceeded downstairs to fix breakfast and get things ready.

The clock kept ticking, and I did not hear any movement upstairs. I did as much as I could in preparation for the hike and sat down to read. The clock kept ticking; I could not concentrate on my reading. I began to think that if she did not move, our day would be spoiled; we would not have time to reach the top and return with daylight to spare. My typical early morning sense of well-being was turning into edginess. I envisioned a frustrating day without time enough to reach the lake or, even worse, not making it out by dark. Suddenly, I noticed signs of movement, which gave me a sense of relief. But soon I realized that things were too slow. These are some of the sentences I was rehearsing: *Why so long to get ready? We are not going to a formal dinner, are we? We are almost one hour late! Didn't we agree last night to leave by six?*

I said, "Stop!" and began to pray, "Lord, help me find calm. Help me to be patient and to be sweet when she comes down. Help me not to pronounce a word of reproach." Afterward, I remained quiet with eyes closed for a few moments to fully gain the blessing of my prayer.

This little prayer was crucial; for when Annette appeared, my own plea of *Not a word of reproach, not a word of reproach* resounded in my mind, and God blessed me with a smile and a topic of conversation other than lateness. We had a pleasant breakfast and a most enjoyable day at Aneroid Lake, high in the

Wallowa Mountains. Departing forty-five minutes late did not make any difference at all. And I'd hate to think what an early argument would have meant to our whole day.

Prayer was the turning point for the day. As I noticed the jitters, I knew that I needed help and God provided it. Prayer was instrumental for interpersonal harmony. As we will see in this chapter, prayer is much more than asking for help in a time of need, but I am thankful for God's availability and willingness to provide simple changes that can lead to patience, wisdom, a suitable attitude, and appropriate words.

The overwhelming majority of believers from all faiths consider prayer as a primary means of spiritual growth and a sure bridge to commune with God. In recent years, research has reported that prayer brings about not only spiritual blessings but also helps keep people away from physical and mental illness. Furthermore, prayer has been correlated positively with subjective well-being (the research term for happiness). This evidence is confirmation that God has designed prayer for the total health of His children.

Prayer benefits

My college days at the University of Madrid, Spain, were marked by social turmoil and deep changes in society. After forty years of living under a dictatorship, most people wanted freedom from the tradition of one single political ideology and one single religious denomination—Roman Catholicism. In the political arena, old parties that had been previously repressed were declared legal, and many more new ones emerged. However, it was not the same for religion. Many people wanted not a plurality of faiths but the rejection of religion altogether. This was probably due to people equating religion with Roman Catholicism; also because the church and state had been intimately blended for decades, many stopped going to church.

Soon prayer and churchgoing were deemed outdated, and many broke from religious practices. But did this mean that people stopped praying? Most likely not. At least that was my impression when I engaged in meaningful conversation with peers. Many continued to pray in the way they did before, but they were less vocal about it. Years later, I found the same thing among students at Newbold College in England, at a time when religion was not "cool" in Europe. I conducted qualitative research about the religious experience of college students. Although the majority of my interviewees were Seventh-day Adventists, there were a number of nonbelievers as well as other Christians. Yet, I did not find a single individual who did not pray with some regularity. It seems that prayer is a necessity and brings enough benefits that most people will not discard it easily. Depending on what survey one looks at over the past four to five years, 50 to 90 percent of Americans report that they pray daily.

And there are sectors of the population that pray more than others: people with limited resources, with little self-control, persons under stress, and those who may have a disadvantage because of gender (women, most typically), age (the elderly), members of minorities (especially oppressed groups), and individuals with low levels of education. This may help us understand Jesus' Beatitudes: those who are poor and humble, who mourn, who are victims of injustice, and who are persecuted for doing right are especially blessed (Matthew 5:3–12). It is the blessing brought by adversity; it is the prayer that takes place when dependence on God is needed. In fact, Jesus is pleased to answer the prayers of those whom He came to help, specifically the poor, the captive, the blind, and the oppressed (Luke 4:18).

Why do people pray? People often pray because they are in some sort of trouble. In my culture, we have a saying: "He prays to Saint Barbara when he hears thunder" (Saint Barbara being the saint of danger from thunderstorms and fire). Others pray because they think they should, praying out of obligation, perhaps pressed by religious prescription. People also pray because they are thankful to God and wish to show gratitude and appreciation. Yet others pray because prayer brings them a sense of closeness to God; they feel His presence and they experience the comfort of being near the Almighty. People also pray for others, asking God to intervene in the life of a friend, a relative, or a person who is struggling with some special need. This can be done because of having been asked or because one is moved by love and compassion.

I pray because prayer has become a habit in my life. I know that habits run the risk of becoming meaningless routines, and that is something I have to watch out for. I pray because I need a connection with God in order for me to keep going, to have the sense that I am not alone and that He surrounds me with His warmth and love. I pray every day when I leave my house to exercise. I thank God for the past night and for the stars (I usually see the stars because, where I live, it is more often clear than not). I thank God for my wife and my children and other people who are part of my life: friends, relatives, colleagues, and students. I thank Him for my job and the opportunities to grow and share experiences with others and learn from them. I praise God for all those provisions and especially for the gift of Jesus Christ and salvation through Him. Petitions come easily in my prayers, so I think of my close family members, one by one, as I know of their challenges. Then I pray for others whom I know are struggling in some way. I pray for myself and for the tasks I have ahead. Invariably, I ask for wisdom in the way I make decisions, treat people, manage my life, my thoughts and actions as well as for health and strength and for understanding on how to preserve them. I also ask for forgiveness for specific sinful thoughts, words, and behaviors as well as for getting bogged down with worthless worries. Lastly, I share my desire to commit my life to Him and for help to do so.

I cherish my prayer life and know that prayer brings me great benefits. I don't need to read empirical studies that show prayer as a good thing. But many people, especially educated ones, may begin to show interest in prayer and religion only because of these studies. Besides, it is helpful to know that the academic community now recognizes prayer and other religious and spiritual factors.

In the last couple of decades, studies have shown differences between those who report they pray and those who say they do not. Results show that people who pray tend to be physically and mentally healthier than those who do not. It is true that we cannot use prayer in the same way we use a pill or an ointment—prayer is the result of a relationship! But it is good to be aware of some of the possible dividends of prayer.

Brain activity

One of the earliest attempts to record brain activity during prayer was conducted by Walter Surwillo and Douglas Hobson at the University of Louisville School of Medicine.[1] It was the modest beginning of neurological studies on Christian prayer before the times of functional magnetic resonance imaging (fMRI). Researchers recruited six adult participants, members of the Church of God in Anderson, Indiana. Their electrocortical activity was recorded via electroencephalograms (EEGs) during prayer. The purpose was to discover whether rhythms during prayer were slower than they normally are in a state of rest. They expected to find these cycles slowing down during prayer time, just as other research had found with transcendental meditation. However, findings did not show evidence of EEG slowing down during the prayers of these three men and three women. In fact, they observed a general speeding up of the EEG.

These findings showed a difference between Christian prayer and transcendental meditation. While Christian prayer is focused on a personal conversation with God, transcendental meditation is centered on a quiet repetition of a mantra—a syllable, word, or group of words. Faster EEGs are the product of a more intense cognitive activity, due to the high concentration displayed by those praying. This was confirmed via one-on-one conversations with participants reporting an intense mental activity as they prayed with fervor.

This is, in fact, not foreign to those who practice Christian prayer as "the opening of the heart to God as to a friend."[2] When I come to God's presence and share a burden with Him, I try to articulate what I think of the issue and ask God to intervene. I talk about my concerns and how I see the problem. Of course, God knows it much better, but that does not stop my conversation because I know that praying will strengthen my faith and help me accept the outcome as directly blessed by the Lord. If I thank God for His blessings, I have to search in my mind for the multiple details that make the blessing special and wonder at the circumstances surrounding the blessing. In doing all this, I need concentration and mental effort. Fervent prayers are not necessarily relaxing. They may, in fact, be rather intense to make the communication more meaningful to me; hence, the faster EEGs observed in the study above. But the real relief comes after prayer: a sense of unloading, of having laid my heavy burden on Jesus as He invites me to do so (Matthew 11:28). This counts among the greatest benefits of prayer.

A more recent study conducted by Dr. Mario Beauregard, a neuroscientist from the University of Montreal, assessed the brain activity of fifteen Carmelite nuns during their mystical experience, of which prayer was a central component.[3] It was not easy for him to convince these women to participate. They live a life of silence and prayer. With the exception of twenty minutes after lunch and another twenty minutes after supper, when they engage in conversation with each other, Carmelite nuns spend their lives working and praying. Their day consists of working in their gardens, sewing, washing, maintaining the convent, and manufacturing crafts and sweets for income. The rest of the time is devoted to prayer and contemplation. Dr. Beauregard estimated that at the time of the study the fifteen participants had spent a combined 210,000 hours of prayer in their lives.[4] Having led this lifestyle for most of their lives, these cloistered nuns in modern-day Montreal were suspicious and thought that the researchers intended to disprove the validity of their devotion. Dr. Beauregard explained that the team was not materialist, and they had the honest purpose of using neuroimaging techniques to identify the electrochemistry of the brain during prayer and meditation. In fact, praying nuns would be among the few individuals in the world able to help. Negotiation with the prioress and a letter from the archbishop made the research possible.

The participants' ages were between twenty-three and sixty-four, with an average of fifty. They had been with the order for an average of nineteen years, and none had a history of psychiatric or neurological disorder. None smoked or was taking psychotropic medications at the time of scanning. Beauregard used fMRI to observe the activity of various brain areas. Mystical experience was a state of closeness to God evidenced by high ratings of statements such as "I have experienced profound joy," "I have had an experience which I knew to be sacred," or "I have had an experience that cannot be expressed with words." During interviews, nuns stated that during the mystical segment they felt "the presence of God, His unconditional and infinite love, as well as plenitude and peace."[5]

These are some of the findings: the caudate nucleus, an area of the brain previous studies have associated with happiness, maternal love, joy, and unconditional love, was found to be very active during the mystical experience. The left brain stem, also associated with the regulation of joy and unconditional love, was especially active during prayer. The insula, which controls the central nervous system and is connected with visceral responses to positive feelings, was also firing during the scanning. Lastly, high levels of activity were observed in the prefrontal cortical region, the area controlling subjective pleasantness, particularly the pleasantness of taste, smell, or music.

Two years later, Beauregard conducted another experiment but with fourteen of the fifteen nuns from the first study.[6] This time he used electroencephalography (EEG) to obtain data during mystical experiences. Several cortical areas were recorded with high activity during the experience as compared with the resting state and with the control condition. These are some of them:

1. The anterior frontal activity, an area related to peace, joy, and unconditional love.
2. The parietal cortex, normally associated with religiously charged visual mental imagery.
3. The right middle temporal gyrus, the area previous studies found quite active during meditation.

In addition, neural coherence (an index of functional connectivity between two or more cortical regions) was found in the following areas:

1. Connectivity between the frontal and the posterior cortices, the connection that has been traditionally associated with positive emotional experiences.
2. Connectivity between the right frontal and the temporal and parietal regions.
3. Connectivity between the right central and the parietal region.

Both 2 and 3 indicate a reduction in sensory processes; in other words, when participants were in the midst of their prayers, sensory stimuli would not be consciously perceived (i.e., they would not be easily affected by noise, light, touch, etc., during prayer), presumably due to the concentration and intimacy of the prayer experience.

Observations like these emphasize the remarkably unique electrochemical activity of the brain during prayer. This helps me understand why the apostle Paul advises us to "pray without ceasing" (1 Thessalonians 5:17). When laboratory observations show prayer putting to work areas of the central nervous system that control emotions such as happiness, well-being, joy, gratitude, love, and compassion, I conclude that God designed prayer to be not only the primary way of communication with His children but also a way to provide refreshing effects in a world of suffering, injustice, and despair. This also teaches me that God communicates with human beings through these intricate neural structures.

At times, these intricate neural structures can become damaged, but there are many stories that illustrate how God works on the human brain despite damage.

For instance, Julie, a schoolteacher who was hit by a car, is a prime example of how an injured brain can work to restore its ability to communicate with God.[7] In her accident, Julie suffered a number of serious head injuries. She was left deaf, with very little speech and poor mobility. She received occupational therapy for several years at the Loma Linda University Medical Center and developed strong ties with the therapists and other staff. She managed to send her messages out via a Dynavox communication device.

After four years of therapy, and in order to honor a family tradition, Julie wanted to host a simple meal for her family, but this posed a serious challenge due to her limitations. Peggy, her therapy assistant, offered to help. They planned the event together; Julie did all she could, and Peggy completed the tasks. On the big day, Peggy drove Julie to her home and helped her with the food and decorations. Then she left for her own home. When Julie's mother and brother arrived, seeing the delightful preparation, they were quite impressed. Julie's mother asked her to pray for the food. Julie recited the entire Lord's Prayer, the longest verbal message she had uttered since the day of the accident.

What a special blessing to be able to pronounce this prayer after struggling for years to speak only small bits! The brain is a wondrous organ with amazing plasticity, and God, at times, chooses to enhance its capacity using a beautiful outcome—this time to pronounce the Lord's Prayer on a special occasion.

Although a person of faith does not need to know the electrochemical processes associated with his or her prayer, it is amazing to glimpse how God designed communication. Awareness of this mechanism may help many realize that prayer is made up of highly positive emotions, and that communion with God is powerful, positive, and life changing.

Calm and serenity

When a burdened person has the chance to converse with a close friend in an atmosphere of warmth, acceptance, and confidentiality, much of the heavy load will be relieved, even when the issue itself remains unresolved. A sincere and fervent prayer to God can have the same results. Those who pray habitually have learned the old hymn by experience:

> Just a little talk with Jesus made me whole. . . .
> Now when you feel a little prayer wheel turning,
> And you know a little fire is burning,
> You will find a little talk with Jesus makes it right.

Claire Hollywell and Jan Walker from the University of Southampton, United Kingdom, confirmed the idea.[8] They conducted a systematic review of research on prayer as an intervention for hospitalized patients. Data from all the relevant peer-reviewed studies found in eight databases showed that the frequency of private prayer was associated with lower levels of anxiety. (They also found the same connection for depression.) Interestingly, when prayers were a result of an emergency, an urgent need not accompanied by a pre-existing faith, prayer increased distress and resulted in less personal function. But when prayer consisted of an ongoing, intimate dialogue with God, optimism, well-being, and the ability to function well were present. In all those studies under review, prayer brought that highly desirable sense of peace and solace.

Amy Ai, from the University of Pittsburgh, together with four other researchers, conducted an exhaustive study in order to assess the role of private prayer in cardiac patients prior to open-heart surgery and its effect on their quality of life.[9] Two hundred ninety-four participants, who were scheduled for nonemergency, nontransplant cardiac surgery, a large majority from Judeo-Christian traditions, were recruited at the Cardiac Clinic of the University of Michigan Medical Center. Patients underwent a face-to-face interview two weeks prior to surgery and then a telephone interview two days before the operation. Lastly, they were interviewed thirty-six days after the operation.

In addition to socio-demographic and clinical data, patients provided information about their use of private prayer to cope with anxiety prior to surgery and its use after surgery for attaining quality of life. They were also administered psychological measures to assess fatigue, mental symptoms, depression, anxiety, coping, social support, post-traumatic symptoms, and prayer coping (using prayer to cope with anxiety).

Results expanded on the findings other researchers had obtained with cardiac surgery patients: Ai's study found that cardiac patients who prayed were able to cope better with the stress and anxiety of the imminent surgery. Furthermore, they were able to attain a better quality of life for weeks after their surgeries. This successful coping was found to be both cognitive and behavioral. In other words, those using systematic and faithful prayer were better able to use their *thoughts and mental processes* to attain a positive and favorable outlook towards surgery and recovery; in addition, they were able *to act* in ways that prevented complications and attained a better quality of life after the intervention.

The studies argue, quite rightfully, that turning to a higher power, such as God, is a suitable mechanism to control crises, and that religion provides a large context in which to fit a personal crisis. Authors also state that private prayer may be superior to the strict support from secular resources because prayer "sheds a bright and unwavering light into a promising future in the presence of adversity."[10]

Prayer, therefore, promotes peace and calm before significant threats, such as hospital surgery. Prayer is an effective antidote for fear and anxiety. It is no wonder that expressions such as "do not fear" and "trust in the Lord" appear so many times in the Scriptures as God invites us to approach Him in prayer, to accept His grace and protection, and to put aside fear and anxiety.

Depression

Barbara Kilbourne, PhD, professor of sociology and social work at Tennessee State University, together with Sherry Cummings, PhD, and Robert Levine, MD, conducted a follow-up study exploring depression and religion among diabetic participants from disadvantaged neighborhoods in a midsize southern city.[11] It is well known that the incidence of depression in diabetics is higher than in the general population; hence, the interest in studying this particular sample. Over a period of two years, the statistical (correlational) analysis showed significant and negative relationships between four indicators of religiosity and levels of depression. In other words, as levels of religiosity went up, depressive symptoms and intensity went down. The four measures of religiosity were prayer, religious reading, religious attendance, and religious belief. Again, the religious component was a protective factor against depression.

Another group with high risk of depression is that of postpartum women. Conservative estimates state that between 15 and 20 percent of women giving birth suffer postpartum depression. The disorder is characterized by anxiety, easy anger, hopelessness, guilt, low appetite, low concentration, decreased interest in the baby, and sleep alterations (either too much or too little sleep). In a study led by Kimberley Zittel-Palamara from Buffalo State College, forty-five women with postpartum depression (current or past), most of them belonging to Christian churches, were questioned about their postnatal depressive symptoms as well as their religious practices and the support they had found from their religion.[12] Sixty-six percent of the women were said to have found strength in religion. Their improvement over depression was found to be greater than in nonreligious women. Prayer was a key component. The remaining elements were spiritual guidance, church-based counseling, congregational support, and spiritual-based support groups.

Jesus assured His disciples that they would weep and mourn (the depressive mood) but their sorrow would be turned into joy. In fact, Jesus illustrated this point referring to a mother's sorrow around birth. Soon after the delivery, "she forgets the anguish because of her joy that a child is born into the world" (John 16:21, NIV). Unfortunately, this is not the case with postpartum depression, but, as those women in Zittel-Palamara's study show, individual prayer, together with the warmth and support provided by a caring church community, can ease the pain of depression.

General health

The Survey of Health, Ageing and Retirement in Europe (SHARE) is one of the most powerful databases; it contains tens of thousands of participants, ages fifty-plus, and covers information on health, socioeconomic status, and social and family networks. Based in Munich, SHARE has collected data from Scandinavia, central Europe, and the Mediterranean since 2004, and it is now a major pillar of the European Research Area. Karsten Hank and Barbara Schaan, from the University of Mannheim, Germany, used SHARE data to study the link between the frequency of prayer and health among some 14,500 men and women from Sweden, Denmark, Germany, the Netherlands, Switzerland, Austria, Italy, Spain, and Greece.[13] The results show that as the frequency of prayer increased, general health also increased. General health was assessed not only by how participants perceived their well-being but also as a count of their chronic conditions. A high frequency of prayer was also linked to a low frequency of depressive symptoms and a low number of functional limitations.

Although correlational results (such as the one above) cannot be used to establish cause-effect relationships (e.g., someone could infer that the correlation may be strong because health causes prayer, rather than the opposite), the study suggests that prayer might be an important resource to help people, especially those in midlife or older, deal more successfully with illness and discomfort.

The Bible offers promises of health related to communion with God and faithfulness. The psalmist writes,

Do not be wise in your own eyes;
    fear the LORD and shun evil.
This will bring health to your body
    and nourishment to your bones (Proverbs 3:7, 8, NIV; emphasis added).

A similar promise of general health, fertility, and long life is given in Exodus 23:25, 26: "Worship the LORD your God, and his blessing will be on your food and water. I will take away sickness from among you, and none will miscarry or be barren in your land. I will give you a full life span" (NIV).

Psychological health

Prayer works not only for physical well-being but also for mental and emotional fitness. Leslie Francis from the University of Warwick, United Kingdom, and colleagues studied more than a thousand Catholic and a thousand Protestant men and women, ages sixteen to eighteen.[14] They were students in sixteen different high schools in Northern Ireland, a highly religious culture. These young people were given measures to identify tendencies to neuroticism and psychoticism, understood as a personality pattern marked by the tendency to aggressiveness and hostility toward people; these are seen as indicators of mental health or proneness to mental disorders. They also inquired about their prayer habits in terms of "daily/sometimes/never" frequency categories. The analysis found a correlation between the frequency of prayer and better psychological health—this was especially evident in the data on psychoticism. The index was negatively strong; in other words, the higher the frequency of prayer, the lower the levels of psychotic tendencies. Psychoticism, taken to an extreme, will make people vulnerable to schizophrenia or other psychotic disorders. Again, consistent prayer was seen in this study as protection against mental disease and as promotion of mental health.

When people are affected by serious mental conditions, they use prayer to cope. This is the main finding of Steven A. Rogers and his colleagues from the Graduate School of Psychology at Fuller Theological Seminary.[15] They studied individuals at a Los Angeles County mental-health facility who had chronic mental illnesses. There were 379 participants (58 percent men, 42 percent women), all firmly diagnosed with psychotic, mood, or anxiety disorders. Results showed that more than 81 percent were using religious beliefs and activities to cope. Those with more severe symptomatology were more inclined to pray than were those with less acute symptoms. Of all religious practices, prayer was by far the main religious coping mechanism. These were the percentages for each coping strategy observed:

Prayer	58.57 percent
Going to religious services	35.62 percent
Worshiping God	34.83 percent
Meditation	32.98 percent
Reading Scripture	31.14 percent
Listening to religious music	21.90 percent
Singing religious songs	19.26 percent
Meeting spiritual leader	15.04 percent

Prayer is the strategy David chose in Psalm 31. He described himself as afflicted, with anguish in his soul; his eyes growing weak with sorrow; and his soul and body full of grief (verses 7, 9, NIV). Anguish, groaning, and affliction consumed his life, and his bones were growing weak (verse 10, NIV). He felt forgotten and fragile, and sensed terror on every side, with many conspiring to take his life (verses 12, 13). As a way out, he calls on the name of the Lord, and he ends up praising His wonders; (verses 14–18, 21, NIV). He concludes by saying,

> Love the Lord, all his faithful people!
>> The Lord preserves those who are true to him,
>> but the proud he pays back in full.
> Be strong and take heart,
>> all you who hope in the Lord (verses 23, 24, NIV).

Prayer and healing

One of the pioneer studies on the healing effects of prayer was conducted by Randolph C. Byrd, a cardiologist at the San Francisco General Medical Center and a professor at the University of California.[16] All patients admitted at the coronary care unit were eligible for entry and those willing to participate signed their informed consent. Three hundred and ninety-three patients (33 percent women and 67 percent men) agreed and were randomly assigned to either the intercessory prayer group (IP) or to the control group (CP). Patients, doctors, and staff at the unit remained "blinded" so that they would not know who had been assigned to which group. Intercessors were individuals who practiced daily devotional prayer and were active worshipers in a local church. Intercessors received their assigned patients' first name, diagnosis, and general condition. Each patient was given to more than one intercessor. They committed to pray for the patients during the patients' hospital stay and to pray for a rapid recovery, no complications, and no death. Once the differences between the two groups were observed, many clinical events came up with no significant differences.

But there were some events where the IP group was at an advantage as compared to the CP group. These were the events: congestive heart failure, diuretics, cardiopulmonary arrest, pneumonia, use of antibiotics, and use of intubation or ventilation. IP participants experienced less of the above than did the CP patients. Furthermore, there was not a single item where the CP group was better than the IP group.

Although there were twenty-three items with no significant difference between the two groups, those with sizable advantages were all in the prayed-for group. This kind of evidence should not be the foundation of belief in prayer. Paul warns us of how deep and rich and wise is the knowledge of God and how unfathomable, inscrutable, and unsearchable are the Lord's judgments (Romans 11:33). Yet, for certain nonreligious people, this may become the gateway to prayer and religious experience.

The promise is certain: "And the prayer of faith will save the sick, and the Lord will raise him up" (James 5:15). Now sometimes you can pray for healing with the best available measure of faith and healing does not come. But this was not the case of my family during our son's illness. My son was working at Sunset Lake Camp when we heard that he was having some digestive problems. We did not give much thought to it because he had always been healthy and strong. But we started to worry when he called and said he needed to go to the emergency room. "No worries," he said, "I just want to be checked up now that we are having a break at work during the weekend."

After various tests the doctor said that the problem was a gastric ulcer and began pharmacological treatment as well as dietary guidelines. However, the symptoms persisted—nausea, vomiting, weakness, and a very strong abdominal pain. He had to be sent home. The pain was so strong that he could not lie down and had to sleep in a sitting position. He slept in the car for a couple of nights as he found that it provided the best support to get some sleep.

His doctor detected a general inflammation and diagnosed gastritis and prescribed the corresponding treatment. However, to rule out major illness, he ordered an endoscopy and a computed axial tomography (CAT) scan. Results from those tests marked the beginning of one of the most fearful experiences in the history of our family. The endoscopy showed no problem in the upper tract, but the CAT scan showed an abnormality in the terminal ileum (the end of the small intestine), which suggested Crohn's disease. This was very scary as this condition is debilitating and serious enough to deeply affect your life, lead to surgery, increase your chance of cancer, and limit your life span.

In spite of this terrible prospect, he was feeling better, and this brought courage to the family. Unfortunately, the symptoms returned with full force a few days later. The worry became more intense when a contrast-enhanced computed tomography (CT) X-ray was ordered, and doctors saw something that looked like a tumor in the bowel. This growth—I was told on the phone by the gastroenterologist—might be some five centimeters in diameter. If we had prayed intensely so far, we began to pray with even more fervor now. The next step was a biopsy to obtain the final, firm diagnosis. We shared the situation only with close friends and family, and, as never before, I prayed for his healing.

He went through the two-day biopsy preparation routine, and the procedure was performed on a Monday. There was no sign of Crohn's disease and no visible tumor, but the doctor told us that we had to see how the tissue would look under the microscope. It was a long week of waiting, for the lab analysis would not be finished until the following Monday. Scores of prayers petitioned that our son would not have to face such an unfair diagnosis in the prime of his life.

When the three of us drove to the doctor's office for the results, we were quiet and reflective. Once in his office, the doctor explained, "All tests we ran are negative. There is no sign of abnormality or pathology anymore. No sign of Crohn's disease. No visible tumor." The doctor explained possible reasons why. I vaguely remember hearing something about the inflamed mesentery possibly due to a virus that had already left the body. But I cannot remember details because my heart was joyous and my eyes tear-filled with happiness because, all medical explanations aside, for me, this was a miracle.

When prayers are not answered

Unfortunately, many times prayers are not answered, at least not in the way we ask. There is a story about two young brothers who had enrolled in a weekend camp and had spent many days planning for the event and dreaming about the wonderful time they anticipated. But when Thursday came, very heavy rain began to pour over the whole region. Fearing a spoiled weekend, the boys turned to God and prayed very hard that the rain might stop. They prayed intensely over Thursday and Friday. But the rain continued and the organizers had to cancel the event. The boys were crushed and did not understand why God had not answered their sincere prayers. Their father explained to them that God, although powerful enough to change the weather instantly, does not always answer our prayers. Farmers may have been praying for needed rain as well. We are just unable to see the whole picture, and God does not normally alter the natural order of events just to suit our comfort.

The Bible gives us hints on why our prayers may not be answered in the way we ask. One very important reason is because it may not be best for us: "we do not know what we should pray for" (Romans 8:26). In the context of healing prayer, Ellen G. White suggested a prayer that includes this thought: " 'Lord, thou knowest every secret of the soul. Thou art acquainted with these persons. Jesus, their Advocate, gave His life for them. His love for them is greater than ours can possibly be. If, therefore, it is for Thy glory and the good of the afflicted ones, we ask, in the name of Jesus, that they may be restored to health. If it be not Thy will that they may be restored, we ask that Thy grace may comfort and Thy presence sustain them in their sufferings.' "[17] This was the case of the apostle Paul after a light brighter than the sun struck him down on the road to Damascus. This left him with a pain that he asked the Lord several times to remove. But God chose not to do so; instead, He gave him reassuring words: "My grace is sufficient for you, for my power is made perfect in weakness" (2 Corinthians 12:9, NIV).

Another reason why we may not see an answer to our prayers has to do with our own lives of sin: "If I regard iniquity in my heart, the Lord will not hear" (Psalm 66:18). This cannot mean that one needs to be free from sin in order to approach God. Jesus clearly stated that He had "not come to call the righteous, but sinners, to repentance" (Luke 5:32). The text in Psalms means that if someone is not sorry for his or her sins and does not want to repent, the Lord will not hear.

I like the idea that prayer is effective in the midst of an intimate relationship. When there is a link between Jesus and me (I remain in Him) and I do the things He asks me to do (His words remain in me), then I can ask whatever I wish, and it will be done for me. That is precisely the language of John 15:7; and, of course, if those above conditions hold true, I would not be asking to satisfy my selfish desire.

It is also crucial to consider that God has put resources and means in our hands for us to do our part; then He will supply the rest, if it is His will. So, my prayer may not be answered if I do not work towards the goal. Again, in the area of healing, Ellen White counsels us to do our share to alleviate pain and to cooperate with God instead of simply sitting idly, praying and waiting for God to do the rest. "When we have prayed for the recovery of the sick, we can work with all the more energy, thanking God that we have the privilege of cooperating with Him, and asking His blessing on the means which He Himself has provided."[18]

Lastly, our prayers may be insincere, mechanical, faithless, or for the wrong reasons: "When you ask, you do not receive, because you ask with wrong motives" (James 4:3, NIV). Jesus censured the hypocrites of His time that loved to "pray standing in the synagogues and on the street corners to be seen by others" (Matthew 6:5, NIV), and I think that this happens today when we pray in public. Some long prayers, exquisitely elaborated, using the finest rhetoric, are designed to impress the congregation but they may not impress God. These prayers are perhaps the modern version of those referred to by Jesus.

I grew up in the Roman Catholic Church during the pre–Vatican II era when the church service was performed in Latin. There was pride in responding to the priest in the correct Latin while looking straight at those next to you in the pew who did not utter the correct words. These prayers were not only meaningless but were spoken with wrong motives. I particularly remember my grandmother who had memorized all the litanies and used to repeat them at home as prayers. I was amazed at her skill, but I soon realized that she did not understand what she was saying, although her intention was probably sincere. In any case, for prayer to accomplish its goal, it must be prayed with the right motive as well as carry meaning, being full of faith.

Conclusion

I have reviewed a number of beneficial effects of prayer upon various important areas of life. It is good to know that prayer may provide us with peace and tranquility and that it can facilitate physical and mental health. Prayer may even make an ill person whole. But beyond those dividends, prayer is the channel that keeps us in touch with the Creator, to talk, to listen, and to deepen our relationship with Him.

The challenge comes in how to pray meaningfully and systematically, how to follow Paul's brief advice: "pray without ceasing" (1 Thessalonians 5:17).

A little book (almost a pamphlet) that has impacted my prayer life the most is *Brother Lawrence: The Practice of the Presence of God*.[19] The original edition was printed in 1692 in French, and it is just a collection of sixteen letters written by Joseph de Beaufort, grand vicar to the archbishop of Paris at that time. The grand vicar visited Brother Lawrence, a lay brother working as cobbler and cook at a monastery in Paris. The high-ranking clergy listened very attentively to Brother Lawrence and went home to write these letters. The document describes how Lawrence experienced the presence of God in his life while he was amid his pots and pans, and how he turned the cake or picked up a stick from the floor for the love of Him. He had a familiar conversation with God all the time. He admitted that the spiritual exercises and the pious methods he was induced to in the community did not work for him, and he learned to apply his mind to the presence of God, even in the middle of his little tasks. In essence, he was in constant touch with the Master, no matter his chore.

This principle has helped me remain in frequent contact with Him. Years back, while preparing a publication on stress management, I suggested that people should be in control of their thoughts, considering what they were thinking in a given moment and reminding themselves constantly of the right choice of thought. One of the tips was, "When your watch beeps at the hour, stop whatever you're doing and spend a couple of minutes analyzing the previous hour and your current emotional state. Scribble down your feelings; try to find out why you feel differently than before. Learn to detect adverse thinking, and dispel it."

Then it occurred to me that in order to lead a life of prayer, I could use the watch-beep method to remind me of prayer. So I began to offer a minute-or-two prayer on the hour. Within a few days, I realized that my companionship with the Lord was reaching a deeper level, and I have tried to keep up with this frequency of conversation with God. Everyone may have their method. But given the necessity of prayer to remain mentally and physically healthy and, above all, to abide in Him, it is important that every child of God prays without ceasing.

Study Questions

- Read Nehemiah 13. Try to understand the prophet's sentiment when he pronounced his brief prayer in verse 14. Read *Prophets and Kings,* chapter 57, "Reformation," in order to understand the context. Reflect on the difficulties of religious leadership and the special need of prayer by leaders.
- Use a concordance or a search feature on an electronic device to locate the word *prayer* in the Bible. Create a list of the most inspiring prayers in Scripture.
- Psalm 6:2 records a prayer for healing. Locate other prayers for healing in the Bible searching for words such as *heal, cure, revive,* or *restore* together with the word *prayer.*

Application Thoughts

- Read the Lord's Prayer (Matthew 6:9–13) in more than one Bible version. What does each statement mean to you? What are some things you can change in your life as a result of practicing this prayer?
- Jesus said, "Ask whatever you wish, and it will be done for you" (John 15:7, NIV). What does this mean? In what context did Jesus say it? How can you, in your personal circumstances, remain in Jesus and Jesus' words remain in you?

- Meditate on the message of Romans 8:26: "We do not know what we ought to pray for, but the Spirit himself intercedes for us through wordless groans" (NIV). Should this change the narrative of your prayers? How?

---

1. Walter W. Surwillo and Douglas P. Hobson, "Brain Electrical Activity During Prayer," *Psychological Reports* 43 (1978): 135–143.

2. Ellen G. White, *Gospel Workers* (Washington, DC: Review and Herald® Publishing Association, 1915), 257.

3. Mario Beauregard and Vincent Paquette, "Neural Correlates of a Mystical Experience in Carmelite Nuns," *Neuroscience Letters* 405 (2006): 186–190.

4. Mario Beauregard, *The Spiritual Brain* (New York: Harper Collins, 2007), 263.

5. Beauregard and Paquette, "Neural Correlates of a Mystical Experience," 187.

6. Mario Beauregard and Vincent Paquette, "EEG Activity in Carmelite Nuns During Mystical Experience," *Neuroscience Letters* 444 (2008): 1–4.

7. Ramona DeGuzman, "A Prayer From the Heart," in *LOV Stories: Living Our Values,* ed. Kathy McMillan (Loma Linda, CA: Loma Linda University Medical Center, 2010), 5.

8. Claire Hollywell and Jan Walker, "Private Prayer as a Suitable Intervention for Hospitalised Patients: A Critical Review of the Literature," *Journal of Clinical Nursing* 18 (2008): 637–651.

9. Amy L. Ai et al., "Private Prayer and Quality of Life in Cardiac Patients: Pathways of Cognitive Coping and Social Support," *Social Work in Health Care* 48 (2009): 471–494.

10. Ibid., 486.

11. Barbara Kilbourne et al., "The Influence of Religiosity on Depression Among Low-Income People With Diabetes," *Health & Social Work* 34 (2009): 137–147.

12. Kimberley Zittel-Palamara et al., "Spiritual Support for Women With Postpartum Depression," *Journal of Psychology and Christianity* 28 (2009): 213–223.

13. Karsten Hank and Barbara Schaan, "Cross-National Variations in the Correlation Between Frequency of Prayer and Health Among Older Europeans," *Research on Aging* 30 (2008): 36–54.

14. Leslie J. Francis et al., "Prayer and Psychological Health: A Study Among Sixth-Form Pupils Attending Catholic and Protestant Schools in Northern Ireland," *Mental Health, Religion & Culture* 11 (2008): 85–92.

15. Steven A. Rogers et al., "Religious Coping Among Those With Persistent Mental Illness," *International Journal for the Psychology of Religion* 12 (2002): 161–175.

16. Randolph C. Byrd, "Positive Therapeutic Effects of Intercessory Prayer in a Coronary Care Unit Population," *Southern Medical Journal* 81 (1988): 826–829.

17. Ellen G. White, *The Ministry of Healing* (Nampa, ID: Pacific Press® Publishing Association, 1942), 229.

18. Ibid., 232.

19. Nicholas Herman, *Brother Lawrence: The Practice of the Presence of God* (Cincinnati, OH: Forward Movement Publications, 1900).

Chapter 2

The Benefits of Scripture Reading and Meditation

"How sweet are your words to my taste,
sweeter than honey to my mouth!"—Psalm 119:103, NIV

G regory* is a successful hospital neuroradiologist of many years. A faithful Christian, he is kind, caring, and hospitable. His conversation goes easily to Bible themes and frequently into its connection with science. He makes deep analyses of scriptural texts and stories and applies these ideas to our times. But he doesn't read the Bible as a thinker only; he also uses it as a source of personal support in difficult times.

One instance in particular stands out. It was in the early days of magnetic resonance imaging (MRI) scanning, when he and his colleagues were experimenting with the newly developed equipment. Nowadays, these machines have become quite standardized and robust, and there is little need of experimentation. But much of the past work in radiology was to test different sequences to find out which ones would yield the best quality pictures. It was common for radiologists to have their own body scanned in order to experiment with the images. This is the time when Gregory had to talk seriously to his colleagues.

"At that time, I was the head of our section," Gregory told me. "I didn't feel I should use my authority to say, 'I don't want to stay after hours and work on the MRI machine.' So, out of duty, I agreed to participate regularly in the testing. But it was not so simple. I am claustrophobic and knew I would very likely experience anxiety symptoms or a panic attack if I had to go into the scanner for more than a few moments because it was a small, long, tight tube. When my colleagues learned about my claustrophobia, they were very understanding

---

* A pseudonym.

and asked me to let them know if at any time I felt out of control and needed to get out so we could stop immediately. With that understanding, I agreed to participate and do my turns.

"To face the challenge, I thought of recalling words from the Bible, verses I committed to memory in my grade-school years. That was my strategy! As I lay in the scanner, I began to feel restless. I would close my eyes and start reciting the complete twenty-third psalm, with strength and fervor. Words became meaningful; it was not a senseless repetition, but I could feel the significance of the words in those difficult moments. Then I would go on with the Lord's Prayer. The verses became well articulated in my mind and, again, the words would take on deep meaning as I mentally recited them. With the Beatitudes, I would challenge myself mentally to remember each and apply them to my life. Sometimes I found that making efforts at retrieving the exact words made time go by quickly and the symptoms did not take over. But most remarkably, these texts were very soothing, comforting, and brought peace to my soul. Most of the time, we did this at night after a full day's work, but in spite of being tired, the strategy kept those nasty symptoms away. I had to do this at least six times, maybe eight. And during every single one, I managed to stay calm.

"Sessions were not short. It took about twenty minutes to do the experiment, try out various sequences until the optimal one was found. The digital information had to be processed to see how the picture looked, and this took twenty to thirty minutes if everything went right. But sometimes we needed to repeat trials, and I had to remain in the scanner for one to two hours. Well, I never had to ask my colleagues to pull me out, partly because they turned their backs and began to work very hard. But most importantly, I felt that the biblical words were the channel God used to bless me and to save me from a very painful experience."

Puritan writer Thomas Brooks wrote, "The Word of the Lord is a light to guide you, a counselor to counsel you, a comforter to comfort you, a staff to support you, a sword to defend you, and a physician to cure you. The Word is a mine to enrich you, a robe to clothe you, and a crown to crown you." Many people have discovered, by their own experience, that the Bible satisfies many needs, and that it has taken a special place in their lives. Only during the past two decades has an extensive effort been made to scientifically observe how reading and meditating on Bible passages affects people's health, behavior, and well-being.

This chapter will review current research on the interface between Scripture reading and meditation and other positive variables. More importantly, we will see how prayerful study of Scripture will yield not only a better mental and physical health but also an abundance of spiritual blessings that will make a difference in the way to salvation.

Scripture and coping

How do you cope? It is an important question that deserves thought. With certain frequency we are confronted with serious difficulties and adversities; other times, we face ongoing, chronic, heavy burdens that pose a continual challenge. At best, we are coping with random issues connected to work, relationships, children, health, money, and so on. How do people cope? Some take immediate action, others wait; some worry, others act; some change their direction, others continue on the same path; some search for solutions from their own resources, others seek help from God via Scripture. And those who opt for this last option tend to get their rewards.

Elderly people are often found to trust more in the divine power through their Bibles than do other age groups. Thomas Arcury and his team from the Wake Forest University School of Medicine in North Carolina studied a group of 145 elderly people, aged seventy or more.[1] Investigators attempted to answer these questions: "How do they use religion to help manage their health status? Are there gender or ethnic differences? Are differences in their use of religion related to their health?"

There were many specific questions about health and lifestyle and also a direct, religious open question offering participants the chance to explain in detail: "Do you use prayer and religious services to help manage your health?" Those who answered affirmatively were given the chance to explain how.

It was interesting that Scripture reading and meditation were not a specific part of the question, but Scripture emerged as the second most important theme, after faith and prayer, to support health management. Reading the Bible, they said, is a way to communicate with God. "That's what I do every night, my last thing is reading Scripture so I can rest. . . . And this morning I said, I'm going to put God first, I'm going to read Scripture this morning," said a woman.

Another woman used Bible meditation to cope with emotional disturbances: "If I feel depressed or anything, I'll probably read a passage of Scripture and, you know, meditate on that. Well, I do pray for good health. And whatever it is I'm doing, maybe, so long as I pray, and I don't do anything, there's always something that we must do that makes sense to keep ourselves healthy." A different participant sought strength from Scripture one day at a time: "The Bible is my guide. It's my guide. I never wake—I am so glad when I wake up in the morning that I laid my Bible on the foot of my bed. And when I wake up in the morning, I read my Bible and my little books. And that's really something—but you know sometime I find out that—exactly what I need for that day, I'll find it in that book or scripture that I read for that day. And it gives me strength. I think that's what gives me the strength to carry on."

Another participant, Bob, was talking when his wife said, "If I may mention a point here. I think one thing that Bob can attribute to the fact that he is [calm and peaceful], is that he so often is reading his Bible or reading his Sunday School material or in communication mentally with the Lord. And you know, that affords you a peace of mind that nothing else can." Researchers made reference to a few Seventh-day Adventist participants who use the Bible for direction in what to eat and how to prevent illness. One Adventist woman said, "The Bible tells us that—folks is coming back to the Bible more so than they was—there's herbs in the woods. God, when He made us, created the world, and created us, He made herbs to cure every disease that they is. And He didn't intend for people to eat this hog meat neither. The Bible tells us that."

After Thomas Arcury read, coded, and analyzed the vast amount of data arising from these interviews as well as the many informal observations reported by interviewers, the conclusion was that prayer and reading the Bible set the pace and the routine of many of these elder participants, who also were given structure by Wednesday night prayer services, Sunday School and church services, choir practice, and church committee meetings.

Another qualitative study was targeted at middle-age women. This was done by Brenda Beagan and her team from Dalhousie University in Halifax, Nova Scotia.[2] African-Canadian women were interviewed on how they experienced issues such as racism, depression, stress, and spirituality. The results revealed that Bible reading (also singing and praying) were the primary means to deal with difficulties, specifically to compensate for racial discrimination. These spiritual means provided a cognitive reinterpretation that allowed them to cope with racism and other challenges. They saw these as tests and trials that they could surmount with God's blessing and protection. Researchers suggest that these practices seem capable to prevent or ameliorate mental-health complications.

Yale University researcher Chyrell Bellamy and her associates studied participants with current mental-health issues (depression, anxiety, alcohol- or drug-related disturbances, and psychotic symptoms).[3] They were given several inventories as well as questions such as, "Is spirituality important to you?" If yes, "What spiritual activities do you participate in?" Spirituality was recorded as either public (church attendance, Bible study groups, etc.) or private (prayer, reading the Bible, and meditation).

Spirituality was important in at least two-thirds of the group, and the most commonly practiced spiritual activity was of a public nature (78 percent), followed by a private nature with 30 percent. Women were one and a half times more likely to be spiritual than were men. Also as age advanced, there were increased chances of more spiritual activities. It was interesting to find that those whose symptoms had exacerbated over the past thirty days reported higher levels of spiritual activities. This goes along with human nature; we feel the need of being closer to our heavenly Father when challenges come our way. Researchers interpret this finding saying that individuals with mental illness tend to experience a loss of control during times of greater symptomatology, and it is in the middle of these crises when spiritual activities can help to soothe the symptoms and provide hope. They conclude by saying that the essence of recovery is believing and having hope that things will get better.

Georgia State University gerontologist Vickie Patterson and her team conducted a study where Bible reading and other private devotional strategies were observed as coping tools.[4] It was found that most deemed religion important and reported that religious practices (specifically, prayer, church attendance, and Bible reading) helped them cope with life in assisted-living facilities. The religious activities used were of multiple modalities: attending church services and devotional meetings, having private devotionals, praying, reading the Bible, reading devotional books or magazines, tuning in to religious radio or TV sermons and religious programs, reviewing church mailings, and listening to cassette tape Bibles. Bible reading was common in the daily routines of residents, some for specific coping purposes. One resident said, "Well, I have a certain amount of that [depression], but I fight it because I pray. And, too, I read my Bible at least one chapter every night." Another resident described her own coping as "putting behind the things that are past," trying to keep busy with everyday life, and, in her own words, staying "busy because, according to the Bible, we're not supposed to put our hand to the plow and look back."

A. Quinn Stanley from the University of Wisconsin–Stevens Point studied a very different kind of group.[5] Participants were teachers of violent students. This study was designed to find out the nature of resources teachers used in order to cope with the stresses of their difficult jobs. Although working with these pupils was very challenging, participants were committed to continue to work with them, using coping mechanisms (part of them religious or spiritual in nature) to maintain efficacy and reduce anxiety. To understand the difficulty of the jobs these teachers were doing, we'll say that they were in charge of special classrooms where threats of death to peers and teacher and assaults from student to student were common. Although the grades were sixth through twelfth, some students were as old as twenty-one. Results show that many of their coping mechanisms were nonreligious (deep breathing, humor, exercise, hiking and camping, relaxation exercise, time with family), but these teachers also used religious methods to cope: Bible reading, prayer, and church attendance. Most residents deemed religion important and reported that religious activities and resources provided an excellent framework for coping with their demanding jobs.

Scripture and health

Scripture reading and meditation can be a powerful stress reducer. This effect is due to the so-called relaxation response, which favors the reduction of the stress hormones cortisol and norepinephrine. Considering that stress can be the cause of a long list of psychosomatic diseases, any relaxing or soothing experience of devotional activities will promote health.

Arthur S. Maxwell, also known as Uncle Arthur, tells the story of Stanley Tefft, an American soldier injured in the South Pacific during World War II. Some friendly islanders guided him and a small group of airmen to a hideout where they remained for almost three months, away from Japanese patrols. Stanley found those natives, far from being savages, were godly, noble, and selfless people. Apparently, a missionary had distributed Bibles in years past, and the divine message had done its work of transforming the hearts of those people. That was amazing in itself. But for Mr. Tefft there was an additional blessing from the Scriptures. His native friends expected to have a religious service every night with the American soldiers. "Those services," explains Tefft, "were the only moments when I forgot my wounds, my tormented nerves, my starving tissues."[6] These Bible-study meetings helped Tefft to completely move his mind away from his wounds, being thus blessed with times of temporary relief.

Leila Shahabi, from the Rush-Presbyterian–St. Luke's Medical Center in Chicago, led a study with healthy American adults in order to see the health variables related to religiosity and spirituality.[7] This study was large and varied enough to be representative of the entire population. Questions about private religious activities were, for example, "How often do you pray privately in places other than at church or synagogue?" "Within your religious or spiritual tradition, how often do you meditate?" "How often have you read the Bible in the last year?" Other questionnaires assessed stress, mistrust, and general health. There were also questions of tolerance and intolerance, such as whether a member of a specific subgroup (e.g., atheist) should be allowed to make a speech, teach at a college or university, or have his or her books in a public library. The results allow us to identify several types of people:

1. Religious and Spiritual. This group was the most intrinsically religious. They reported more Bible reading, more private prayer, more meditation, more frequent service attendance, and more daily spiritual experience. Compared to people in the spiritual-only group, they had a higher frequency of meditating, feeling deep inner peace or harmony, and being spiritually touched by the beauty of creation—essential characteristics of the spiritual person. They seemed to take the best of the spiritual side and the best of the religious side. They were subject to less distress and less mistrust, and emerged as more politically conservative and more inclined to believe that life has a purpose. Together with the religious-only participants, they enjoyed the lowest levels of morbidity and mortality, and the highest health. However, this group came up as the least tolerant in judging the cases presented.

2. Spiritual Only. This group responded affirmatively to language that represented spiritual experiences with no religious terminology (inner peace, harmony, spiritually touched, etc.) They were found more politically liberal and more likely to have no religion than any other group, even the neither-nor group. They participated in religious activities to some extent but not as much as the two groups with a religious element, but they were more tolerant than the religious groups. According to Zinnbauer and colleagues, this group would perhaps fit the label of "New Age."[8]

3. Religious Only. People who responded affirmatively to items with language that represented spiritual experiences with religious terminology: Jesus, church, prayer, religious service, Holy Bible, and so on. They showed higher levels of distress and of mistrust than the religious and spiritual group and, as mentioned before, together with them, displayed the highest levels of health.

4. Neither Religious nor Spiritual. People in this group reported no religion, using the least religious and the least spiritual resources. They reported the highest tolerance and the most liberal outlook. In terms of health, they were comparable to the spiritual group and significantly behind the religious and spiritual as well as the religious-only groups.

This study clearly showed the religious advantage in terms of health, both mentally and physically. Yet being intolerant was a distinctive feature that does not speak well of religious people. As a general principle, it would do us all good to remember Mrs. White's assertion: "If we but knew the evil of the spirit of intolerance, how carefully would we shun it!"[9] The study also gives us light into the issue of religiosity and spirituality. Some people say that religion is not important and that being spiritual is what matters. However, this study shows that blessings are maximized when spirituality happens in a religious context. The authors write that spirituality is likely to thrive amid religiosity, and that "going each week to a serene place that encourages reflection, listening to sermons that advocate love and service to others, and experiencing the joy of joining in song and in praise of faith may provide direct, ongoing, and reinforcing experiences of the virtues enjoyed by highly spiritual people."

A unique study by Marsha Wiggins, the University of Colorado at Denver, and her team was published in the *Journal of Spirituality and Mental Health*.[10] It was done among men who had tested positive for human immunodeficiency virus (HIV), and it had the purpose of observing the effects of religious coping on stress, depression, and risk behaviors. The results indicate that the religious variables (Bible reading, prayer, and church attendance) were unrelated to stress but were significantly and inversely related to depression and to the use of hazardous alcohol and illicit drugs; in other words, men who read the Bible, prayed, and attended church were less likely to experience depression and to use the mentioned substances.

A study done at Duke University, led by Hughes Helm, focused on whether private religious activity prolonged survival in older adults.[11] The results show that those engaged in private religious activities (Bible studies, prayer, and meditation) before the onset of impaired daily living had a survival advantage over those who didn't.[12] Females reported a much higher level of private religious activities than did males. And those with little or no private religious activities reported a higher use of alcohol and tobacco than did those with higher levels of private religious activity.

A significant finding of this study, therefore, was the high survival advantage of those involved in private devotions in the unimpaired daily living group. However, this was not the case in the impaired group, who did not have any advantage associated with private religious activities. The explanation given by the authors is that an ill, elderly population may not be able to overcome the force of impending mortality even when using adaptive measures that have a positive effect on the survival of healthy populations. This study also found the benefits of private devotions was not just for those practicing it daily but the protection also reached to those who reported participation in religious activity only a few times a month. The trend really started to reverse when people reported private devotions taking place "rarely" to "never."

Scripture and young people

Leslie Francis from the University of Wales in Bangor, United Kingdom, studied an unusually large sample of 25,888 thirteen- to fifteen-year-olds (13,300 boys and 12,588 girls) from 128 secondary schools throughout England and Wales with the main purpose of observing the relationship between Bible reading and purpose in life.[13] They were asked about their Bible reading habits with the question "How often do you read the Bible?" and the options were "never," "sometimes," "at least once a week," and "nearly every day." They were also given measures of mental health. The study was performed with only

Christians; those who claimed affiliation to a non-Christian religion (1,089 students) were omitted from the analysis.

Now, when we refer to Christians here, we need to understand the sociological context where this study was conducted. People of the United Kingdom consider themselves "Christian" because they don't belong to, say, the Muslim religion, but they may not believe in God or be members of any church. This is evidenced by the demographic results of this study: one-third (34 percent) of the participants defined themselves as agnostics, 25 percent as atheists, and 41 percent as believers in God. Nearly half (48 percent) of these students never attended church, compared with 19 percent who attended once or twice a year, 14 percent who attended several times a year, 4 percent who attended monthly, and 15 percent who attended most weeks. Two-thirds (66 percent) of these young people never read the Bible, 29 percent read it occasionally, 3 percent weekly, and 2 percent daily. Given the sample size of this study, even very small percentages of boys and girls reading the Bible or going to church represent hundreds of individuals, and thus the results of the analysis are trustworthy.

The findings showed those who believed in God, attended church often, and read the Bible frequently, yielded low psychoticism scores and low social conformity scores. Also, these three private religious behaviors were found to be the best predictors of having a greater sense of purpose in life. In fact, in this study, the highest correlation indexes of the three was Bible reading over church attendance and belief in God, but all three were high. This means that, in a statistical sense, Bible reading conveys additional unique predictive power of purpose in life.

Kelly Davis and Catherine Epkins, professors of clinical psychology at Texas Tech University, studied children of a similar age range in the U.S.[14] They examined the role of private religious practices of twelve-year-olds on the conflict they encountered in their families. The participants took a survey of religiosity and spirituality, including questions about private religious activities such as praying and reading the Bible. They also took a family environment scale to examine the family conflict (e.g., "We fight a lot in our family," "Family members sometimes hit each other," were statements rated from "strongly agree" to "strongly disagree"). Then the preadolescents took a depression inventory and an anxiety scale. The results are multiple, but private religious practices had moderated the relationship between family conflict and symptoms of depression. In other words, families with abundant conflicts tend to have higher levels of child depression and child anxiety than did families where conflicts are rare. In this study, the link between conflict and depression and anxiety became very weak when youth were involved in private devotions such as Bible reading. This indicated that even though Bible reading and study did not eliminate the conflict, it provided refuge and protection from depression and anxiety in children caught in family quarrels.

The benefits of Bible study even touch general academic achievement and school behavior. This is what William Jeynes found.[15] A professor of teacher education at California State University–Long Beach, Jeynes studied a random sample of 140 students, seventh to twelfth grade, in a large Christian school. The research goal was to observe how knowledge of the Bible related to general academic performance. He assessed Bible literacy via three tests: a test of Bible knowledge, the ease with which students could recite the sixty-six books of the Bible in order, and the final grade from the last Bible course taken. Results show that secondary students with high Bible literacy also tended to have a high grade point average (GPA). In contrast, those with low levels of biblical knowledge tended to have low GPAs. Additionally, those with good biblical knowledge tended to display the best school behavior, while the group with the lowest level of Bible literacy had the worst school behavior. This was true for males and females and for whites and nonwhites.

To explore the effect of the Bible in public schools is not easy because of the schools' secular nature, but an ongoing project by the American Bible Society, together with the Salvation Army, is an exception. In order to help inner-city children with their reading skills, these organizations have been implementing the so-called Literacy Plan for a number of years. The project consists of helping kids improve their reading ability with the Bible as their reader.

Anna is a schoolgirl in Philadelphia benefiting from this program. She had a speech impediment that caused her peers to laugh. As a result, she became scared of reading aloud. The adverse social effects were bad enough; but then there was the added risk of being functionally illiterate for life. The program provided a caring tutor to work one-on-one with Anna and it proved successful to the point that Anna overcame her impediment.

As often happens in cases like these, her self-esteem remained ruined and she took some time to recover. It was the reading of the Bible that helped significantly. Knowing more about the Bible characters, about God's love for her and His promises, and about Jesus was critical. This program reports that as students improve their reading skills, while discovering the joy of reading God's Word, they also recover from their self-esteem issues. Anna was so excited at her progress that she kept saying, "When I read the Bible it makes me feel stronger and not scared!"[16]

Imagery, reflection, and meditation on the Bible

The word *meditation* in the Western world has been historically connected to religious activities, generally linked to silent prayer and profound reflection on the Scriptures. But in the last few decades, with the explosion of Eastern religions in many Christian countries, meditation has become almost a synonym of transcendental meditation and other like practices. The first edition of *Webster's Dictionary* defines meditation as "close or continued thought; the turning or revolving of a subject in the mind; serious contemplation." But the eleventh edition, in addition to the original definition, presents another: "To engage in mental exercise (as concentration on one's breathing or repetition of a mantra) for the purpose of reaching a heightened level of spiritual awareness." Thus, many Christians are afraid to say that they meditate out of the fear that other believers will think that they are into following heathen practices. Others don't do it at all, and thus miss out on the benefits. Etymologically, *meditate* (from the Latin *meditari*) simply means "to think over, reflect, and consider." It denotes an intense focus on a topic as to become partially unaware of the surroundings. I think we believers would get many more divine blessings out of the Scriptures if we studied them with such intensity more often. It would also open our minds for God to speak more clearly to us.

Transcendental meditation (TM) is a very different concept. TM refers to reaching the goal of wakefulness by means of a mantra—a word or sound with no meaning that is repeated over and over until the mind reaches "inner wakefulness," a silent state of mind with "inner peace" being the goal. TM insists that the mantra must be void of meaning. By contrast, Bible meditation is full of meaning as the object of meditation is made up of actual words, thoughts, and ideas with a clear significance based on the Word of God. Bible meditation brings not only inner peace but also a better understanding of God's messages, more wisdom to discern between good and evil, guidance in our next steps, and motivation to do right. That powerful agent is vividly described in these terms: "For the word of God is alive and active. Sharper than any double-edged sword, it penetrates even to dividing soul and spirit, joints and marrow; it judges the thoughts and attitudes of the heart" (Hebrews 4:12, NIV).

In my sixteen years as a Roman Catholic, I never heard of Hebrews 4:12. When I learned about this text in my first Bible study with Adventists, it touched me in such a way that I became mysteriously curious, eager, and thirsty for the Word of God. What a powerful image to use in times of Roman military dominance! A sword, but not a steel sword to kill but to impart life; a divine sword, a living and active one that would touch the innermost intricacies of the human soul and impart so many rich dividends to the believer.

Yes, it is enriching to meditate on the Bible. Every pious Bible reader does it in a different way and God will bless those who honestly search for Him through the Word. How do I meditate? I put aside a good block of time and follow these steps:

1. Choose a brief passage, either a single verse, a group of related verses, or a story.

2. Read it several times to gain increasing understanding, to feel the impact of the words until those words are almost memorized or, if the text is short, fully memorized.

3. If a verse, I think about how its idea fits the context and the rest of the Bible and how it can translate into real action.

4. If a story, I unleash my imagination to see as much detail as possible in my mind. It helps me to read a good commentary or encyclopedia and close my eyes to try and see in my mind the action of the people involved, their looks, their feelings, the environment, the message (see the box below as an example of a helpful commentary on the text when Jesus drove out an unclean spirit at the Capernaum synagogue [Luke 4:31–37]). I feel emotionally involved in the story and experience a flow of compassion, love, zeal, thankfulness, sadness, and hope.

5. Allow quiet time for the Holy Spirit to work. This doesn't mean that I hear words, but I often experience peace and solace. I may become imbued with trust in the Lord and sense that things will be all right because God is in charge. "The Spirit fills the mind and heart with sweet hope and courage and Bible imagery."[17]

6. Close with prayer, making the Bible passage the center of the prayer.

Text to amplify the Sabbath episode at Capernaum synagogue
(Luke 4:31–37)

At Capernaum Jesus dwelt in the intervals of His journeys to and fro, and it came to be known as "His own city.". . .

The deep depression of the lake gives to the plain that skirts its shores the genial climate of the south. Here in the days of Christ flourished the palm tree and the olive, here were orchards and vineyards, green fields, and brightly blooming flowers in rich luxuriance, all watered by living streams bursting from the cliffs. The shores of the lake, and the hills that at a little distance encircle it, were dotted with towns and villages. The lake was covered with fishing boats. Everywhere was the stir of busy, active life.

Capernaum itself was well adapted to be the center of the Saviour's work. Being on the highway from Damascus to Jerusalem and Egypt, and to the Mediterranean Sea, it was a great thoroughfare of travel. People from many lands passed through the city, or tarried for rest in their journeyings to and fro. Here Jesus could meet all nations and all ranks, the rich and great as well as the poor and lowly, and His lessons would be carried to other countries and into many households. . . .

In Capernaum the nobleman's son whom Christ had healed was a witness to His power. And the court official and his household joyfully testified of their faith. When it was known that the Teacher Himself was among them, the whole city was aroused. Multitudes flocked to His presence. On the Sabbath the people crowded the synagogue until great numbers had to turn away, unable to find entrance. . . .

Jesus in the synagogue spoke of the kingdom He had come to establish, and of His mission to set free the captives of Satan. He was interrupted by a shriek of terror. A madman rushed forward from among the people, crying out, "Let us alone; what have we to do with Thee, Thou Jesus of Nazareth? art Thou come to destroy us? I know Thee who Thou art; the Holy One of God."

All was now confusion and alarm. The attention of the people was diverted from Christ, and His words were unheeded. This was Satan's purpose in leading his victim to the synagogue. But Jesus rebuked the demon, saying, "Hold thy peace, and come out of him. And when the devil had thrown him in the midst, he came out of him, and hurt him not."

The mind of this wretched sufferer had been darkened by Satan, but in the Saviour's presence a ray of light had pierced the gloom. He was roused to long for freedom from Satan's control; but the demon resisted the power of Christ. When the man tried to appeal to Jesus for help, the evil spirit put words into his mouth, and he cried out in an agony of fear. The demoniac partially comprehended that he was in the presence of One who could set him free; but when he tried to come within reach of that mighty hand, another's will held him, another's words found utterance through him. The conflict between the power of Satan and his own desire for freedom was terrible. . . .

The man praised God for his deliverance. The eye that had so lately glared with the fire of insanity, now beamed with intelligence, and overflowed with grateful tears. The people were dumb with amazement. As soon as they recovered speech they exclaimed, one to another, "What is this? a new teaching! with authority He commandeth even the unclean spirits, and they obey Him." Mark 1:27, R. V. (Excerpts from Ellen G. White, *The Desire of Ages* [Mountain View, CA: Pacific Press®, 1940], 252, 253, 255, 256.)

Ellen G. White and the power of Scripture

There are a large number of personal blessings obtainable from the Bible, according to Ellen G. White. Here are a few examples:

The Bible builds character. In offering advice to parents, White writes, "The lessons of the Bible have a moral and religious influence on the character, as they are brought into the practical life. . . . A noble, all-round manhood does not come by chance. It is the result of the molding process of character building in the early years of youth, and a practice of the law of God in the home. God will bless the faithful efforts of all who teach their children as He has directed."[18] The text especially targets parents and teachers of children who need counsel in the Word of God and the example of men and women of character. Listening and reading about exemplary individuals (heroes) can transform children and adolescents into adults of character.

The Bible gives intellectual vigor. As we have seen, research is only the beginning. Links between Bible reading and academic achievement are numerous. "There is nothing more calculated to strengthen the intellect than the study of the Scriptures. No other book is so potent to elevate the thoughts, to give vigor to the faculties, as the broad, ennobling truths of the Bible."[19] In fact, current CognitiveGenesis findings show that students in Adventist schools—where the Bible has a prominent place—are performing much higher academically than expected, according to standardized test results.[20]

The Bible banishes fears. Words such as *fear, afraid, terrified, fret,* or *frightened* appear hundreds of times in the Bible. Many of them represent God's urges: "Do not fear," "Fret not," "Don't be afraid," because He knows that fear can happen any time over the course of human life. "Only the sense of God's presence can banish the fear that, for the timid child, would make life a burden. Let him fix in his memory the promise, 'The angel of the Lord encampeth round about them that fear him, and delivereth them.' Psalm 34:7. Let him read that wonderful story of Elisha in the mountain city, and, between him and the hosts of armed foemen, a mighty encircling band of heavenly angels. Let him read how to Peter, in prison and condemned to death, God's angel appeared; how, past the armed guards, the massive doors and great iron gateway with their bolts and bars, the angel led God's servant forth in safety."[21] Bible stories and promises are proven safeguards for the fearful experiences of children and grown-ups alike.

The Bible teaches how to attain happiness. "Through the study of the Scriptures we obtain a correct knowledge of how to live so as to enjoy the greatest amount of unalloyed happiness."[22] Indeed, the Scriptures offer convincing values and principles by which to live and to relate successfully with others and with God, to serve, to forgive, to obey God, to rejoice, to be free from guilt, and to have the assurance of salvation—all key elements of happiness.

The Bible makes minds clear and sound. "The clearness of our views of truth will be proportionate to our understanding of the Word of God. He who gives the Scriptures close, prayerful attention will gain clear comprehension and sound judgment, as if in turning to God he had reached a higher grade of intelligence."[23] This can happen, not only because of the high value of Bible content, but also because of its miraculous power as expressed in Hebrews 4:12.

The Bible provides the means to reject temptation. "The reading and contemplation of the Scriptures would be regarded as an audience with the Infinite One. . . . When Satan presses his suggestions upon our minds, we may, if we cherish a 'Thus saith the Lord,' be drawn into the secret pavilion of the Most High."[24] Overcoming temptation by means of the Scriptures will take us ever closer to God. Ellen White uses the expression "secret pavilion," the King James Bible's term for the presence of God in the tabernacle (Psalm 18:11; Psalm 27:5). It depicts a very reassuring figure of maximum protection and comfort, as near to God's presence as our human nature allows.

The Bible nourishes our spiritual dimension. The spiritual experience during and after some time of reading, meditation, and reflection upon the Holy Scriptures is that of profound peace and inexpressible joy—so much so that it cannot be but a gift from God. White says, "Fill the whole heart with the words of God. They are the living water, quenching your burning thirst. They are the living bread from heaven. . . . Our bodies are built up from what we eat and drink; and as in the natural economy, so in the spiritual economy: it is what we meditate upon that will give tone and strength to our spiritual nature."[25]

The Bible can guide the scientific mind. "God has permitted a flood of light to be poured upon the world in discoveries in science and art; but when professedly scientific men lecture and write upon these subjects from a merely human stand-point, they will assuredly come to wrong conclusions. The greatest minds, if not guided by the word of God in their research, become bewildered in their attempts to investigate the relations of science and revelation."[26] This text could be seen as a chastising message for scientists to take the Bible literally. It has not been so in my experience. The passage confirms that scientific theories and applications, even those rooted in nontheistic presuppositions, can serve as a source of learning and application as long as they are filtered through the Word of God.

The senior psychologist at my first job in Spain attended a psychoanalytic workshop on how to help clients retrieve early memories. Being a Christian, she returned in a state of shock. She had witnessed a session where a therapist induced a client to awareness of memories from when the client was a young child, and even earlier. At some point, the client curled into a fetal position. The therapist began to ask for memories of the time when she was in her mother's womb! And she responded to the prompt in her semiunconscious state! To my mentor and to me, it was clear that this was forbidden territory. In an optimal state of mind, nobody can recall content from the first two years of life, let alone from the prenatal stage. The Bible tells us that "the secret things belong to the Lord our God, but the things revealed belong to us and to our children forever" (Deuteronomy 29:29, NIV). To us, this technique was attempting to enter into the "secret" realm, and it was not for us to explore. We understood that those practices were dangerous enough to become Satan-led. We committed to use strategies that would be compatible with biblical tenets—and there are plenty of them, even though many are from a purely secular origin.

This is how I see the Scriptures guiding my academic search and professional practice. As the psalmist puts it, the Word is "a lamp unto my feet, and a light unto my path," not the answer to scientific questions, but the guide and reference for the seeker to move on (Psalm 119:105, KJV). "I will instruct you and teach you in the way you should go; I will counsel you with my loving eye on you" (Psalm 32:8, NIV). Cherishing this biblical promise, one can press on in whatever endeavor, including Bible meditation, knowing that God is helping us at each crossroad of our lives.

Conclusion

Kevin was a college student who decided to study a few years after the typical college age. He told me his experience; it goes like this:

"I grew up in a Christian family, but I was not interested in religion at all. I attended church with my parents, not because I had any desire but to avoid their lectures. I believed in God but rejected Him. Many years went by like this. When I reached the age of twenty-four, an opportunity opened to work in New Zealand and I left home. There I had my true encounter with the Bible. I started from the beginning and began to feel a strong desire to keep reading. Soon I was leaving aside any other activity to read on. I remember that many days I was reading for seven and eight hours—nonstop, absorbing everything written there. When I reached the Gospels and I read about Jesus' agony at the Garden of Gethsemane, I started to cry like a child. It was at Calvary's episode when I fell on my knees with my tear-sodden face and asked God to take lead of my life. That was the moment of my conversion.

"Then everything changed in my life. The interaction I had with the biblical message transformed me. Up to that point, the most important things for me were tobacco, alcohol, drugs, sexual activity, and very specially motorcycling. I had a motorbike that cost more than twenty-thousand dollars—the most important thing in my life. I cleaned it and polished it every two or three days. All that I earned I put it into the bike to make it prettier and faster. Now with this new understanding I did not have any desire to keep on with that life. I admit that I had to struggle between that machine and Jesus of Nazareth. But when the time to sell came, I did not regret it at all. The bike seemed something insignificant to me. I am glad to have chosen Jesus; if I had to choose again, my choice would be the same."

As we have reviewed the multiple advantages of the Word of God and especially its transformational power, we need to commit to a daily reflection of the best source to find out God's will for our lives. Through prayerful reading, reflection, and meditation, we will reach a better understanding and a transformation by the power of the Spirit. And when this becomes a continuous part of our lives, Christ, the Word (John 1:1, 14), may dwell in our hearts by faith, as promised in Ephesians 3:17.

Study Questions

- Have you have tried to read the Bible in a year and failed? Why not try reading a book at a time? Start with a small New Testament book, such as James, Philippians, or the letters to Timothy, then you can move on to others. Ask yourself, What is the main point of the book? When was it written and in what circumstances? (This may require consulting a Bible commentary.) What does this message tell me? How can I put its messages into practice? How can I share my blessings with my friends, family, and others I encounter?

- The expression "the Lord's Word" or the "Word of the Lord" appears all over the book of Psalms. Search for it in several locations and reflect on how the Word of God has helped you in the past and how you can ensure its blessings for the future.

- Use your concordance to find entries for *meditate*. What are the different contexts in which the word is used? How can you enhance your meditation in the Holy Scriptures?

Application Thoughts

- Read Psalm 139 twice; the first time, read at a good pace in order to feel the entire message as a whole; the second time, verse by verse, pausing, reflecting on each word and expression and connecting the message to you personally. What feelings does the reading bring to you? What are some decisions and behaviors that may be the result of your reading?

- The power of God's Word can be seen in the life of Jesus. What specific story or stories come to mind where the Word of God is active in His ministry? Where can the Word bless your life?

- Using your concordance or digital device, search for one Bible character whose life attracts you (e.g., Sarah, Joseph, Moses, Ruth, Jonathan, Solomon, John, Peter, etc.). Read every verse where the name appears and the verses around them to see the context. Try to imagine the situation from the viewpoint of your character and from others' viewpoints. What lessons can you learn from what the Scriptures say about him or her? Pray to God for His leading in your own life.

---

1. Thomas A. Arcury et al., "Faith and Health Self-Management of Rural Older Adults," *Journal of Cross-Cultural Gerontology* 15 (2000): 55–74. Participants in this study came from two rural counties in North Carolina and were diverse (33 percent African Americans; 37 percent European Americans; and 30 percent Native Americans; with a 40/60 male to female ratio). In order to get a good representation of a variety of backgrounds, participants were recruited from home health-care agencies, senior centers, senior clubs, churches, social service agencies, and veterans' organizations. Researchers collected data via four in-depth, semistructured, quarterly, personal interviews over the course of one year. The initial interview took about three hours spread over two or three days.

2. Brenda L. Beagan et al., "With God in Our Lives He Gives Us the Strength to Carry On," *Mental Health, Religion, & Culture* 15 (2012): 103–120. Participants in the study were fifty African-Canadian women living in Nova Scotia. Researchers gathered data via four standardized instruments and also by means of qualitative, in-depth interviews designed to probe discussion on how they experienced issues such as racism, depression, stress, and spirituality.

3. Chyrell D. Bellamy et al., "Relevance of Spirituality for People With Mental Illness Attending Consumer-Centered Services," *Psychiatric Rehabilitation Journal* 30 (2007): 287–294. The study was quantitative, thus allowing for a larger sample of 1,835 participants drawn across the state of Michigan in day centers for people with mental illnesses.

4. Vickie L. Patterson et al., "Coping With Change: Religious Activities and Beliefs of Residents in Assisted Living Facilities," *Journal of Religious Gerontology* 14 (2003): 79–93. The study was among fifty-five elderly residents from seventeen assisted-living facilities in suburban Atlanta. Data were collected via extensive interviews about their religious practices. The sample was made up of people no less than seventy-five years of age (89 percent women, 98 percent Caucasians).

5. A. Quinn Stanley, "Benefits of Teacher 'Connections' in Stressful Educational Settings," *International Journal of Children's Spirituality* 16 (2011): 47–58. These special-education teachers came from four schools and reported their coping experiences via eight in-depth interviews that were tape-recorded, transcribed, coded, and analyzed.

6. Arthur S. Maxwell, *Your Bible and You* (Washington, DC: Review and Herald®, 1959), 59.

7. Leila Shahabi et al., "Correlates of Self-Perceptions of Spirituality in American Adults," *Annals of Behavioral Medicine* 24 (2002): 59–68. Study participants were 1,422 persons of eighteen years or older, living in noninstitutionalized settings, 46/54 percent men to women, with an average age of forty-six. This was a reliable and representative sample of the adult population across the United States.

8. Brian J. Zinnbauer et al., "Religion and Spirituality: Unfuzzing the Fuzzy," *Journal of the Scientific Study of Religion* 36 (1997): 549–564.

9. Ellen G. White, *Gospel Workers,* 302.

10. Marsha I. Wiggins et al., "The Longitudinal Effects of Spirituality on Stress, Depression, and Risk Behaviors Among Men With HIV Infection Attending Three Clinics in the Southeastern United States," *Journal of Spirituality and Mental Health* 10 (2008): 145–168. This study sample of 226 men

living in the southeast U.S. was followed up for two years.

11. Hughes M. Helm et al., "Does Private Religious Activity Prolong Survival? A Six-Year Follow-up Study of 3,851 Older Adults," *Journal of Gerontology: Medical Sciences* 55A (2000): 400–405. This project was strong in that it included a large sample (3,851), was longitudinal (six years), and had a good response rate (80 percent). Participants were older adults (sixty-five and older) who lived in five contiguous counties of North Carolina (Durham, Granville, Vance, Warren, and Franklin). They were asked about their private religious activities (Bible study, prayer, and meditation), public religious activities, impaired daily activities, and their lifetime history of chronic conditions: cancer, stroke, heart attack, diabetes, hip fractures, other fractures, angina pectoris, bronchitis, cardiac glycoside use, and antihypertensive use. They were also given a short mental status questionnaire, two blood pressure measurements, a depression measure, and a negative life events inventory. The six-year follow-up consisted of a yearly telephone interview.

12. A majority of researchers have adopted the use of a single variable called private religious activity or nonorganized religious activity (NORA) as well as public religious activity or organized religious activity (ORA). This makes it difficult for us to always isolate "Bible reading or study" *per se*, as many studies cluster Bible reading and study with prayer and private devotion.

13. Leslie J. Francis, "The Relationship Between Bible Reading and Purpose in Life Among 13-15-year-olds," *Mental Health, Religion & Culture* 3 (2000): 27–36.

14. Kelly A. Davis and Catherine C. Epkins, "So Private Religious Practices Moderate the Relation Between Family Conflict and Preadolescents' Depression and Anxiety Symptoms?" *Journal of Early Adolescence* 29 (2009): 693–717. The participants in this study were 160 preadolescents (seventy-five boys and eighty-five girls) and their mothers. They were recruited via oral presentations in sports events, educational programs, and other community gatherings. They were contacted via phone to set individual meetings with one of the investigators or a research assistant. The meeting was to explain the project and to administer the instruments.

15. William H. Jeynes, "The Relationship Between Bible Literacy and Academic Achievement and School Behavior," *Education and Urban Society* 41 (2009): 419–436.

16. Liz Smith, "The Bible Makes Me Feel Stronger," American Bible Society Record, accessed May 28, 2013, http://record.americanbible.org/content/usa /%E2%80%98-bible -makes-me-feel-stronger%E2%80%99.

17. Ellen G. White, *Christ's Object Lessons* (Washington, DC: Review and Herald®, 1941), 131, 132.

18. Ellen G. White, *Child Guidance* (Washington, DC: Review and Herald®, 1954), 41, 42.

19. Ellen G. White, *Steps to Christ* (Mountain View, CA: Pacific Press®, 1893), 90.

20. See the CognitiveGenesis study at http://www.cognitivegenesis.org.

21. White, *Child Guidance,* 42, 43.

22. Ellen G. White, *Testimonies for the Church* (Mountain View, CA: Pacific Press®, 1948), 3:374.

23. Ellen G. White, *Review and Herald,* November 10, 1905, 7, para. 5.

24. Ellen G. White, *Testimonies for the Church* (Mountain View, CA: Pacific Press®, 1948), 6:393.

25. Ellen G. White, *Steps to Christ,* 88.

26. Ellen G. White, "Science and Revelation," *Signs of the Times,* March 13, 1884, 1, para. 3.

Chapter 3

The Benefits of Forgiveness

"Then I acknowledged my sin to you. . . . And you forgave the guilt of my sin."
—Psalm 32:5, NIV

*A*fter having completed graduate studies at Andrews University, Pastor Ruimar DePaiva, his wife, and his two children moved to the island of Palau. He served as the pastor of a large Seventh-day Adventist church there and also coordinated mission work on the island. They were originally from Brazil and had become United States citizens a few years before.

Many people on the island loved this family. They were kind to everyone, and they always welcomed anyone to visit their home. Student missionaries working as teachers at the local Seventh-day Adventist secondary school took the DePaivas as their adoptive family and were planning to spend Christmas Eve at their house during the 2003 holiday season. But the event never took place because on December 22, a nighttime robber entered their house and killed Ruimar, his wife, and their eleven-year-old son. He assaulted their ten-year-old daughter, took her in his car, and threw her down a ravine.

In a relatively small community and with the description offered by the young victim, the assassin was located and arrested immediately as he was trying to commit suicide. His name was Justin Hirosi, and he had been taking drugs prior to the murder. Soon after the tragedy, Pastor DePaiva's parents arrived to attend the funeral and take their granddaughter back to America to decide about her future. During the following days, Pastor DePaiva's mother met the man who killed her son, her daughter-in-law, and her only grandson. Her behavior was absolutely unprecedented. This woman, torn apart by grief, talked lovingly with Justin and prayed with him. Then she told him that she had already forgiven him. Justin wept.

On the day of the funeral, Mrs. DePaiva, having learned that the perpetrator's mother was at the funeral, took the microphone and invited her to come close. Ruimar's mother embraced her dearly. Then she said, "Both mothers are grieving for their lost sons." She delivered a little speech appealing to the Palauan community not to hold grudges against Justin's family and assuring them that her family does not blame their family and that no one else should either. She said that both mothers tried to educate their children and teach them right from wrong and that this is all mothers can do.

This kind of attitude caused the high chief of the island to praise the generosity of the victims' family and express shame, regret, and sorrow on behalf of Justin's family. He also announced that Justin's family and clan, although very limited in resources, had sold their possessions and gave the DePaiva family ten thousand dollars toward the young girl's college education. The entire island population was forever changed through the forgiving attitude shown by Mrs. DePaiva.

Commenting about the positive changes in the community, a local villager said that the DePaiva family had done "more good after their death than before!" John P. Rutledge, legal counsel for the Koror state government was at the funeral. His words portray the magnitude of his experience: "I'm now a proud member of the DePaiva clan, and we do things a little differently. Love and forgiveness, that's what it's about. It's taken me 31 years and one hell of a tragedy to learn that. But . . . can you hear me Ruimar? I've finally got it . . . we've finally got it through our thick heads."[1]

The value of forgiveness

Forgiveness is, perhaps, the single most studied moral quality from the psychological perspective. Guilt, oftentimes resulting from unforgiveness, is a monumental barrier to mental health and psychological well-being. This is the reason why professionals have felt the need to study forgiveness and how it relates to, depends upon, and causes a variety of events and experiences. As we will see in this chapter, apart from the extraordinary spiritual blessings of granting forgiveness to offenders, research shows that people who extend and are prone to receive forgiveness are physically and mentally healthier than those who do not.

Receiving forgiveness (from God and from those who have offended us) and extending forgiveness to others are experiences of high psychological value. Forgiveness is such a central theme in the Bible because it is a necessary healing experience in our sin-scarred lives.

There are two kinds of messages about forgiveness in the Bible: (1) those showing the necessity of seeking forgiveness from a loving God who has provided the channels to eliminate guilt and attain moral cleansing, and (2) those encouraging people to forgive each other. Both processes are essential, and the second is a condition to the first: God's forgiveness is not viable without having extended forgiveness to others (Matthew 5:24; 6:14, 15; Mark 11:25; Luke 6:37). This is not a capricious condition. It is clear that, in order to obtain God's forgiveness, one needs to repent and abandon all sin, even if one will sin again in the future. But not forgiving an offender is like praying, "Father, forgive all my sins, except my grudge against so-and-so." Full forgiveness simply cannot happen. It is not that God does not wish to forgive; it is that the person is not willing to give up a state of immorality.

The importance and urgency of reconciliation (which carries forgiveness implicitly) is portrayed in Jesus' sermon on the mount: "Therefore, if you are offering your gift at the altar and there remember that your brother or sister has something against you, leave your gift there in front of the altar. First go and be reconciled to them; then come and offer your gift" (Matthew 5:23, 24, NIV).

The theme of forgiveness runs through both Testaments. Before his death, Jacob left a message for Joseph to forgive his brothers (Genesis 50:17). Saul asked Samuel to forgive him for not having followed his instruction (1 Samuel 15:24, 25). Abigail asked David to forgive her for her presumption (1 Samuel 25:28). When people please God, He "causes their enemies to make peace with them" (Proverbs 16:7, NIV).

But it is in the New Testament when the emphasis on forgiveness becomes strongest. Jesus found a culture where human forgiveness was not considered a virtue, and hatred was sometimes encouraged: "You have heard that it was said, 'Love your neighbor and *hate your enemy*' " (Matthew 5:43, NIV; emphasis added). Through His example and precept, Jesus does not leave any doubt about the virtue of forgiveness: "Lord, how many times shall I forgive . . . ?" And Jesus replied, "I tell you, not seven times, but seventy-seven times" (Matthew 18:21, 22, NIV).

But forgiveness is not understood in the same way across religions. Buddhism's foundational concepts are forbearance and compassion. Forgiveness is not necessarily a part of that, although Buddhists who are willing to forgive may also be quite willing to reconcile. Islam values and encourages forgiveness, but it is a prerogative of the victim to grant it. Judaism also values and encourages forgiveness but does not consider it desirable to grant forgiveness to offenders who do not acknowledge the injury. Comparatively, Christians hold a very high standard (Matthew 6:12; 18:22; Mark 11:25; Luke 23:34), although it is unclear that Christian people forgive more than do non-Christian or nonreligious people.

A tool for healing

The power of forgiveness has been rediscovered, and it has received a great deal of attention in the last two decades. Psychologists, counselors, and social workers have noticed that a major portion of cases seeking psychotherapy are related to interpersonal problems: marital conflict, offenses, crises at work or with friends, litigation, and so on. They have also realized that forgiveness lies at the foundation of relationships and that not forgiving is detrimental to human interactions and to mental and physical health.

As a result, many psychotherapists are using forgiveness as a tool for healing, a process built into their therapy to free people from certain burdens. A number of therapeutic procedures or models are now in place. One widely accepted protocol used by many clinicians is the model proposed by Dr. Robert Enright, a professor of educational psychology at the University of Wisconsin–Madison and pioneer in the scientific study of forgiveness.[2] It is based on the assumption that forgiveness does not happen instantly but requires time and involves steps. It also assumes that, even though many clients understand that they should forgive (because it is a religious mandate or because it is the moral thing to do), they do not know how to proceed. The model consists of four phases.

1. Uncovering. Clients are helped to understand how the offense is causing pain and anger toward the offender. This may be the time to learn thought-stopping techniques and the organization of daily routines that will help manage such anger. The counselor and counselee discuss the effects of the injury, not only on oneself, but on other closely related individuals (e.g., family and dear ones) who may feel the effects of anger, animosity, and other adverse emotions. The Christian counselor, in alliance with a Christian client, may suggest meditation on Bible promises as well as God's power to help in the understanding and on the path to forgiveness. Jesus' words, such as, "Whenever you stand praying, if you have anything against anyone, forgive him" (Mark 11:25), or "Love your enemies and pray for those who persecute you, that you may be children of your Father in heaven" (Matthew 5:44, 45, NIV), can be used to set up goals.

2. Decision. The counselor teaches the client the benefits of forgiveness, both physical and mental, as well as the dangers of not forgiving. The first goal is deciding to abandon resentment and drop any degree of hatred. The most important goal is to decide to forgive the offender. Depending on the degree of damage and the client's personality, this process can go quickly or excruciatingly slow. Some will take days or weeks to reach these goals; others may need months or years. The person of faith should understand that it may be humanly impossible to forgive certain egregious offenses and that the Divine Power must be called upon to intervene in a supernatural manner, according to the promise: "And I will give them one heart, and I will put a new spirit within you; and I will take the stony heart out of their flesh, and will give them a heart of flesh" (Ezekiel 11:19, KJV).

3. Work. The main goal of the third phase is to arrive at forgiveness. Much of the time is spent discussing the transgressor's life circumstances that may have led to the offense. The purpose is not to justify wrongdoing but to gain an understanding that helps differentiate between the person and the deed. When the transgression can be seen in context (e.g., the offender may have used drugs, been affected by a mental disorder, or have been the victim of abuse in early life), the client may be able to separate the person from the misdeed, empathize with the transgressor, and grant forgiveness. A Christian therapist may make reference to biblical accounts, such as Jesus praying to the Father: "Father, forgive them, for they do not know what they do" (Luke 23:34), in order to indicate that a great offense may be carried out by someone who does not comprehend the magnitude of the pain or effect incurred. This may be the time when the client offers a moral gift to the offender, for instance, communicating (orally or in writing) forgiveness to him or her.

4. Deepening. Clients at this level work on the challenging task of finding meaning in the suffering produced by the process. This tends to be easier for the person of faith, particularly a Christian who understands that there is a role for pain and suffering. Jesus did not guarantee a pain-free life to His followers, although He left an authentic peace with them (John 14:27). A consequent goal is to realize that, after the offense-pain-forgiveness experience, life can take a new turn and have a better purpose than before.

After having granted full forgiveness, people experience emotional and psychological healing, liberation from the burden of the past, more love and trust, and less anger and hostility. They also sleep better, perform better at work, and in the long run, prevent physical and mental illness. Above all, the path to forgiveness pleases God and takes people increasingly closer to the kingdom.

With the exception of highly complex situations, or in cases of very resistant persons, there is no need to follow a systematic model guided by a professional therapist. It is sufficient to understand a few useful principles. For example, forgiving does not mean that the person who hurt you is right or that you are condoning the acts of the offender; instead, you are letting go of your anger, frustration, and bitterness. You are following the Master's advice, generously and altruistically loving your enemy, whether or not reconciliation is possible. Mark Twain once said, "Forgiveness is the fragrance the violet sheds on the heel that has crushed it." Another principle is that forgiveness is not about changing the past but about the present and the future; because, when you forgive, you are transforming your own attitude and freeing yourself from the burden that prevents you from functioning well. Corrie ten Boom wrote, "Forgiveness is to set a prisoner free, and to realize the prisoner was you."

It is also important to remember that true forgiveness comes only through God's influence. It is not in the sinful nature of human beings to take insult, humiliation, slander, disdain, and mockery and to then lovingly think and say, "I forgive you." The same Jesus who invited His people to turn the other cheek, can "grant you, according to the riches of His glory, to be strengthened with might by His Spirit in the inner man" (Ephesians 3:16). But it is your responsibility to do your part while allowing God to act. Your part is to work on dispelling feelings of anger and hatred. This is best done while understanding that adverse feelings come from thoughts. Therefore, harbor thoughts that don't leave room for the adverse ones. When thoughts of anger and bitterness arise, some people say "Stop!" and occupy their minds with some pleasant memory; others sing aloud; others go for a run; others call a friend. An excellent way to vary adverse thoughts and feelings is to thank God for how far you have gotten and commit yourself to continue in the path of forgiveness with His help.

Lastly, forgiveness can be a blessing to a repenting perpetrator. It can help complete God's forgiveness and attain moral cleanliness.

General health and well-being

Quite a number of studies conducted in various locations with an array of participants have set a trend: health and well-being go together with the practice of forgiveness. And when forgiveness decreases, health also decreases. Kathleen Lawler and her team from the University of Tennessee at Knoxville conducted a well-designed and reliable study on forgiveness and health.[3] They gathered extensive data on forgiveness, health, social skills, spirituality, affect, and stress. Much of the health data was based on physiological measures such as blood pressure, heart rate, mean arterial pressure, and rate-pressure product. To ensure that the demographic variables were not intervening, researchers verified that scores on the forgiveness measures were unrelated to gender, cigarette smoking, age, height, weight, ethnicity, or marital status. Their correlations between forgiveness and health measures include thirty-eight statistically significant results. These are some of the most relevant:

- *Sleep quality and forgiveness.* The higher the tendency to forgive, the better the sleep. It makes sense to think that those who practice forgiveness enjoy a peaceful conscience and are able to enjoy a more uninterrupted and restorative sleep.
- *Revenge and medication.* Participants' data yielded a significantly high correlation between these two variables. Specifically, the higher the desire to

seek revenge, the higher the number of medications used in the past month.

- *Avoidance and medication.* There was also a strong correlation between these two variables, meaning that high levels of avoidance of the transgressor were found together with high numbers of medications taken over the past month.
- *Avoidance and physical symptoms of illness.* This correlation indicates that those with a high determination to avoid their offender exhibited a high number of symptoms of illness; likewise, those with low levels of avoidance had a fewer number of pathological symptoms.
- *Fatigue and forgiveness.* This was a negative correlation indicating that, as the tendency to forgive went up, the intensity and frequency of fatigue went down. Likewise, resistance to forgiveness was accompanied by high fatigue.
- *Medication and forgiveness.* This was also a negative correlation. The higher the willingness to forgiveness, the lower the number of medications used in the past month.
- *Revenge and sleep quality.* These two items were also significantly correlated, also in an inverse manner: The higher the levels of revenge feelings, the poorer the quality of sleep.

Findings seem consistent across various ages. For example, college students have participated in a number of studies like that of Tobi Wilson and colleagues.[4] Wilson's investigation was done at a university in Ontario, Canada. Students were administered a forgiveness scale to assess forgiveness toward others and toward themselves as well as a subjective appraisal of their physical health. The correlational analysis showed that those reporting greater forgiveness of others tended to have a more positive health status. This was consistent with what previous studies had found. Lastly, the study results indicated that the health status was linked to not only forgiveness of others but also to forgiveness of themselves.

A similar design by Jon Webb and Ken Brewer obtained consistent results with a sample of college students from southern Appalachia who were problematic drinkers.[5] After having removed the effect of all demographic variables (including religiosity), they confirmed that forgiveness (and especially self-forgiveness) played a major role in their health. It is interesting to find similar results with quite different samples—ordinary students and students with drinking problems. It is also interesting that both benefited the most when they forgave themselves.

However, the idea of self-forgiveness as understood in most professional literature does not fit biblical teachings on forgiveness. Self-forgiveness is understood like this: *I hurt or offend someone, or I commit a great mistake that results in pain to others and to me. As a result, I feel the burden of guilt and my thoughts and behaviors are deeply affected. Those I hurt may forgive me, but I still feel the burden: I am not forgiving myself! I must self-forgive!* But God's forgiveness is left out of the equation. The professional literature tends to place too much emphasis on me forgiving myself when, in reality, it is God who has to forgive me, so that I am cleansed morally and I do not experience shame and guilt anymore.

In addition to young participants seen in the previous studies, other age ranges have been found to benefit from forgiveness. Dealing with forgiveness is one task that deeply affects people involved in automobile accidents: forgiveness of the other party, if the person in the other car is perceived as the offender, or forgiveness of self, if one is deemed responsible for the accident. A team of researchers from East Tennessee University, Luther College, and the University of Michigan studied a sample of individuals with spinal cord injury to find the connection between forgiveness and health.[6] Participants had either quadriplegic (48 percent) or paraplegic (52 percent) spinal cord injuries as a result of motor vehicle accidents and violence. After controlling for demographic variables, forgiveness of self was significantly associated with health behavior and life satisfaction; and forgiveness of the other party was significantly associated with overall general health. In all cases, the higher the presence of forgiveness, the higher the levels of health and satisfaction.

Studies with elderly individuals tell us that they also experience the benefits of forgiveness. This was the case with a study conducted by Berit Ingersoll-Dayton, from the University of Michigan–Ann Arbor, and her associates.[7] They gathered a small group of twenty elderly women and men to provide them with psychological help and support and then to observe the results. Participants had to have been emotionally hurt by someone, had something to forgive, not be psychiatrically vulnerable, and be sixty years of age or older. They had them participating in eight weekly sessions with a four-month follow-up session in order to teach them about the benefits of forgiveness and to teach them how to forgive following Enright's steps (see above). Offenders were a parent, a spouse, a child, a relative, a friend, or other. Participants were asked to keep a journal with notes and questions about their processes of developing compassion for and forgiveness toward those who had been hurtful. By comparison of pre- and post-tests (before and after the eight weeks of seminars), they not only confirmed that their ability to forgive had been enhanced in all areas of forgiveness (affective, behavioral, cognitive, and general) but their health score also had risen significantly and, where present, depressive symptoms had been reduced during the training period.

The quality of forgiveness is so important that it might be the most relevant element of the entire religiosity factor affecting health. This was the major finding of Kathleen Lawler-Row's research.[8] Her report entitled "Forgiveness as a Mediator of the Religiosity-Health Relationship" includes three studies with the participation of 938 middle-age and older adults. In all three investigations, forgiveness appeared as a partial or full mediator of the religion-health relationship. This means that the effect of religion upon health is significantly attenuated or eliminated when the forgiveness mediator is added to the model. None of the other religion variables (frequency of attendance, frequency of prayer, and belief in a watchful God) had as much weight on health in these studies as did forgiveness.

Chronic fatigue and fibromyalgia

Loren Toussaint from Luther College in Decorah, Iowa, together with his colleagues from the Mayo Clinic and Stanford University, reviewed the medical literature on fibromyalgia and chronic fatigue syndrome as well as the psychological studies on forgiveness, in order to develop a model to mitigate the symptoms of these disorders.[9] Fibromyalgia is a chronic syndrome of generalized pain that affects at least three body quadrants as well as eleven or more standard tender points. Chronic fatigue syndrome is characterized by ongoing (lasting six months or more) debilitating and unexplained fatigue that does not improve with rest.

Because fibromyalgia and chronic fatigue are known to produce anger, frustration, stress, fear, and resentment, which in turn cause higher levels of pain, weakness, and a lower quality of life, and because research points out the salubrious effects of forgiveness upon general health and specifically on anger, stress, and other negative emotional consequences, it is proposed that the use of forgiveness as a coping strategy will compensate for the negative emotions accompanying fibromyalgia and chronic fatigue and mitigate their painful symptoms.

In reading studies like this, I cannot but think of David's statements:

> Blessed is he whose transgression is forgiven. . . .
> When I kept silent [or when I did not confess my sin and therefore did not obtain forgiveness], *my bones grew old*
> Through my groaning all the day long (Psalm 32:1, 3; emphasis added).

> Have mercy on me, LORD, *for I am faint;*
> heal me, LORD, *for my bones are in agony* (Psalm 6:2, NIV;
> emphasis added).

Although we cannot know whether this is a figure of speech or rheumatic pain, we can certainly relate to the great trouble of not obtaining forgiveness. It is true that David's agony comes from the sense of not being forgiven and most studies focus on the problems of not granting forgiveness. Either case seems strong and painful enough to do something about the situation.

Cardiac conditions

Forgiveness may even benefit cardiac conditions. Several studies found that forgiving individuals (whether hypertensive or normal) experience significantly higher reductions in blood pressure levels than those not committed to forgive. A later study went a step further to assess the forgiveness connection in hospitalized patients with diagnosed cardiac conditions.

Jennifer Friedberg and her team from the New York University School of Medicine gathered data from eighty-five hospitalized coronary artery disease (CAD) patients to observe the relationship between forgiveness, psychological well-being, and physiological indices.[10] The researchers obtained various measures of forgiveness, stress, anxiety, depression, and physiological data on total cholesterol, high-density lipoprotein (HDL or "good" cholesterol) and low-density lipoprotein (LDL or "bad" cholesterol). Higher levels of forgiveness were associated not only with lower levels of anxiety, depression, and stress but also with a lower total cholesterol to HDL ratio as well as a lower LDL to HDL ratio. This was true even after controlling for age and gender.

Mental health

Not forgiving is an adverse mental state that produces stress. Forgiveness is a logical and adaptive way to deal with it; to grant forgiveness, to forgive the offender, even when in human terms, the victim is right and the offender is responsible for the damage. But many people do not find this step to be easy, so they attempt to reduce their distress in a variety of ways. Some attempt to take revenge, to get even, or to take "an eye for an eye." Others seek justice and may appeal to an external source of authority to restore what is right. Others develop a new narrative about the transgression ("It should have been done differently," or "A much better way is . . ."). Some deny what happened, some avoid it, some become defensive, and some remain forever victims.

Alternatives that avoid forgiveness do not go without a toll. Maybe that is the reason for the warning: "Do not say, 'I'll pay you back for this wrong!' Wait for the LORD, and he will avenge you" (Proverbs 20:22, NIV). Likewise, one of the purposes of the following message may be to preserve the mental health of Jesus' followers: "Do not take revenge, my dear friends, but leave room for God's wrath, for it is written: 'It is mine to avenge; I will repay,' says the Lord. On the contrary: 'If your enemy is hungry, feed him; if he is thirsty, give him something to drink. In doing this, you will heap burning coals on his head' " (Romans 12:19, 20, NIV).

While forgiveness is not granted, stress is experienced to a greater or lesser extent. Everett Worthington and Michael Scherer consider the lack of forgiveness a stress reaction to a transgression; in contrast, they see forgiveness as a coping strategy that can reduce health risks and promote health resilience.[11] In their analysis of research, they refer to studies that use functional MRI technology, blood analyses, and salivary cortisol measurement to show the following:

- Not forgiving is correlated with anger, and anger inhibits cognitive activity in the prefrontal cortex and increases limbic-system activity—which is the nucleus of stress.
- Hormonal changes, namely cortisol variations, occur when participants think of the lack of the forgiveness toward their partners, as observed in a study with participants that had recently ended a romantic relationship.
- There are significant changes in sympathetic nervous-system activity (evidenced by facial tension, heart rate, mean arterial pressure, and skin conductance) when participants imagine the transgression or the person against whom they hold a grudge.
- Blood chemistry is very similar when not forgiving or when facing stress and/or other negative emotions.
- When experiencing a favorable disposition to forgive, people reduce their chances of blood viscosity (a risky physiological activity) and increase toxicity-preventive activities in their blood.
- Forgiveness reduces the stress of not forgiving as it is associated with lower blood pressure.

All of the above presume the mental-health benefits of an ongoing forgiving attitude (forgiveness trait), and they also reveal the benefits of the willingness to forgive a single offense (forgiveness state). In the previously mentioned study by Jennifer Friedberg and her colleagues, the cardiac patients' forgiveness scale scores could reliably predict their levels of stress and anxiety.

Sonia Suchday, from Yeshiva University in New York, studied a sample of 188 college students from Mumbai, India, and reported similar findings.[12] Participants here were local students at a college affiliated with the University of Bombay. Thirty-five percent were Christians and the rest were Hindu, Jain, Muslim, Parsi, and Buddhist. In spite of this diversity, forgiveness made a significant difference to their mental health. Results indicate that lower levels of forgiveness were associated with high rumination and high stress, although this study did not find a connection between forgiveness and physical health. Studies like these talk about the universality of the effects of forgiveness across cultures and religions.

Charlotte Witvliet and colleagues provided additional support on the effects of forgiveness on emotion, physiology, and health.[13] Their study design was focused on one group that imagined granting forgiveness and another that mentally rehearsed hurtful memories and grudges. Participants were asked to think of a specific offender in a real-life situation and spend time rehearsing the corresponding theme. The "forgiving" participants showed significantly higher improvements in cardiovascular measures (heart rate, blood pressure) and in sympathetic nervous system functioning (skin conductance, corrugator electromyogram) than did the "nonforgiving" participants. Findings of this nature remind us of how powerful our thoughts are and how simple imagination of right or wrong puts various physiological mechanisms to work that enhance healthy or unhealthy organic reactions. When a lack of forgiveness, resentment, grudges, and so on, are rehearsed over and over again, a habit is created and illness may take over.

Gayle Reed and Robert Enright, from the University of Wisconsin–Madison, observed the effects of forgiveness therapy on depression, anxiety, and post-traumatic stress disorder (PTSD) in women after they had suffered emotional abuse from their husbands.[14] Women reported a variety of the following: criticizing, ridiculing, jealous controlling, purposeful ignoring, threats of abandonment, threats of personal harm, threats of harm to property or pets, and ridicule or threats followed by demands for sexual favors. These women had been separated for two or more years. They were randomly assigned either to a therapy group where forgiveness (FG) was the central focus of training or to an alternative therapy group (AG) where anger validation, assertiveness, and interpersonal skills were the topics of focus. Therapy in both groups was one hour weekly for eight months. The FG therapy women experienced significantly greater improvement not only in depression, anxiety, and PTSD but also in self-esteem, environmental mastery, and the ability to find meaning in suffering. This study demonstrated that forgiveness treatment plays a central role in the prevention and reduction of the typical psychological sequels of abuse.

In another study dealing with post-divorce adjustment, Mark Rye, from the University of Dayton, and his colleagues found forgiveness to be a beneficial variable in recovery.[15] The participants were 199 women and men who attended one of twenty-five community organizations for divorced individuals in several midwestern cities in the United States. They reported that their ex-spouses committed wrongdoings including infidelity, verbal abuse, emotional abuse, wrongdoing to children, lying, physical abuse, false accusations, unfair distribution of assets, use of drugs or alcohol, and other bad acts. They were asked their degree of forgiveness to their ex-spouses: *already forgiven, trying to forgive, not trying to forgive, did not know if they will choose to forgive, no intention of forgiving.* Several questionnaires were administered on demographics, religiousness, hope, depression, anger, spiritual well-being, and two forgiveness scales. After statistically removing the effect of demographic variables, forgiveness of their ex-spouses was positively correlated with well-being (including religious well-being), and negatively correlated with depression and anger. The results were predictable: the more forgiveness, the less depression and anger. Results point to the mental-health benefits that come from forgiving an ex-spouse.

Interestingly, this study made a differentiation between forgiveness that develops into letting go of negative thoughts, feelings, and behaviors toward an ex-spouse and forgiveness that develops into a positive response toward an ex-spouse. With this particular data, the health benefits were clearer for the first type of forgiveness than they were for the second. The authors recognize that the second type of forgiveness might have other benefits. However, their data may be encouraging for those who want "to forgive, but who believe that it is unrealistic for them to respond positively toward their ex-spouse."[16]

Forgiveness training has helped people manage their own emotions, control anger better, and manage their stress successfully. This is the essence of the Stanford University study led by Alex H. S. Harris.[17] Two hundred and fifty-nine adult participants (ages twenty-five to fifty) who had experienced an interpersonal affront were randomly assigned either to a six-month forgiveness training seminar or a no training control group. Those in the forgiveness group were taught to cultivate a more relaxed state of mind, to reduce the arousal to anger when overtaken by unpleasant memories of the offense, to reduce physiological unrest from the thoughts and emotions of not forgiving, and, in sum, to gain control of their own emotions and learn about the application of both general and specific forgiveness. Participants in the forgiveness training exhibited significantly greater degrees of forgiveness toward their transgressors, attained more positive emotions toward any offenses, experienced higher degrees of recovery, were more inclined to forgive beyond their target offense in the study, and improved significantly in the areas of stress and anger.

Forgiveness is definitely a decisive factor in all areas of mental health. The adverse emotions that the lack of forgiveness produces cannot remain alive for too long without affecting our sanity. But there is more than sanity; Jesus Christ of Nazareth made it very plain through His life and words that without forgiveness there is no divine forgiveness, and without divine forgiveness there are eternal consequences.

Substance-use disorders

Forgiveness has also been found to have salutary effects on the mental health of a special population: those with alcohol problems. Jon Webb, from East Tennessee State University, and Elizabeth Robinson and Kirk Brower, from the University of Michigan, conducted a follow-up study with 157 adults recruited from a community-based substance-abuse treatment center located in southeastern Michigan.[18] They were given several measures of forgiveness and mental health. The study lasted six months. After data analysis, dozens of significant correlations between forgiveness and specific indicators of mental health were found. Specifically, high forgiveness scores were linked to low levels of depression, anxiety, somatization, obsessive compulsion, hostility, phobia, paranoid ideation, and psychoticism. The majority of these significant correlations remained true after six months, indicating that forgiveness can be a good predictor of mental health among those who struggle with substance abuse.

Relationships

It seems natural that a forgiving attitude toward others' mistakes and offenses should bring about an enhanced quality of relationship. And this has been confirmed by research. Two examples follow: one dealing with adolescent-parent relationships, the other with married and dating relationships.

Loren Toussaint and Kimberly Jorgensen, from Luther College in Decorah, Iowa, and the University of North Dakota respectively, recruited 260 college students who identified themselves as Christians and who completed a number of questionnaires on interparental conflict, parent-child relationship quality, and mental health and well-being.[19] Like several other studies before, there were associations between forgiveness and mental health and well-being. But in addition, a parent-child relationship enhancement was observed: higher forgiveness levels as a trait (ongoing, stable, consistent tendency to forgive) were associated

3—T.B.O.B.

with lower interparental conflict and with a higher parent-child relationship quality. Forgiveness as a state (willingness to forgive a particular offense committed by a father or mother) was even more substantially correlated with the quality of the relationship with the respective parent. This finding emphasizes the role of forgiveness in the quality of family relations. Children and adolescents can be taught that their parents' offenses, as well as their own offenses toward their parents, can be forgiven. This enhances not only the physical health of everyone in the family, but it also makes the relationship much stronger.

In the area of marital relationships, Peggy Hannon, from the University of Washington, and colleagues, from the University of Vrije, Amsterdam, and the University of London, published a paper based on three studies, one with married couples as participants.[20] Researchers asked couples to identify an unresolved "betrayal" or a "rule-breaking" incident.[21] Then each of the seventy-five married couples discussed the matter, and trained observers video-recorded and rated the discussion. The analysis of the recordings showed that a perpetrator making amends promoted a victim's forgiveness and that a victim's forgiveness promoted a perpetrator making amends. Both hypotheses were confirmed and the study concluded that an interaction-based analysis of issues is more likely to bring forgiveness. When both partners are able to enact constructive behaviors following the betrayal and to plan for the next steps in their interaction, they are likely to reap the rewards of an enhanced relationship. In sum, it is much easier to forgive when the perpetrator makes amends and the next steps are discussed together.

Even when the perpetrator is not always willing to make amends, forgiveness can take place. This was the experience of Fred Luskin.[22] Fred grew up with a dear friend named Sam. They were like brothers—the brother Fred never had. And that continued for years until Sam met a young lady in college who did not like Sam being friends with Fred. Through her persistent influence, she made Sam ignore and even reject Fred. They married and did not even inform Fred of their marriage. Fred did not take this easily and experienced pain for years. He carried this burden, and it became increasingly worse after his own wedding. The situation became burdensome enough that he describes it in this way: "Holding on to resentment is like drinking poison and expecting the other person to die. That was me." One day his wife said to him, "Fred, I love you, but I don't like the person you've become."

This was a turning point in his life, and he began to study the topic of forgiveness, as he was a psychology graduate student. In his extensive study, he became convinced that he had to forgive Sam, and so he let go of his anger toward him. His trouble with Sam, in his own words, seemed more like a blessing. He is now Dr. Fred Luskin, director of the Stanford University Forgiveness Project, and his work consists of coordinating research on forgiveness and helping people forgive and overcome resentment, an example being men and women from both sides of the violence in Northern Ireland. He has helped organizations and trained lawyers, doctors, church leaders, congregations, hospital staff, teachers, and other professionals to enhance forgiveness. His own experience was crucial in the choice and development of his work.

Conclusion

Forgiveness is becoming a new form of medicine. Medical and psychological research is finding that forgiveness, a central theme in Christianity, is a highly efficacious factor in health, both physical and mental. A recent review of literature on forgiveness by Barbara Elliott, from the University of Minnesota Medical School, concludes that forgiveness intervention will become a powerful tool in the arsenal for personal and public health.[23] This seems particularly true with the treatment of chronic illnesses with etiologies in interpersonal and societal past experiences: addictions, mental-health circumstances, obesity, chronic obstructive pulmonary disease (COPD), chronic bronchitis and emphysema, and cirrhosis. How exactly do these apparently unrelated camps connect? According to Elliott, etiologies are very complex and many diseases are confounded with early life events, such as physical, emotional, and sexual abuse; or with growing up in a household where someone was in prison; the mother was treated violently; a family member was an alcoholic or drug user; someone was chronically depressed, mentally ill, or suicidal; or one of the parents was lost to the patient during childhood.

When past experiences cause mental and physical illness, and when certain individuals intentionally or unintentionally inflicted long-lasting pain, forgiveness becomes a necessity for physical, mental, and spiritual healing. It is not wise to resist forgiveness and to keep blaming the past and others (albeit wholly responsible) for our troubles of today. And remote experiences are not only at the root of problems. Current relational problems with a spouse, children, parents, relatives, friends, neighbors, supervisors, employees, brothers and sisters in the church, civil authorities, and so on, necessitate forgiveness. Sometimes it is easy to forgive, but other times offenses can touch the innermost sensitive points of one's soul, and then forgiveness does not come so easily. Only the Lord can make the difference, "for it is God who works in you both *to will* and *to do* for His good pleasure" (Philippians 2:13, NIV; emphasis added). It is definitely pleasing to God that we grant true forgiveness to others, and He promises to place within our hearts the *will* to forgive as well as the *act* of granting forgiveness.

Study Questions

- Find passages in the New Testament that say if you don't forgive, the Father will not forgive you either. Why is the forgive-then-be-forgiven principle necessary?
- There is a sin that has no forgiveness (Matthew 12:30–32). What is this sin and what does it mean? Read *Testimonies for the Church,* volume 5, page 634, to learn what Ellen G. White said to a brother who asked her whether he had committed the sin that has no forgiveness.
- Read the parable of the prodigal son (Luke 15:11–31). What are some evidences of the father's extremely generous forgiveness? How is the son transformed by his father's forgiveness?

Application Thoughts

- Is forgiveness a mental state or a series of actions? Or is it both? Reflect on Colossians 3:13.
- Forgiveness is interpreted differently by different religious traditions. How can you show a Muslim or a Jew that the Christian understanding is more complete?
- Jesus said, "If your brother or sister sins against you, rebuke them; and if they repent, forgive them" (Luke 17:3, NIV). What would you do if they don't repent? Jesus then added, "Even if they sin against you seven times in a day and seven times come back to you saying 'I repent,' you must forgive them" (verse 4, NIV). What is the principle behind this passage?

---

1. "Murder and Forgiveness," Squidoo, accessed May 28, 2013, http://www.squidoo.com/murder.

2. Robert Enright and Catherine T. Coyle, "Researching the Process Model of Forgiveness With Psychological Interventions," in *Dimensions of Forgiveness: Psychological Research and Theological Perspectives,* ed. Everett L. Worthington Jr. (London, England: Templeton Foundation, 1998), 139–161.

3. Kathleen A. Lawler et al., "The Unique Effects of Forgiveness on Health: An Exploration of Pathways," *Journal of Behavioral Medicine* 28 (2005): 157–167. They assessed by multiple means eighty-one adults with a mean age of 42.6 years.

4. Tobi Wilson et al., "Physical Health Status in Relation to Self-Forgiveness and Other-Forgiveness in Healthy College Students," *Journal of Health Psychology* 13 (2008): 798–803. The study included 266 undergraduate students, 81 percent female.

5. Jon R. Webb and Ken Brewer, "Forgiveness, Health, and Problematic Drinking Among College Students in Southern Appalachia," *Journal of Health Psychology* 15 (2010): 1257–1266.

6. Jon R. Webb et al., "Forgiveness and Health-Related Outcomes Among People With Spinal

Cord Injury," *Disability and Rehabilitation* 32 (2010): 360–366. The study assessed 140 people ages nineteen through eighty-two.

7. Berit Ingersoll-Dayton et al., "Enhancing Forgiveness: A Group Intervention for the Elderly," *Journal of Gerontological Social Work* 52 (2009): 2–16.

8. Kathleen A. Lawler-Row, "Forgiveness as a Mediator of the Religiosity-Health Relationship," *Psychology of Religion and Spirituality* 2 (2010): 1–16.

9. Loren Toussaint et al., "Implications of Forgiveness Enhancement in Patients With Fibromyalgia and Chronic Fatigue Syndrome," *Journal of Health and Care Chaplaincy* 16 (2010): 123–139.

10. Jennifer P. Friedberg et al., "Relationship Between Forgiveness and Psychological and Physiological Indices in Cardiac Patients," *International Journal of Behavioral Medicine* 16 (2009): 205–211. There were fifty-six male and twenty-nine female coronary patients.

11. Everett L. Worthington Jr. and Michael Scherer, "Forgiveness Is an Emotion-Focused Copying Strategy That Can Reduce Health Risks and Promote Health Resilience: Theory, Review, and Hypotheses," *Psychology and Health* 19 (2004): 385–405. The study involved ninety-two males and ninety-six females.

12. Sonia Suchday et al., "Forgiveness and Rumination: A Cross-cultural Perspective Comparing India and the US," *Stress and Health* 22 (2006): 81–89.

13. Charlotte V. Witvliet et al., "Granting Forgiveness or Harboring Grudges: Implications for Emotion, Physiology, and Health," *Psychological Science* 12 (2001): 117–123. Participants included thirty-six male and thirty-five female psychology students.

14. Gayle L. Reed and Robert D. Enright, "The Effects of Forgiveness Therapy on Depression, Anxiety, and Posttraumatic Stress for Women After Spousal Emotional Abuse," *Journal of Consulting and Clinical Psychology* 74 (2006): 920–929. The group was composed of twenty abused women between thirty-two and fifty-four years of age.

15. Mark S. Rye et al., "Forgiveness of an Ex-spouse: How Does It Relate to Mental Health Following a Divorce?" *Journal of Divorce and Remarriage* 41 (2004): 31–51. Participants included 199 women (75 percent) and men (25 percent).

16. Ibid., 48.

17. Alex H. S. Harris et al., "Effects of a Group Forgiveness Intervention on Forgiveness, Perceived Stress, and Trait-Anger," *Journal of Clinical Psychology* 62 (2006): 715–733.

18. Jon R. Webb et al., "Forgiveness and Alcohol Problems Among People Entering Substance Abuse Treatment," *Journal of Addictive Disease* 25 (2006): 55–67.

19. Loren Toussaint and Kimberly Jorgensen, "Inter-parental Conflict, Parent-Child Relationship Quality, and Adjustment in Christian Adolescents: Forgiveness as a Mediating Variable," *Journal of Psychology and Christianity* 27 (2008): 337–346. Study participants were 73.5 percent women and 26.5 percent men.

20. Peggy A. Hannon, "In the Wake of Betrayal: Amends, Forgiveness, and the Resolution of Betrayal," *Personal Relationships* 17 (2010): 253–278.

21. The word *betrayal* was not used in the instructions because it connotes infidelity. Instead, these incidents were described as "breaking the rules," such as telling a friend something that should have remained private, doing something hurtful behind one's back, or flirting with another person.

22. Fred Luskin, "The Power of Forgiveness: Forgiveness 101," *Guideposts,* November 2011, 62–66.

23. Barbara A. Elliott, "Forgiveness Therapy: A Clinical Intervention for Chronic Disease," *Journal of Religion and Health* 50 (2011): 240–247.

Chapter 4

The Benefits of Commitment

"My son, pay attention to what I say; turn your ear to my words."
—Proverbs 4:20, NIV

*M*y friend Francesc Gelabert was in prison for fourteen months in Madrid for refusing to kneel down before the holy host at his boot camp's closing Mass. This was in 1974–1975. For four decades after the Spanish Civil War (1936–1939), there was no religious freedom in Spain. Being a non-Roman Catholic was illegal and followers of other faiths encountered problems. For example, attending public school required a Roman Catholic baptismal certificate; a small group meeting together for a Bible study could be taken to the police station for interrogation; and someone distributing books without the Roman Catholic *imprimatur* could be arrested. Seventh-day Adventists were particularly exposed because of Sabbath keeping: they had to deal with examinations on Sabbath; most jobs became unavailable because of the Sabbath; and the compulsory military service that often conflicted with their faith.

My friend was a man of courageous and noble qualities and determined to be faithful to his religious convictions. Being a few years my elder, Francesc was my role model of a loyal Seventh-day Adventist Christian of contemporary times. He was incarcerated immediately after his refusal and accused of a crime of disobedience of the military authority. He was deprived of all his books (including a Roman Catholic Bible) and placed in a cell where visitation was very restricted. His fiancée was not allowed to see him for two months after her first attempt. The Seventh-day Adventist Church religious liberty department attempted to mediate but without success. After eight months of pretrial jail, a court-martial sentenced Francesc to three years of military prison and, after serving his term, to complete the rest of his service in a disciplinary battalion.

It was hard to take, but he found refuge in prayer, his Bible, and his God. Many times he repeated to himself the promise he memorized as a child in

Sabbath School: "And we know that all things work together for good to those who love God, to those who are the called according to His purpose" (Romans 8:28). He also later found another text that became especially dear to him: "For I reckon that the sufferings of this present time are not worthy to be compared with the glory which shall be revealed in us" (verse 18, KJV). It was not without temptation that he went through these hard times. He often felt guilty of bringing unnecessary pain to his family, friends, and church, and especially to his mother and fiancée. He also felt defeated because of the taunts, mockery, loneliness, and mistrust he experienced.

Through some high-level negotiations of the Adventist Church and his wife (he married his fiancée in the midst of his sentence), a very frail General Franco signed his pardon on May 23, 1975, exactly six months before Franco's death. After fourteen months of jail, Francesc was set free only to be forced into his pending thirteen months of military service. Fortunately, this time his religious principles were respected and he was discharged on June 12, 1976.[1]

One could ask, Was it worth it to refuse to kneel for ten seconds at the closing Mass? For him, it was well worth it. I recently talked to him, and he told me, "Although I would not recommend prison to anyone, I can see the enriching aspects of my experience today."[2] He told me that he learned more about politics, sociology, economics, and religion in prison than out of it. "Behind bars, I learned patience, the virtue I lacked the most. I also learned that there are people with a heart even among those prisoners and military chiefs. But above all, my faith grew and was confirmed. At that time, I called it a 'victory' and I still consider it a victory today . . . not a Pyrrhic victory but a decisive and solid one that brought me closer to God, made me a better and happier Christian, and led me to live the blessed hope more intensely."

Being loyal and obedient to God is not always easy; it may even bring unpleasant consequences in the short run. But the Lord is faithful in His promise: "Obey me, and I will be your God and you will be my people. Walk in obedience to all I command you, that it may go well with you" (Jeremiah 7:23, NIV). At times, one can see this in perspective only after years of waiting to see what the Lord means by "it may go well with you."

This chapter is about the benefits of being faithful and obedient to God and of living by the principles that a person of faith has decided to adopt. The professional literature calls this concept "religious commitment" and it is defined as "the degree to which a person uses and adheres to his or her religious values, beliefs, and practices and uses them in daily living."[3] Individuals committed to their religious principles and ideals not only internalize the doctrines and teachings of their religion but also abide by the rules and codes of conduct that go with them. Commitment goes beyond the attendance of services to more proactive actions—faith becomes central to their lives and is ever present in all aspects of existence.

That experience is rewarding in itself: a pleasant sensation of having done what one believes to be right. But the consequences go beyond that warm feeling; the Lord is generous and promises a more lasting blessing: "Keep his decrees and commands, which I am giving you today, so that it may go well with you and your children after you and that you may live long in the land the Lord your God gives you for all time" (Deuteronomy 4:40, NIV). Research today confirms the benefits of faithfulness—benefits that have to do with trouble-free behavior, better relationships, better mental and physical health, and longer life.

A blessing to young people

Reading current research on the effects of religious commitment, I found several areas where it pays to be committed to your beliefs; but the most repeatedly studied were the blessings of religious commitment for young people. Research shows that youth who do not just attend church but adhere to their beliefs and put them into practice perform better academically, don't get into risky behaviors, end up marrying rather than cohabiting, and have a balanced attitude toward life issues.

William Jeynes, from California State University–Long Beach, studied data from the U.S. Department of Education's National Education Longitudinal Survey on 18,726 twelfth-graders.[4] He asked the question, Do religiously devout teenagers perform better academically than their less religious counterparts? He found that twelfth-graders who are highly committed to their faith scored, by and large, significantly higher than their less committed counterparts. As the data included students both in public and private, religious and secular schools, the following question was asked: Are these results explained by the fact that very religious teens are more likely to attend private religious schools with a higher academic expectation? The results remained constant across all types of schools. Within gender, racial, and socioeconomic status subgroups, he found again, a robust association between high religious dedication and high academic achievement.

Beau Abar from Pennsylvania State University studied a sample of college students, thirty men and fifty-five women, randomly selected from Oakwood University in Alabama.[5] Ninety-three percent were African American and 86 percent Seventh-day Adventists. Results show that students with a high level of deep-seated religiosity had a higher GPA, fewer risk behaviors, better academic self-regulation, and better study skills than their counterparts. Those with a firm commitment to their religious beliefs tended to be more competent in their study skills and were able to attain a better academic performance.

But the findings about risky behaviors have more transcendental effects. According to the behavior index used, participants were asked about their frequency of smoking marijuana and other drug use, including alcohol and tobacco. Also included were behavior problems such as lying, fighting, skipping classes, and bigger issues such as stealing, shoplifting and damaging property. Those committed to their religious beliefs acted out in these behaviors the least.

Jessica Burris and other researchers from the University of Kentucky found similar results at a public university with a Caucasian majority (89 percent).[6] She studied a total of 344 eighteen- to twenty-year-olds. Students adhering to statements such as, "My religious beliefs lie behind my whole approach to life," "I enjoy working in the activities of my religious organization," or "Religion is especially important to me because it answers many questions about the meaning of life" were the least likely to use alcohol. The sample group consisted of mostly alcohol users: 73 percent reported having had an alcoholic drink at least once a month, and half of them said they drink at least one to two times each week, while most had two to three drinks per occasion. As many as 59 percent said they get drunk once a month, with 37 percent of these getting drunk about once a week. It is comforting to know that students standing firm for their religious convictions were in the opposite extreme.

Byron Johnson and his team from the University of Pennsylvania performed a nationwide study that found a distinction between devoutly religious adolescents who attend church out of their own convictions and those who attended church out of an obligation.[7] This was done to see whether the connection between religious commitment and delinquency is spurious. The study also intended to see whether the link was direct or via other nonreligious variables. Being committed to a religion, they found, was a safeguard against delinquency. And this was true for both "minor" (damage to property, lying about age, buying liquor for a minor) and "major" crimes (stealing a motor vehicle, stealing objects of more than fifty dollars, aggravated assault, gang fights, sexual assault, armed attack, or breaking into a building or vehicle).

A different study explored the effect that religious commitment has on the formation of a family in terms of marriage versus cohabitation. David Eggebeen and Jeffrey Dew, from Pennsylvania State University and the University of Virginia, respectively, studied a national sample of 13,895 adolescents and followed up to see how religious fervor affected the choice of cohabitation or marriage.[8] They found that the stronger the religious fervor, the higher the probability of marriage and the lower the chance of cohabiting. Further, they observed two kinds of cohabitation: (1) those entering into it as a form of advanced courtship with the intention to marry later, and (2) a cohabiting union where individuals indicated they have no desire to marry.

A comparison between conservative Protestants and conservative Catholics showed that the latter were the least likely to cohabitate. However, once Catholics were in a cohabiting state, they were less likely to end up in marriage than were conservative Protestants, demonstrating that Protestants had a concept type 1 and Catholics a concept type 2 idea of cohabitation.

Another study explored a different issue related to family: attitudes toward having a child out of wedlock. William Jeynes used the two sets of data from the U.S. Department of Education's National Education Longitudinal Survey of about twenty thousand students each.[9] He drew from across the whole nation. One of Jeynes's goals was to find out how twelfth-graders felt about having a child outside of marriage. The results were very clear: most religiously devout teens, in comparison with their less religious counterparts, were opposed to having a child out of wedlock and considered it very important to be married before being a parent. While it is sensible to assume that very religious people would not approve of having children outside of marriage, the important lesson to learn is that this attitude comes from being religiously committed. Too often adults teach adolescents that religion is completely irrelevant, that religion is something of the past, when, in actuality, religion could help fix many social problems. William Jeynes states that "adolescent religious involvement should be encouraged rather than discouraged," and he also recommends that psychologists, social workers and counselors work together with clergy to attempt to solve this issue and prevent childbirth outside of marriage.

Religion and religious commitment do make a difference in the lives of young people. Even those who grow up in a completely secular environment may benefit from a glimpse of Jesus' presence in their lives. Doug Brown, the associate pastor of my church, ran a ministry for local public high-school students. With the assistance of ministerial students from Walla Walla University, Pastor Brown invited these kids to participate in various activities and to discuss current issues and spiritual matters. Many came from nonreligious families, had never prayed or attended church, and believed that Jesus was a good man who lived many years ago. Although the students were hesitant at first, they started to build trust as the weeks went by. They began to show interest in Bible stories and characters and came to the leaders to seek out counseling and even prayer. One of the ministerial trainees told of his experience: "I prayed with [a student], and blessed him and after I finished I looked at him to see if he might be interested in praying as well. And he looks at me and says 'OK, here goes,

I've never done this before!' What a blessing to be a part of helping unchurched, uninterested, unmotivated youth start to get a taste of hunger after God!"

As important as being religious is to young people, how does it happen? How can the adult world be more successful in instilling these values so that the next generation may adopt them and receive the blessings promised by God? Emily Layton and two other researchers, all from Brigham Young University, led a qualitative study.[10] She interviewed eighty religiously diverse adolescents from families in northern California and New England. They were between ten and twenty-one years of age, with a medium age of fifteen. Studies like these allow kids the freedom to express themselves rather than answering Yes or No questions or other similar close-ended questions.

This method is called intensive interviewing; it consists of a list of open-ended questions that do not force the interviewee to select pre-established responses. For example, "Does your religion guide your life? How? What challenges arise from being a religious family in the surrounding culture?" and so on. This study made a great attempt to listen to a broad array of denominations and included six Baptist, ten Catholic, one Christian and Missionary Alliance, three Christian Scientist, two Congregationalist, three Episcopal, two Jehovah's Witness, sixteen Jewish (Conservative, Modern Orthodox, Reform, and Ultra Orthodox), eleven Latter-day Saint, three Lutheran, two Methodist, seven Muslim, five Orthodox Christian, one Pentecostal, three Presbyterian, and five Seventh-day Adventist members. The interviewer was always the same, David C. Dollahite, one of the authors of the study. He went personally to each home and used twenty-six open-ended questions to guide the conversation. Often follow-up questions were used to clarify responses. No less than one hour was spent in each interview. The analysis of the massive content brought about the following themes the authors call "Anchors of Commitment":

1. Commitment to religious traditions. Traditions and rituals may just be shadows of the more meaningful things of religion, but youth seem to appreciate them very much. Jewish young people brought their positive statements about Sukkot, Hanukkah, Purim, and Pesach; Christians talked about such routines as church attendance and how special it was that everyone in the family got together and went to church. An eighteen-year-old Seventh-day Adventist young man even referred to a Feast of Tabernacles in his church in which everyone participated. He was sorry that those things were not done more often.

2. Commitment to God. God was seen as the Source of authority, Someone who is near and with whom we can have a personal relationship. Some referred to God like "a friend," but also as Someone toward whom you have responsibility.

3. Commitment to faith tradition or denomination. For all these young people, religious life was not possible without an organization. They found a personal identity in their faith tradition, and together with this identity came a sense of faithfulness to the particular affiliation.

4. Commitment to other members of the denomination. The young informants enjoyed a sense of community, a sense of belonging, and a strong feeling of family where they could find personal support. They saw strength in the possibility of sharing communion with other believers. And they appreciated the intergenerational relationship.

5. Commitment to parents. These young believers displayed a very firm anchor of commitment to their parents. They saw with affection parents as a source of religious authority. Trusting, respecting, and honoring parents were the primary forms of positive expression. A fourteen-year-old Latter-day Saint male explained why he doesn't drink alcoholic beverages: "Because my parents taught me not to do that and I respect them."

6. Commitment to Scripture or sacred texts. They often referred to the Bible, or their corresponding sacred writings, as a source of authority and truth. An eighteen-year-old Baptist young woman said, "I just remember sitting in English class last year, and we were discussing a lot of things; and I just remember sitting there thinking how confused I'd be on this earth if I didn't have the Bible and God's standard and morality to live by."

7. Commitment to religious leaders. The informants referred to ministers, rabbis, youth leaders, bishops, and so on as sources of spiritual authority. They followed these authorities because of their prominent positions, although this understanding was noticeably more common for younger than for older youth.

Because of reports like this, and informal observations of religious congregations, we see an obvious sense of community that is fundamental to promoting religious faithfulness in youth. The findings of another study, this time on a smaller scale, confirm that commitment is attained through community. Mervyn Wighting and Jing Liu from Regent University in Virginia, and Northfield Mount Hermon School in Massachusetts, conducted the study respectively.[11] Data was gathered at a small Christian high school in southeastern Virginia from eleventh- and twelfth-graders. These students demonstrated how a group mentality helped with their religious commitment. The findings show that a faithfulness to religious principles was very closely tied to a sense of school community, both academically and socially. The strength of this link was high for all participants but highest for females. It is as if it were virtually impossible for young people to gain a firm foundation in their religion without the presence and support of other young people who also walk with Jesus. Consequently, the authors of the study suggest multiple activities to enhance the sense of community—the ideal environment to promote adherence and devotion to religion—activities such as mission trips, opportunities to help with Vacation Bible Schools, participation in community services, spiritual retreats, group Bible studies, Bible classes, debates on controversial topics, preaching, special guest speakers, and prayer groups.

It is certainly good news that young people who are committed to their religious and moral ideals are blessed in a variety of ways, many of eternal consequence. As Ellen White puts it: "By the fireside and at the family board, influences are exerted whose results are as enduring as eternity. More than any natural endowment, the habits established in early years decide whether a man will be victorious or vanquished in the battle of life."[12]

Marital success

The marriage scandals of public religious figures are popular in the headlines today. "Unchristian Witness: Pro-Life Congressman Asks Mistress to Abort Their Child" (referring to Rep. Scott DesJarlais, a renowned Christian Right U.S. congressman, doctor, and defender of family values). Or "Dinesh D'Souza Caught in Cheating Scandal" (referring to best-selling author, filmmaker, and Christian college president Dinesh D'Souza who delivered a speech at a religious conference and, instead of taking his wife, went with a young woman and introduced her as his fiancée). Or "TV Evangelist Benny Hinn Caught in Torrid Affair: Fling With Fellow Preacher Rocks Christian Community" (referring to an alleged affair that the famous pastor had with televangelist Paula White).

Are these cases representative of the general population? Do they reflect the lives of the majority of people of faith that entered the marriage covenant with the blessing of a church? Most likely not! These are the "juicy" vignettes that people seem to enjoy reading, but these accounts do not explain the true role of sacred married life. When one looks at data coming from large numbers of ordinary people scattered over the nation, one must conclude that religion, by and large, is a blessing to married couples. True, it does not guarantee happiness and does not render immunity against divorce, but it works better than the absence of faith in a home.

Annette Mahoney, a professor at Bowling Green State University, and colleagues have carried out a great deal of research showing that religious married adults are more likely to stay married over time and have high levels of marital satisfaction and commitment than their nonreligious counterparts.[13] In addition, individuals who are religious tend to have better marital outcomes than nonreligious people.

To mention an example from a qualitative, in-depth study, I'll outline the findings of Nathaniel Lambert and David Dollahite from Florida State University and Brigham Young University respectively.[14] These researchers recruited fifty-seven husband-and-wife couples from Jewish, Muslim, and Christian communities, including Seventh-day Adventists, with a mean age of forty-eight (men) and forty-five years (women). They carried out intensive one-hour interviewing, couple by couple, asking them questions about their religiosity and covenant making in their marriage. After analyzing and coding all those hours of recorded accounts, a core concept clearly appeared: *including God in marriage enhanced and stabilized marital commitment.* Further, the analysis identified three major themes. Religious beliefs and practices helped couples to do the following:

1. Have God in their marriage. They believed that God was present from the beginning of their relationship, bringing them together. They saw their wedding vows as a covenant that united each to the other and also united them to God. These vows were remembered periodically after their marriage ceremony. Several said that God was an ongoing Partner in their marriage, and several others said that God was the center of their marriage.

2. See marriage as a religious entity designed to last. Couples had a clear perception that the institution of marriage can and should be permanent. Many referred to the statement in Matthew 19:6: "Wherefore they are no more twain, but one flesh. What therefore God hath joined together, let not man put asunder" (KJV). Having made a decision not to divorce seemed to give couples an increased motivation to work through their problems. Also, knowing that God disapproves of divorce served as an incentive for them to avoid it.

3. Find meaning in their marriage. Religiosity helped these participant couples to find meaning in their marriage in that they saw their union not as an unpleasant obligation for life, but rather a powerful, sacred calling. Being committed to each other in a religious manner helped them cope with arising difficulties and misfortunes.

These spiritual concepts of marriage may be incomprehensible to the contemporary secular human—"they are foolishness unto him" (1 Corinthians 2:14) but make a great deal of sense to someone imbued with the biblical concept of marriage, all of which leads to a higher chance of remaining happily married.

The process, however, is not of human design. Says the preacher,

If two lie down together, they will keep warm.
   But how can one keep warm alone?
Though one may be overpowered,
   two can defend themselves.
A cord of three strands is not quickly broken
   (Ecclesiastes 4:11, 12, NIV; emphasis added).

The second half of Ecclesiastes 4 is devoted to the positive aspects of relation-ships. The togetherness of two can cause a great deal of emotional support, protection, and mutual satisfaction. But the final sentence of verse 12 brings an abrupt element to the pair: "A cord of three strands is not quickly broken." Although many see this as a statement about the strength that can be attained by adding more human resources to any project, I like the interpretation given by many pastors at wedding ceremonies: couples may choose to allow Jesus (the Third Strand) in their marriage to bring in abundant blessings to married life and to prevent the rope from breaking.

Faithfulness to their religion instills in couples a sense of union that gives them increased incentives to work out difficulties together and to include God and His principles in the process. Belonging to a church also helps, especially if the organization strongly discourages divorce. On the contrary, nonreligious couples have a much higher chance of cohabiting, and when they marry, a higher risk of divorce than do their religious equivalents.

Motivation to forgive

We have already looked at forgiveness, but it comes into play in this context as well. The question of why people do not forgive has attracted the attention of many experts who, being aware of the importance of forgiveness in interper-sonal relationships, intend to remove those obstacles. Mary Beth Covert and Judith Johnson from Regent University, on the other hand, wanted to find answers to the question of why people *do* forgive, and they found out that the majority of forgivers were *loyal to their religious principles*.[15] They drew a sample of ninety-seven individuals from a mid-Atlantic Christian university commu-nity. They used a Web survey to answer the following questions:

1. Briefly describe a hurtful situation within the past five years where you were hurt or injured by another person.
2. Did this person intentionally hurt you in a vengeful way or for purposes of revenge?
3. Were you motivated to forgive the person?

4. Describe your motivation to forgive. What were the reasons behind your motivation?

These data in the form of a semistructured self-report permitted both qualitative as well as quantitative analyses, adding both objectivity and depth to the results. The results show that the most common offenses were hurtful words or actions, betrayal, rejection, lack of support, blame, lies, and abuse. The most common perpetrators were friends, partners, colleagues, and mothers. When those willing to forgive were asked for their motivation to forgive and the reasons behind it, the number one reason was "religious," which was present in 43 percent of the responses. The next reasons were "relational" (30 percent), "desire for well-being" (29 percent), "feelings of sorrow for" (21 percent), "unintentional offense" (16 percent), "self-blame" (16 percent), "moral reasons" (12 percent), and a few others of insignificant size. It is interesting to note that religion played a role that was even superior to moral reasons.

Nathaniel Wade and his team from Iowa State University found that Christian college students extended more forgiveness than did their non-Christian counterparts.[16] They also confirmed the dangers of rumination about offenses. The observed sample was made up of 249 college students, 90 percent of which were single, 50 percent Protestant, 20 percent Catholic, and the rest were Hindu, Muslim, Jewish, Buddhist, other, and nonreligious. The study focused on rumination about offenses and particularly the offender. Rumination is the compulsive rehearsal of a past unpleasant memory, and it is a trait that contributes to depression. Rumination about offenses has been found to transform into bitterness, vengefulness, and grudges. It is also a known fact that the more one ruminates, the less likely one is to forgive. In this study, results showed that Christians endured rumination significantly less than non-Christians. Furthermore, participants who displayed religious commitment were more likely over time to change feelings of revenge into neutral sentiments and into forgiveness than did those, even religious participants, without such commitment.

Dr. Aaron Beck, the founder of cognitive-behavioral therapy, tells that early in his psychiatric career, wanting to test psychoanalytic claims in his interviews with depressive patients, he found the issue was really their thinking style—they exhibited patterns of negative thoughts about themselves, about the surrounding world, and about the future. Working on changing those thought patterns was the path to changing their behaviors, and that is how cognitive therapy began. The principle might be very useful for Christians, for temptation works similarly. Ruminating, for example, on how nasty my old friend was to me and the recurring rehearsal of our incident definitely takes me far from forgiveness.

But if I develop the good habit of catching myself early enough in the process of rumination and direct my thoughts to a topic of distraction, better yet, to a moment of prayer, begging God to take my thought away from that path, I will have gone closer to forgiveness and reconciliation.

I was about five when I began to fathom the importance of thought. As a Catholic boy, I was taught to make the sign of the cross following a series of three small crosses with my right thumb—one small cross on my forehead, one small cross on my lips, and one small cross on my chest. As I was told, the sign on the forehead was to protect me from bad thoughts, the sign on the lips from bad words, and the sign on the chest from bad acts. I still remember my silent reflection on the ritual: *Not only being naughty, but planning to be naughty is no good!* The Bible also points out the close-knit connection between thinking and doing and being: "For as he thinketh in his heart, so is he" (Proverbs 23:7, KJV).

Health and longevity

Guinness World Records recognized Gertrude Baines (1894–2009) in 2009 as the world's oldest person. She was born and grew up in Shellman, Georgia, lived in Connecticut, Ohio, and eventually in California. She lived on her own until 1999 when she was 105, and then resided at the Western Convalescent Home in Jefferson Park, Los Angeles, until her death. At 112, she was interviewed by a CNN correspondent and she was asked to explain why she thought she had lived so long. She replied, "God. Ask Him. I took good care of myself, the way He wanted me to."

The Seventh-day Adventist health message is another example of God's intervention in health and longevity—this one affecting millions of individuals. It goes back to when Ellen G. White received the first comprehensive health-reform vision on June 6, 1863. Since then, abiding by a few simple health principles has brought much health and well-being to many. As it could be expected in the nineteenth century, ideas of a diet based on plant food, abstemiousness, and the attention to pure air, cleanliness, adequate clothing, sunshine, and exercise as the means of attaining health were generally rejected. But, by and large, people following those principles have been greatly blessed with longer and healthier lives.

Today, there is enough evidence to show that those simple concepts were correct. The Loma Linda University School of Public Health Web page lists, up to the summer of 2012, 335 scientific studies indexed in Medline,[17] plus another seventy-two that are indexed elsewhere, mostly because of their international location. All are scientific publications from Adventist Health Studies as well as about Adventists from other studies from around the world. The large majority of these reports reveal an advantage in the physical and mental health of Adventists over other groups.

The Adventist Health Study (later known as the Adventist Mortality Study) began in 1958 and included 22,940 Adventist participants residing in California.[18] The project was hosted at Loma Linda University and consisted of an intense five-year follow-up plus an informal twenty-five-year follow-up. Results were compared with data from a similar study done with the general population by the American Cancer Society (ACS). Both samples were similar in demographic characteristics. Public health experts cautioned them to look closely at the levels of education, because educated people tend to have better health compared to those who are less educated, but in this particular comparison the ACS participants had a slightly higher level of education than did the Adventists. Results showed that cancer mortality was consistently less frequent in Adventists than it was in ACS participants. In some types of cancers, the difference was vast, and it favored Adventists especially in lung and colorectal cancers (most likely due to lifestyle); and the differences became less notable when comparing data on breast, prostate, lymphoma or leukemia cancers, where lifestyle has a lesser role.

Deaths due to other causes (such as coronary heart disease and stroke) were also compared. Again, Adventists were at an advantage. Because smoking is not part of the Adventist lifestyle, it could be argued that the differences are really attributable to tobacco use; but when researchers compared the mortality rates of nonsmokers from both populations, it was clear that, although the difference narrowed, Adventists still enjoyed a lesser mortality rate.

Subsequent phases of the Adventist Health Study continue to confirm these differences and offer greater lifestyle choices linked to the prevention of specific types of cancer. For example, consuming fruit regularly was found as highly protective against lung cancer and stomach cancer; eating legumes, vegetarian meat products, dates, raisins, or other dried fruits was protective against pancreatic and colon cancers; eating beef doubled the risk of contracting bladder cancer; dried fruits, tomatoes, and beans diminished the risk of prostate cancer. No dietary factor was found associated with breast cancer.

Being vegetarian is a highly protective factor, not just because of the diet, but because vegetarians tend to perform additional healthy behaviors that nonvegetarians do not. For instance, vegetarians tend to be less obese, drink less coffee, and exercise more frequently than do nonvegetarians. Many Adventists are vegetarian, and being Adventist poses comparison difficulties (according to some researchers) because Adventist populations are so unique that certain pieces of data cannot be compared to non-Adventist populations. In other words, being a Seventh-day Adventist Christian is far, far more than following a list of dos and don'ts. It entails a whole package of beliefs, behaviors, and attitudes so that it is hard to single out the differentiating factors. That is why those interested in health look at the ultimate test: longevity.

Perhaps the strongest, most solid evidence on the topic of death rates and longevity of a population of Adventists is the study conducted by Gary Fraser and David Shavlik, which was published by the American Medical Association's prestigious Archives of Internal Medicine.[19] They followed up with 34,192 Seventh-day Adventists from California between 1976 and 1988, the partcipants' ages being between 30 and 104 years. Comparisons were made with non-Adventist residents of California. All participants completed a detailed lifestyle questionnaire, including medical history, diet, physical activity, and a number of psychosocial variables. They were contacted yearly thereafter, and the study obtained current data and clinical information when any of the participants were hospitalized.

Deaths were also recorded and compared to the control age groups. Results show that Seventh-day Adventists had a higher level of survival than did the non-Adventist control group, namely, an additional 7.3 years for men and 4.4 years for women. This data refers to the entire population. When the subgroup of Adventist vegetarians (defined as eating meat "never or less than once a month") was studied alone, two more years of life expectancy were added to men, and three more to women. When the researchers analyzed other variables, they noticed that the life expectancy varied. For example, those vegetarians who exercised three or more times a week, ate nuts five or more times a week, and never smoked had a life expectancy of 10.8 years higher (men) and 9.8 years higher (women) than the average Californian. For that reason, the study was named "Ten Years of Live: Is It a Matter of Choice?"

The above results must tell us something about the confirmation of the divine promise: "If you listen carefully to the LORD your God and do what is right in his eyes, if you pay attention to his commands and keep all his decrees, I will not bring on you any of the diseases I brought on the Egyptians, for I am the LORD, who heals you" (Exodus 15:26, NIV). Today, for a conscientious seeker, adhering to the best health behaviors proven by science may be a matter of logic, but we must remember that some of the participants in Fraser and Shavlik's study were born in the nineteenth century and most in the first half of the twentieth century, when there was no conclusive scientific data about diet, smoking, sunshine, exercise, attitude, religiosity, and other elements of the proposed Adventist total health strategies. The majority of participants in the study followed those principles by faith, in the understanding that God entrusted a young and frail woman with a health message for the benefit of His people, regardless of what medical science said at the time. Although it is good to have our principles confirmed by external, objective, and scientific tools, oftentimes reasons to obey God may not be available, and so we cannot simply wait until proof comes.

There are other sources, outside Adventist populations, which also show extended life spans for people committed to religious beliefs and who want to obey the Lord. One example is the data from the cohort initiated in 1921 by Stanford University psychologist Lewis Terman. I recall my days as a psychology student at the University of Madrid in the 1970s. I was aware of this group of highly intelligent children that were studied along various stages of their lives; they were beginning to retire when I was earning my degree. Various reports were released over the years about their professional achievements, family life, adjustment, health, and so on, but what I didn't imagine is that connections between their religiosity and longevity would become available in the twenty-first century. This is what Howard Friedman, a health psychologist and professor of psychology at the University of California–Riverside, and Leslie Martin, professor of psychology at La Sierra University, have done in their book *The Longevity Project*.[20]

The book tells the story of the research, which tracked the life of some fifteen hundred Americans who were children when invited by Terman to participate in this historic lifelong study. Recently, Friedman and Martin studied the data accumulated over the decades and interacted with a few of the participants still living. They reviewed information about variables such as personality, ability to adjust, family life, professional paths, social life, and there was also information about their religious beliefs and practices. These individuals, approaching one hundred years of age, had remarkable traits such as persistence, sociability, or resilience. But a large proportion had also a firm commitment to their religious principles. This was particularly true in women who seemed especially strong in social skills. They had led busy and balanced lives, were deeply religious, and had been active in church environments. On the other hand, the least religious women were less likely to reach advanced ages. They were intelligent, active, and productive but did not manage to remain married and to have children as often as those women faithful to their religious beliefs. They were less extroverted and less trusting than were the religious women. The researchers' explanation for these differences was that factors associated with longevity are part of religious involvement: fellowship, family life, connection between young and old, mutual support, and trust.

Conclusion

After searching for quite a long time, Farmer Hassell found a young man who seemed to be the best farmhand available. Hassell seemed puzzled by something the applicant said with a big smile, "I can sleep when the wind blows!" But the young fellow got the job anyway. Days later, a strong windstorm woke up Mr. and Mrs. Hassell. As it was of unusual strength, they checked various points on the property to ensure that the wind would not cause damage. They found the farmhouse shutters well fastened, the porch clear, the shed securely fastened with all the tools inside, the barn properly locked, and the animals in place with sufficient food. When they checked the young man's room, they found him soundly asleep. Then they understood the words "I can sleep when the wind blows." Their helper had understood early in his life that he did not need to do anything spectacular and out of the ordinary—just do his job faithfully and loyally in a consistent manner, and he could rest in peace even when the wind blew.

The Bible contains promises for the obedient and the faithful. They can be sources of encouragement:

- "A faithful person will be richly blessed" (Proverbs 28:20, NIV).
- "Let love and faithfulness never leave you; bind them around your neck, write them on the tablet of your heart. Then you will win favor and a good name in the sight of God and man" (Proverbs 3:3, 4, NIV).
- "Obey me, and I will be your God and you will be my people. Walk in obedience to all I command you, that it may go well with you" (Jeremiah 7:23, NIV).

In this chapter we have reviewed specific blessings from being faithful, loyal, and committed to the Lord. The list of benefits presented here was limited because the blessings of obedience to God are beyond counting. But still, more important are the blessings of eternal consequence that are promised to the faithful: "Be faithful until death, and I will give you the crown of life" (Revelation 2:10).

Study Questions

- Read the story of Hezekiah in 2 Kings 18–20. We are told that he "trusted in the LORD, the God of Israel. There was no one like him among all the kings of Judah, either before him or after him" and that "he held fast to the LORD and did not stop following him; he kept the commands the LORD had given Moses" (2 Kings 18:5, 6, NIV). Yet he had to endure a good share of problems and faced a serious illness. How do you reconcile this apparent inconsistency? What would you say to a friend who, having been faithful to God, experiences misfortune?

• Read Jeremiah 35 about the faithfulness of the Rekabites. Not being from the chosen people, they were nevertheless used by God as a teaching lesson to Judah. Think of what you can learn from other groups of people, even unbelievers, from their loyalty, faithfulness, and coherence to their chosen ideals.

• Use your concordance to find texts that mention "obedience" and "faithfulness." What is similar and what is different between God's faithfulness and man's faithfulness? What can you learn about the results of following the Lord's commands?

Application Thoughts

• Can you think of times in your past experience when obedience brought about blessings? Was the blessing obvious at the time or did it become clearer once time had elapsed? What lessons can you learn about not seeing things clearly at present?

• As it is so crucial for young people to find support in their church communities in order to remain faithful, what can you do to help your local congregation's youth?

• How can you use the experiences and blessings of your commitment to God in order to witness to others?

---

1. Francesc X. Gelabert, "439 días de prisión," *Revista Adventista,* July 1976, 6, 7.

2. F. X. Gelabert, personal communication with the author, October 10, 2012.

3. Everett Worthington et al., "The Religious Commitment Inventory-10: Development, Refinement, and Validation of a Brief Scale for Research and Counseling," *Journal of Counseling Psychology* 50 (2003): 84–96.

4. William H. Jeynes, "The Effects of Religious Commitment on the Academic Achievement of Urban and Other Children," *Education and Urban Society* 36 (2003): 44–62.

5. Beau Abar et al., "The Effects of Maternal Parenting Style and Religious Commitment on Self-Regulation, Academic Achievement, and Risk Behavior Among African-American Parochial College Students," *Journal of Adolescence* 32 (2009): 259–273.

6. Jessica L. Burris et al., "A Test of Religious Commitment and Spiritual Transcendence as Independent Predictors of Underage Alcohol Use and Alcohol-Related Problems," *Psychology of*

Religion and Spirituality 3 (2011): 231–240. The study included 344 eighteen- to twenty-year-olds with a 40/60 male to female ratio.

7. Byron R. Johnson, "Does Adolescent Religious Commitment Matter? A Reexamination of the Effects of Religiosity on Delinquency," *Journal of Research in Crime and Delinquency* 38 (2001): 22–44.

8. David Eggebeen and Jeffrey Dew, "The Role of Religion in Adolescence for Family Formation in Young Adulthood," *Journal of Marriage and Family* 71 (2009): 108–121.

9. William H. Jeynes, "The Effects of Religious Commitment on the Attitudes and Behavior of Teens Regarding Premarital Childbirth," *Journal of Health and Social Policy* 17 (2003): 1–17.

10. Emily Layton et al., "Anchors of Religious Commitment in Adolescents," *Journal of Adolescent Research* 26 (2010): 381–413. The study included forty-one females and thirty-one males.

11. Mervyn J. Wighting and Jing Liu, "Relationships Between Sense of School Community and Sense of Religious Commitment Among Christian High School Students," *Journal of Research on Christian Education* 18 (2009): 56–68.

12. Ellen G. White, *Mind, Character, and Personality* (Nashville, Tenn.: Southern Publishing Association, 1977), 1:134.

13. Annette Mahoney, "Religion in Families, 1999–2009: A Relational Spirituality Framework," *Journal of Marriage and Family* 72 (2010): 805–827. Annette Mahoney et al., "Religion and the Sanctification of Family Relationships," *Review of Religious Research* 44 (2003): 220–236. Annette Mahoney et al., "Religion in the Home in the 1980s and 1990s: A Meta-analytic Review and Conceptual Analysis of Links Between Religion, Marriage, and Parenting," *Journal of Family Psychology* 15 (2001): 559–596.

14. Nathaniel M. Lambert and David C. Dollahite, "The Threefold Cord—Marital Commitment in Religious Couples," *Journal of Family Issues* 29 (2008): 592–614.

15. Mary Beth Covert and Judith L. Johnson, "A Narrative Exploration of Motivation to Forgive and the Related Correlate of Religious Commitment," *Journal of Psychology and Christianity* 28 (2009): 57–65. The study group sample included ninety-seven individuals, about thirty men and seventy women.

16. Nathaniel G. Wade et al., "Predicting Forgiveness for and Interpersonal Offense Before and After Treatment: The Role of Religious Commitment, Religious Affiliation, and Trait Forgiveness," *Journal of Psychology and Christianity* 27 (2008): 358–367. The study included twenty-eight men and seventy-two women, with an average age of twenty-one.

17. "Scientific Publications About Adventists," Loma Linda University School of Public Health, accessed May 30, 2013, http://www.llu.edu/public-health/health/pubs.page.

18. "The Adventist Health Study: Mortality Studies of Seventh-day Adventists," Loma Linda University School of Public Health, accessed May 30, 2013, http://www.llu.edu/public-health/health/mortality.page.

19. Gary E. Fraser and David J. Shavlik, "Ten Years of Life: Is It a Matter of Choice?" *Archives of Internal Medicine* 161 (2001): 1645–1642.

20. Howard S. Friedman and Leslie R. Martin, *The Longevity Project* (New York: Hudson Street Press, 2011).

Chapter 5

The Benefits of Service

"Blessed is the one who is kind to the needy." —Proverbs 14:21

I have seen scores of young people serving as taskforce or student missionaries, at home or abroad and in a variety of positions such as teacher, nurse, pastor, dormitory dean, builder, maintenance, and so on. Because of my connection with the teaching profession, most typically I have had the chance to talk with those who worked as teachers.

This was the case of Sarah,* who served as a teacher assistant on a South Pacific island. Being at an international school with English as the medium of instruction, Sarah didn't need to learn the local language, but she had to learn a whole world of things from her host culture. Although she had started a different major in college, upon returning home she was firmly committed to teaching. That's why she came to see me about the education degree with teacher certification. When I asked her about her service abroad, her face lit up and she began talking freely: "The mission field has changed my life, I am a different person altogether. I can understand people so much better . . . and myself! My mind was so narrow before last year, but now I can see the world from a different perspective—a much more fulfilling one. My personality has changed; I used to be an introvert, now I approach others confidently and initiate conversations with ease. I rarely am afraid of anything anymore."

Her positive experience was not just limited to herself and her connection to others. She had gone through a spiritual revival: "When I was working there, I learned to truly depend on God and to become a close friend of Jesus. I prayed with such fervor and faith unknown to me before. You see, when you lack things or skills and do not have your parents or your usual means of support, you seek God so eagerly. This religious experience has transformed me spiritually."

Listening, I said to myself, *What excitement! She comes back from her mission happier than if she were coming home from receiving the Nobel Prize!* Then the

* A pseudonym.

words of Paul exhorting the Ephesian elders came to mind; quoting Jesus, he said, " 'It is more blessed to give than to receive' " (Acts 20:35).

It was obvious that Sarah had been blessed by serving others. Unlike her, many people cannot take a year of their lives to provide help to people in a distant land. But there are endless ways to provide service locally. The experience of joy, as promised by Jesus, can be similar for someone volunteering just two hours a week.

Service to others has been proven as one of the greatest blessings to people at large and particularly to those suffering from physical and mental illness. This chapter is about the evidence showing that those who offer themselves to help others in need can be blessed, as promised in Proverbs 14:21, Acts 20:35, and other biblical passages. The activity of supporting, assisting, and helping others is central to Jesus' doctrine and thus is encouraged by His church. That is why religious communities offer multiple opportunities to bring hope, help, and relief of others' pain and suffering. And the benefits of service are great for the recipient, but they are even greater for the giver.

A source of happiness

Sarah seemed ecstatic when she kept talking about her teaching experience in the Pacific Islands. And so was our daughter, Claudia, when she returned from Haiti after having done a Christian veterinary service mission trip to that country. Her face glowed when she reported about this family who had a horse with a sore on its back. They needed the animal to work the land in order to survive, and they were so grateful for the help. She seemed utterly joyful as she showed photos of the many pets and farm animals treated. Bringing relief to both the animals and their owners was sufficient to lift her spirits and experience that peculiar glow of having rendered a good service.

What are the true sources of happiness? Looking at human behavior, one would conclude that power, money, and everything that can be obtained with them must be the way to happiness, but we know from the Bible that this is not so. Recently, theory and research are coming to a less materialistic understanding of happiness. Stephen G. Post, a professor of preventive medicine at Stony Brook University in New York, in his book *The Hidden Gifts of Helping*, identifies three types of happiness:[1]

1. Happiness based on power over others. In their search for happiness, many try to reach positions of power and influence. This is so real that the race to the top can become ruthless among competitors. Yet, this kind of "happiness" is always incomplete—no matter what position one reaches, there will always be someone not submitting. As a result, this modality of happiness is unsatisfying and leaves the person wanting higher power.

2. Happiness rooted in desire. This is a commonly practiced path. It is the pursuit of money and everything we crave. It is temporary, uncertain, and leaves people with a desire for more. Polls about happiness conducted in the 1940s and 1950s show higher scores than sixty years later when the income and possessions had tripled! Mihalyi Csikszentmihalyi, a leading researcher in the study of happiness, asks himself, "If we are so rich, why aren't we happy?" If we look at the happiest states on the Gallup-Healthways Well-Being Index, we find Hawaii, North Dakota, Minnesota, Utah, and Alaska at the top, in that order.[2] Then we find out the personal income per capita in those states showing them as the eighteen, the twenty-ninth, the eleventh, the forty-fifth, and the fifteenth, respectively.[3] None of the ten richest states made it to the top of the list. A satisfying life does not depend on wealth. Jesus Christ already said it: "For one's life does not consist in the abundance of things he possesses" (Luke 12:15). And in fact, riches may be a barrier to enter the kingdom (Mark 10:25).

3. Deep happiness. This is the happiness obtained by contributing to the lives of others. Serving others provides a boost in personal well-being. And when this becomes a habit, the maximum happiness possible in this imperfect world will take place. This is becoming clearer to happiness experts, as we will see in a sample of studies below.

The difference between the first two types and the third is their direction: happiness number one and number two flow from the outside to the inside (myself) and allow me only partial control, whereas number three flows from the inside to the outside (others) and allows me to have choice and control. In fact, the apostle Paul connects this inside-outside direction with the freedom to choose helping others: "You, my brothers and sisters, were called to be free. But do not use your freedom to indulge the flesh; rather, serve one another humbly in love" (Galatians 5:13). The text affirms the idea that freedom, will, personal initiative, and choice are best used to help others than to please oneself.

Doing good makes us feel good and, if the good deed is for someone else, then happiness becomes complete. This is what Sonja Lyubomirsky has been finding over the years in her psychology laboratory at the University of California–Riverside. Dr. Lyubomirsky and her doctoral candidates are studying the architecture of sustainable happiness. Through their studies with human participants, and the analysis of external research and data, they are identifying the mechanisms that facilitate long-term positive affect, the benefits of being happy, the differences in happiness across cultures, the barriers of happiness, the ripple effect of generosity in social networks, and other such topics. Results from twin studies have led Professor Lyubomirsky to the conclusion that 50 percent of a given human's happiness level is of genetic origin (basic temperament, constitution, and personality traits), 10 percent is affected by life circumstances (people, surroundings, etc.), and the remaining 40 percent depends on each individual's choice and control (deciding to change mode of thinking, starting an exercise plan, setting up an objective and pressing forward to reach it, etc.). The goal of this team is to target that 40 percent, so that people lead their lives to a reasonably satisfying existence, avoiding the choices that will make them miserable.

Sonja Lyubomirsky's book, *The How of Happiness,* displays the practical application of her research findings.[4] Again, "having" is not what makes people happy, but rather "choosing to act" in certain ways. Dr. Lyubomirsky suggests, based on scientific studies, that activities that lead to happiness express gratitude, cultivate optimism, nurture relationships, grant forgiveness, and so on. One of utmost importance is to practice kindness. Acts of kindness, doing good things for others, can be relatively simple in everyday life. Yet it makes a huge difference. People who commit acts of kindness on a regular basis become significantly happier over time. People involved in altruistic behaviors think of themselves as good persons and do further service. Then the recipients show appreciation and this, in turn, reinforces the behavior and builds up more happiness.

In the process of providing help to others, there is always the risk of adopting an attitude that may bring a curse rather than a blessing; it can imply a patronizing descent, a condescending air to those being helped. Complete humility is the only solution.

Princess Wilhelmina of the Netherlands was born in 1880 in The Hague. When the princess was four, her half-brother died and she became heiress to the throne. On November 23, 1890, her father King William III died. The girl became the queen instantly and was crowned in a ceremony that attracted thousands who cheered the new queen. Seeing the multitude and, without quite understanding the weight of the occasion, she looked at her mother, saying, "Mother, do all these people belong to me?" With a gentle smile her mother replied, "No, my dear child, you belong to all these people."[5]

Jesus talked about the blessings of being charitable. He promised rewards for this behavior. "Be careful not to practice your righteousness in front of others to be seen by them. If you do, you will have no reward from your Father in heaven. . . . But when you give to the needy, do not let your left hand know what your right hand is doing, so that your giving may be in secret. Then your Father, who sees what is done in secret, will reward you" (Matthew 6:1, 3, 4, NIV).

It is clear that acts of charity are rewarded. The arrogant will receive immediate reward from the look of the observer; but what is the authentic reward, the reward from the Father? It cannot be eternal life, for salvation is only by faith and not by works (Ephesians 2:8, 9). The reward that Jesus promises (at least part of it) may have to do with the natural consequences of doing good: a tender feeling, a desire to do more, closeness to the Creator, and a lasting pleasant memory.

The story is told of a mother and her teen daughter living in a rural area of Montana in the times of the Great Depression. As the mother saw her daughter reading a love novel, she said, "Soon after you have read the story, you will forget it. But I'll tell you what you can do and remember for many years to come." Then she talked about Mrs. Eberhart, the elderly lady next door, and her meager means and how she would benefit from a warm wool sweater. "Knit one for her and deliver it secretly at her door." The young woman followed her mother's suggestion, and, once she had finished it, she wrapped it up and left it at the neighbor's doorstep with a note: "A gift from someone who cares for you." For several winters, this young woman and her mother could see Mrs. Eberhart wearing her knit sweater. That teenager still fondly remembered the event forty years later—this was a blessing after the Matthew 6:4 promise.

Some criticize college-age young people of today for being too self-centered. Well, that criticism may as well go for the entire human race, but coming to the time of developing personal strategies for authentic happiness, many a student might be right, as the study by Chris Tkach and Sonja Lyubomirsky shows.[6] A total of five hundred undergraduate students provided written data about their state of happiness and about their strategies to attain better well-being, to maintain it, and to enhance it. The analysis of the multiple responses revealed that social affiliation strategies were the first factor and the most frequently used strategy. This included activities such as helping others, supporting and encouraging friends, communicating/relating with friends, and savoring the moment.

Two important things can be learned from this study. First, people themselves, not luck or fate, construct their happiness; second, when interested in attaining happiness and well-being, people tend to choose social affiliation and, more specifically, their support to others.

This is precisely what Paul wrote to the believers in Philippi: "So if there is any encouragement in Christ, any comfort from love, any participation in the Spirit, any affection and sympathy, complete my joy by being of the same mind, having the same love, being in full accord and of one mind. Do nothing from selfish ambition or conceit, but in humility count others more significant than yourselves. Let each of you look not only to his own interests, but also to the interests of others" (Philippians 2:1–4, ESV). Paul wanted happiness for the community of faith, advising them to practice precisely the core of the gospel: Love your neighbor (Mark 12:31) and even your enemy (Matthew 5:44).

What happens inside?

Scientists have studied the biochemical processes associated with helping behaviors. What happens in our brains when we help an elderly person purchase groceries for a week? What are the neurological steps taking place while we empathically listen to a close friend telling us about an unfortunate event? Are our brains working in unique ways while we babysit the children of a single mother so she can run necessary errands?

Helping someone elicits a number of organic responses that are beneficial to our physical and mental health. For instance, involvement in a charitable project lights up the mesolimbic system of the brain (the center of motivation, pleasure, reward, and partly of learning) and it begins releasing specific chemicals. Dopamine is one; it has a soothing effect and communicates a general sense of well-being. It is known that sufferers from Parkinson's disease do not have enough dopamine activity (due to the loss of the neurons secreting it). Likewise, it is a bad sign to have excessive activity, as schizophrenia involves elevated levels of dopamine activity in the mesolimbic pathways.

Serotonin is another chemical released by certain neurons when performing helping behaviors. This neurotransmitter is associated with a good mood. In fact, many of the drugs used for the treatment of depression are designed to increase its concentration and enhance its activity. Oxytocin also becomes more abundant and active with charitable actions. It has been called the "compassion hormone" or the "love hormone."

Oxytocin is released profusely in mothers giving birth, which makes them strengthen the mother-child bond. This hormone also interferes with the stress response, preserving a state of calm, and preventing aggressive manifestations and the loss of one's own control. All of the above hormones and neurotransmitters push aside negative emotions such as hatred, revenge, hostility, fear, and resentment.

Using magnetic resonance imaging (MRI), Jorge Moll of the National Institutes of Health and a team of international researchers obtained MRI scans from the brains of nineteen healthy adult participants given $128 for participating in the study.[7] In addition, funds were made available for donations to charitable organizations. They could also give part of their allowance to charity and decide in all cases which charities would receive their donations. Researchers observed that the brain activity was affected, not just by the act of donating, but also when discussing specific alternatives to grant or not to grant the money to charities. Again, the mesolimbic system was especially active when donating, and less active when refusing to donate. Remarkably, the prefrontal cortex (the most distinctively human area of the brain that controls decision-making, planning, adjustment to actions or reactions in changing situations, etc.) was distinctively engaged when altruistic, rather than selfish, choices prevailed.

David McClelland of Harvard University and Carol Kirshnit of Loyola University–Chicago studied the variations of salivary immunoglobulin A (S-IgA) in subjects being exposed to two different movies.[8] S-IgA helps the body build immunity. They discovered the power of compassion over internal secretion. One hundred and thirty-two college students divided into small groups were shown either a film depicting power motivation (political scenes) or a film showing affiliation motivation (Mother Teresa of Calcutta caring for people). Changes in S-IgA were monitored before and after the viewing. S-IgA levels did not change significantly with the first film, but they rose significantly in those watching the second film. This difference remained one hour after the experiment.

It is amazing to learn of the beneficial internal processes taking place in the human body when performing altruistic deeds. But is altruism built into our own nature? What moves someone to be altruistic? Understanding altruism represents a great challenge to evolutionary biologists. If survival is central in continuing the species, why should an individual carry out an altruistic behavior that may be risky, costly, or painful in order to favor another individual who is not kin? Why not use those resources to outfit oneself in the tough environment of the survival of the fittest?

For me, the explanation is clear: the Creator has placed mechanisms that bring a transitory reward for honest and good behaviors. It is true that with generations of sins and a deviation from God's original plan, the system has become imperfect and may not work consistently, but it is satisfying to see that God has made it possible for humankind to preserve occasional desires to do good.

Volunteering and psychological well-being

Well-being and happiness are different terms but are oftentimes used interchangeably, even by scientists. Well-being refers to optimal conditions with regards to someone's health, wealth, and the social and physical environment. Happiness, on the contrary, is the state of mind that a person experiences about him or herself. Objective well-being does not imply that the person is happy, and adverse circumstances don't always mean unhappiness. A patient with a chronic disease might be happy even in the midst of poor conditions; likewise, someone perfectly healthy—with an enviable profession and a good social network—can be miserably unhappy. One definition of happiness accurately puts these concepts together: happiness is perceived well-being.

Because many research studies use the concept of well-being to see its connections with service, altruism, and helping behaviors, I will outline a number of those studies to emphasize the benefits of helping others.

There is one new development in the psychological arena that seems quite compatible with the Christian worldview. It is the concept of eudaimonic versus hedonic well-being. Aristotle was the originator of the term *eudaimonia* (true nature of well-being). In his time, *hedonia* (seeking pleasure) was referred to as happiness. So Aristotle deemed happiness-*hedonia* to be a vulgar idea. As he rightfully argued, *hedonia* may yield pleasure but not necessarily wellness. So he coined the term *eudaimonia* to refer to a nobler goal: living a virtuous life leading to true satisfaction. Now, this concept has been retaken in the twenty-first century to differentiate between the self-centered and the others-centered well-being. In that way, types 1 and 2 of Professor Post's classification of happiness (seen above) would be hedonic, and type 3 would be eudaimonic.

Michael Steger, a psychologist at the University of Louisville in Kentucky, and his associates, tested this theory asking a group of sixty-five undergraduate students to keep an online diary in which they entered daily annotations about the nature of their behavior—hedonic (or pleasure seeking) versus eudaimonic (meaningful acts).[9] Examples of the first would be purchasing something for myself or eating my favorite food; examples of the second would be giving a hand to someone in need or listening to my friend's problems. Participants regularly recorded their perceived level of well-being. Results showed that the more they engaged in helping and meaningful activities, the happier they felt and the more meaning they saw in their lives. Furthermore, the study found a temporal sequence whereby altruistic activities were related to greater well-being the next day. The conclusion of Steger and his colleagues is that "doing good" is an effective way for people to create meaningful and satisfying lives.

In these findings, I see again the imprint from our Creator: He has put in us the mechanism by which doing good brings us fulfillment and satisfaction. And, naturally, when we incur evil deeds, our consciences let us feel the burden of sin. It is true that there are exceptions—those who have freely chosen to walk away from the Lord. But for those who choose to listen to Him, there is both the ability to discern and to notice the consequences:

> Then you will understand what is right
>   and just and fair—every good path.

> For wisdom will enter your heart,
>   and knowledge will be pleasant to your soul.
> Discretion will protect you,
>   and understanding will guard you (Proverbs 2:9–11, NIV).

Taking a look at how much people volunteer and observing their state of well-being has been one of the preferred ways for researchers to study the connection between these two factors. David Mellor, from Deakin University in Melbourne, and his associates collected data across Australia from 1,289 participants.[10] These people were interviewed via phone and followed up with a survey, including questions about their standard of living, feeling of safety and security, life achievements, availability of resources, relationships, self-esteem, optimism, and volunteer status. Results revealed that, for all ages, volunteers had a higher level of well-being than did nonvolunteers, and this continued to be true after accounting for psychosocial and personality factors. In addition, it was found that volunteers were more extroverted, less neurotic, more optimistic, and had greater perceived control than did nonvolunteers. These findings, as well as other similar ones obtained repeatedly elsewhere, made the authors conclude that the relationship between volunteering and well-being is robust.

Volunteering has been found to have a particular strength: it moderates the risk of developing functional limitations as people grow older. This is a unique finding from Emily Greenfield and Nadine Marks, from the Department of Human Development and Family Studies at the University of Wisconsin–Madison, who studied a sample of 4,646 people.[11] In this study, groups normally under-represented were in fact over-represented: African Americans, Puerto Ricans, Mexican Americans, single-parent families, families with stepchildren, cohabiting couples, and recently married persons. Results were quite positive for those engaged in voluntary activities with recreational entities, religious groups, and civic initiatives. Because of the longitudinal (follow-up) nature of the methodology, this study confirmed a cause-effect relationship between volunteerism and well-being: engagement in voluntary tasks caused a better psychological well-being and were affected less by functional limitations associated with age.

A different study shed light on the precise balance of the amount of work invested. The Center for Mental Health Research at the Australian National University sponsored a study led by Timothy Windsor aimed at seeing how the quantity of hours invested in community service affected well-being.[12] This study was conducted in the Australian capital, Canberra, with 2,551 participants between the ages of sixty-four and sixty-eight. Results were atypical, in that the correlation between the time of volunteering and psychological well-being was a nonlinear, U-shape curve, between time invested and well-being gains. This meant that any change in well-being was unnoticeable to people who spent less than two hours a week in altruistic service. As they invested more time, their well-being became increasingly higher, reaching an optimal level between three and fifteen hours a week. In the moment that participants spent more than fifteen hours a week volunteering, there was a significant increase in negative affect and a decrease in life satisfaction.

These kinds of results remind us of the necessity of *balance*. Something as good as being helpful to others may reach an extreme where our own well-being becomes jeopardized. The realization of a great need may drive well-meaning people to help incessantly. It happens to professional as well as volunteer helpers. But that is an unwise path; some preventive measures to avoiding reaching the limit include learning to say No without feeling guilty, setting up clear limits, becoming aware of when you are doing too much, respecting breaks, learning to refer tasks to another person when necessary, improving one's time management skills, and gaining the spiritual blessings of prayer and meditation on the Word of God.

On repeated occasions, Ellen G. White counseled the ministry, a good example of a helping profession, to limit their work: "I have been shown that at times those in the ministry are compelled to labor day and night and live on very meager fare. When a crisis comes, every nerve and sinew is taxed by the heavy strain. If these men could go aside and rest a while, engaging in physical labor, it would be a great relief."[13]

Research on service and well-being focuses on the status of service and the self-perception of well-being, but the process should not stop at a warm, fuzzy feeling—even joy is not the ultimate goal. It is true that Christians should be joyful consistently (1 Thessalonians 5:16), but their behavior should make an impact on others, as when Peter and John were seized and taken to the Sanhedrin and those present "took note that these men had been with Jesus" (Acts 4:13, NIV). The tradition of standing up and applauding at the *Messiah*'s "Hallelujah Chorus" comes from an early performance of the piece in London in 1743. King George II was so transported that he stood up, and the rest of the auditorium did the same and remained so until the end of the chorus. Some days later, Mr. Handel went to visit George Henry Hay, 8th Earl of Kinnoull, a British diplomat and former member of the parliament, who congratulated the composer warmly for the outstanding oratorio providing such noble entertainment to the town. "My lord," said Handel, "I should be sorry if I only entertained them; I wish to make them better."[14]

Acts of kindness and depression

Mario,* a high school student, came to see me at the counseling center where I worked as a school psychologist. The pressure from studies, heartbreak, and a family issue caused several depressive symptoms, enough to diagnose it as a major depressive episode. After two counseling sessions, a treatment plan was agreed upon in consultation with Mario, his parents, his anchor teacher, and a medical doctor. The plan included a number of short-term goals (master problem-solving skills as learned in therapy, dispel self-harm ideations and replace them with positive thoughts, master communication skills with the family, and sharpen study skills as monitored in counseling sessions). The plan also contained important activities like enrolling in a sport club, and participating in a ministry to help immigrant elementary students with reading difficulties. Mario agreed to carry out all the assigned tasks and signed an agreement together with the rest of us. The least arduous task, according to Mario, was tutoring the elementary kids. It required little effort and the reward was sizeable; every time he worked with these youngsters, Mario's mood improved, and he enjoyed a state of well-being that lasted for days.

According to the World Health Organization, depression is a serious global disorder that affects over 350 million people.[15] Fewer than 25 percent (10 percent in the developing countries) affected receive treatment because of a lack of resources and social stigma. However, there are positive activity interventions capable of relieving the symptoms at little cost, and this has been tested, at least in cases of minor depressive disorders. Kristin Layous of the University of California–Riverside, with colleagues from her same university and Duke University, made an analysis of research studies (all randomized) dealing with self-administered interventions on minor depression.[16] The two leading and most successful interventions were "Counting Blessings" and "Acts of Kindness." If only people with mild depression (some on their way to major depression) knew that counting their blessings and performing acts of kindness would notably alleviate their symptoms, they would set themselves to such tasks on a daily basis.

But things may not be so simple as to prescribe, "Rx: two acts of kindness daily." In fact, divine power must be allowed to intervene. For those acts of kindness to yield their proper dividends, they have to be performed with the right attitude and commitment. When someone engages in helping behaviors out of obligation or because someone is watching, or does it with resentment or a feeling of being taken advantage of, the biochemical steps that bring relief do not work as well as when the acts of kindness come from the heart. In fact,

* A pseudonym.

such phony attitudes may be detrimental. It is, therefore, necessary to be truly honest about this process.

And in order to do so, the power of the Holy Spirit is essential, according to Ellen G. White in her commentary of the Beatitudes. Jerry D. Thomas's adaptation of the original *Thoughts From the Mount of Blessing* reads like this: "The human heart is naturally cold and selfish. Whenever someone shows kindness or mercy, it is because of the Holy Spirit's influence whether or not that person realizes it. God Himself is the Source of all mercy. He doesn't treat us as we deserve to be treated; He doesn't ask if we deserve to be loved. He just loves us, and that love gives us value and self-worth."[17]

Altruism, health, and longevity

Everybody knows that diet, exercise, pure air, abundant water, and good sleep add health and years. But few consider the positive impact that helping others might have on health and longevity because research results on the effects of service to others have emerged only in the last few years.

Work- and home-related stress creates burnout, a great concern for public mental health. When demands become intense for an extended period of time, many reach physical and emotional exhaustion, depersonalization, and a lack of accomplishments. It would make sense to think that if people afflicted by burnout added altruistic service and care to their agendas, it would equate to adding fuel to the fire. However, Clark Campbell, a professor of psychology at George Fox University, found the opposite.[18] He monitored a group of thirty-six physicians and nurses going on a medical missionary trip to South America. This group of professionals took three burnout scales prior to embarking and gave information about their stressful medical incidents, such as lack of control over time and the pressure to see more patients in less time. Upon return, their burnout scores were reduced and continued to reduce after the mission trip, as evidenced by a six-month follow-up.

Altruistic deeds are beneficial to the health of people of all ages. For example, Carolyn Schwartz from the New England Baptist Hospital in Boston led a study of 457 teenagers from the Presbyterian Church.[19] Altruistic practice had been found to be beneficial to the health of adults by these researchers, and now they wanted to find out the effect on teens. Participants were given questionnaires about altruistic practices and health-related quality of life, among other areas. Altruistic practices were found beneficial to females' physical health and to males' mental health. One of the main conclusions of this study is to lead teens toward helping those in need, as this could enhance their quality of life for a short term.

In the context of more advanced ages, data from the Wisconsin Longitudinal Study (WLS) were able to reveal several beneficial effects from the practice of helping others. The WLS is a long-term project to follow up and study a random sample of 10,317 men and women who graduated in the high schools of Wisconsin in 1957. This database, managed by the University of Wisconsin–Madison, has provided an excellent opportunity to explore life course, intergenerational relationships, family interactions, physical and mental health, well-being, and morbidity and mortality from adolescence into late adulthood. Data have been collected consistently over the years from the participants, their siblings, spouses, widows, and their widowers.

Jane A. Piliavin and Erica Siegl used this databank to study the relationship between volunteering and health.[20] They were asked about their volunteering status (whether they volunteered, its intensity, diversity, and consistency) and about their health. The sample under analysis was of approximately four thousand from the WLS. Consistent with other studies, service and health were linked. Furthermore, the more diversity and consistency of service they rendered, the better levels of health they had. Because of its longitudinal nature, the study was successful in finding a causal relationship—helping behaviors in 1992 were good predictors of both psychological and physical health in 2004. Researchers also found out that mattering ("people need my assistance," or "people are aware of my presence") was a good mediating factor. In other words, service was more beneficial health-wise when there was a sense of mattering. Finally, this study was able to differentiate between social engagement and others-oriented activity, revealing that the effect of the first on health was negligible but the second significant.

These results are replicated in various parts of the world, such as in China or in Europe. Chau-Kiu Cheung and Alex Yui-Huen Kwan from the Chinese University of Hong Kong and the City University of Hong Kong, respectively, conducted their study with elderly participants, 719 Chinese men and women, older than sixty with an average age of 79.9.[21] As hypothesized, results revealed significant positive effects of volunteering upon the older person's self-esteem, life satisfaction, and health. Researchers also observed that when social workers, using a loving and kind manner, invited them to join in the service, the benign effects on the elderly were magnified.

On the other side of the world, a large-scale study found consistent results. The Survey of Health, Ageing, and Retirement in Europe (SHARE) is a database of twenty European nations on health, socioeconomic status, and social and family networks of more than fifty-five thousand individuals, aged fifty or over. Using these data, Debbie Haski-Leventhal made an analysis of volunteerism and health in Western Europe, including Israel.[22] Using 30,023 individuals, she found out that people who volunteered reported higher rates of physical health, life satisfaction, less depression, and more optimism about living longer.

William Brown of Rutgers University and his associates from Long Island University explored whether giving or receiving help and social benefit would have a stronger health benefit.[23] Participants were 1,118 ethnically diverse, community-dwelling older adults living in Brooklyn, New York. Data were collected via interviews, and results showed that those giving care and help to peers enjoyed low levels of morbidity, whereas those receiving the support did not. These relationships held even when controlling for other important variables. Again, these observations are in full agreement with Jesus' words: " 'It is more blessed to give than to receive' " (Acts 20:35).

Finally, Stephanie Brown from the VA Health Services Research & Development Center of Excellence in Ann Arbor, Michigan, conducted a longitudinal study designed to assess variations in mortality with a large sample of 3,376 elderly married couples.[24] Criteria for selection were couples living in the community, in a two-person home, where one would have to care for the other according to spousal need. She followed up on participants for seven years; they provided information about hours of care to the spouse, spousal need, and health, and death of spouse, if and when it happened—909 participants died during the years of the study. These data revealed that those spending fourteen hours or more per week providing care to their spouses had their mortality rate significantly decreased in comparison with those providing less than fourteen hours. This remained true regardless of the limitations of the care-receiving spouses and other demographic and health variables.

It is a great sacrifice to care for a critically ill loved one, but the Lord is fair and provides the necessary help to the helper so that he or she may gain renewed strength, better health, and a longer life. And for those trusting in the Lord, the guarantee is firm:

> "But those who hope in the LORD
>   will renew their strength.
> They will soar on wings like eagles;
>   they will run and not grow weary,
> they will walk and not be faint" (Isaiah 40:31, NIV).

Other benefits of service

In addition to the wide array of mental and physical health benefits, there are other miscellaneous advantages. These are some:

101

- Provides optimal social connection. Service opportunities are accompanied by the chance to meet new friends and strengthen social ties and connections. This work is usually performed in the midst of a family-like atmosphere with people who tend to be sociable, good-hearted, and have solid principles. When service is done in the church context, the quality of relationship is even better, with the possibility of establishing solid, long-lasting friendships with people who share a similar faith and similar values.
- It is fun. Organized service tends to be enjoyable and, even when at the beginning one may not enjoy the task, practice makes helping tasks increasingly pleasurable.
- May open professional opportunities. Service can enhance one's abilities and skills and open paths otherwise not available. Many employers, especially those searching for young people, want to find out previous hands-on experiences. They also prefer those with volunteering attitudes, often evidence of a faithful commitment to high standards and principles.
- Not limited to helping persons. According to the study by Liz O'Brien, Mardie Townsend, and Matthew Ebden, various benefits can be obtained from environmental volunteering with no needy people involved.[25] Researchers spent time with volunteer groups in northern England and southern Scotland who cared for nature, and respondents reported gains such as improved fitness, keeping alert, meeting other volunteers, and reducing stress levels. The overall analysis revealed that the activity provided a range of physical, social, and mental well-being, in spite of the fact that volunteers in the study were from all walks of life.

Conclusion

A king placed a heavy rock on a highway and hid to see who would remove it. Some wondered how that rock got there; others loudly blamed the government for their lack of care; still others simply dodged it and kept going. None took the time and effort to remove the obstacle. At last, a humble peasant noticed the rock and patiently rolled it out of the way to permit the traffic to go by. As he looked back at the position where the stoned had lain, he saw a purse full of gold coins. The king congratulated him and told him it was the reward for the person willing to perform the needed service.

As we have seen in this chapter, the benefits of lovingly serving others are not material, but gold can represent the greatness of the rewards: health, well-being, longevity . . . and above all, the blessing of following the example of Jesus Christ, who will lead us closer to God as we serve others.

Study Questions

- Read random portions of the book of Proverbs and search for maxims calling for love, support, help, and care for others. Reflect on the results of putting the advice into practice.
- Reflect on the message of Leviticus 23:22 and imagine how you could apply that Old Testament practice in the twenty-first century.
- Read Deuteronomy 15 and imagine the results of putting this in practice today.

Application Thoughts

- Mark 1:34, 35 tell us of Jesus taking care of many in need of healing to then go to a solitary place to pray. How can you practice this example in your life?
- What suggestions could you offer to a friend coming to you, saying, "I would like to offer help to people, but I am very inhibited, shy, and introverted . . ."?
- Make a list of your personal gifts and skills and another of needs of people in your immediate surroundings. How can you match the two? What could you do to provide support to those people?

---

1. Stephen G. Post, *The Hidden Gifts of Helping* (Hoboken, NJ: John Wiley & Sons, 2011), 90.

2. Jeanna Bryner, "Happiest States of 2011: The List," Live Science, accessed June 25, 2013, http://www.livescience.com/18666-happiest-states-2011-list.html.

3. U.S. Census Bureau, "Personl Income Per Capita in Current Dollars, 2007," U.S. Census Bureau, accessed June 25, 2013, http://www.census.gov/statab/ranks/rank29.html.

4. Sonja Lyubomirsky, *The How of Happiness* (New York: Penguin Press, 2008).

5. Paul Lee Tan, *Encyclopedia of 15,000 Illustrations,* entry 11491.

6. Chris Tkach and Sonja Lyubomirsky, "How Do People Pursue Happiness?: Relating Personality, Happiness-Increasing Strategies, and Well-Being," *Journal of Happiness Studies* 7 (2006): 183–225.

7. Jorge Moll et al., "Human Fronto-Mesolimbic Networks Guide Decisions About Charitable Donation," *Proceedings of the National Academy of Sciences* 103 (2006): 15623–15628.

8. David C. McClelland and Carol Kirshnit, "The Effect of Motivational Arousal Through Films on Salivary Immunoglobulin A," *Psychology and Health* 2 (1988): 31–52.

9. Michael F. Steger et al., "Being Good by Doing Good: Daily Eudaimonic Activity and Well-Being," *Journal of Research in Personality* 42 (2008): 22–42.

10. David Mellor et al., "Volunteering and Its Relationship With Personal and Neighborhood Well-Being," *Nonprofit and Voluntary Sector Quarterly* 38 (2009): 144–159. Age of participants ranged from eighteen to eighty-eight years with a median age of fifty-three.

11. Emily A. Greenfield and Nadine F. Marks, "Continuous Participation in Voluntary Groups as a Protective Factor for the Psychological Well-Being of Adults Who Develop Functional Limitations: Evidence From the National Survey of Families and Households," *Journals of Gerontology* 62B (2007): S60–S68. The sample of 4,646 people ranged from ages thirty-five to ninety-two.

12. Timothy D. Windsor et al., "Volunteering and Psychological Well-Being Among Young-Old Adults: How Much Is Too Much?" *Gerontologist* 48 (2008): 59–70.

13. Ellen G. White, Evangelism (Washington, DC: Review and Herald®, 1946), 661.

14. Paul Lee Tan, *Encyclopedia of 15,000 Illustrations,* entry 11488.

15. World Health Organization, "Depression," World Health Organization, accessed June 25, 2013, http://www.who.int/mediacentre/factsheets/fs369/en/index.html.

16. Kristin Layous et al., "Delivering Happiness: Translating Positive Psychology Intervention Research for Treating Major and Minor Depressive Disorders," *Journal of Alternative and Complementary Medicine* 17 (2011): 675–683.

17. Jerry D. Thomas, *Blessings* (Nampa, ID: Pacific Press®, 2008), 27.

18. Clark Campbell et al., "Reduction in Burnout May Be a Benefit for Short-Term Medical Mission Volunteers," *Mental Health, Religion & Culture* 12 (2009): 627–637.

19. Carolyn E. Schwartz et al., "Helping Others Shows Differential Benefits on Health and Well-Being for Male and Female Teens," *Journal of Happiness Studies* 10 (2009): 431–448. The study included 457 teenagers between the ages of twelve and seventeen (mean age of 15.6).

20. Jane A. Piliavin and Erica Siegl, "Health Benefits of Volunteering in the Wisconsin Longitudinal Study," *Journal of Health and Social Behavior* 48 (2007): 450–464.

21. Chau-Kiu Cheung and Alex Yui-Huen Kwan, "Inducting Older Adults Into Volunteer Work to Sustain Their Psychological Well-Being," *Ageing International* 31 (2006): 44–58.

22. Debbie Haski-Leventhal, "Elderly Volunteering and Well-Being: A Cross-European Comparison Based on SHARE Data," *Voluntas* 20 (2009): 388–404.

23. William M. Brown et al., "Altruism Relates to Health in an Ethnically Diverse Sample of Older Adults," *Journal of Gerontology* 60B (2005): P143–P152.

24. Stephanie L. Brown, "Caregiving Behavior Is Associated With Decreased Mortality Risk," *Psychological Science* 20 (2009): 488–494.

25. Liz O'Brien, Mardie Townsend, and Matthew Ebden, " 'Doing Something Positive': Volunteers' Experiences of the Well-Being Benefits Derived From Practical Conservation Activities in Nature," *Voluntas* 21 (2010): 525–545.

Chapter 6

The Benefits of Churchgoing

"I rejoiced with those who said to me, 'Let us go to the house of the LORD.' "
—Psalm 122:1, NIV

When first attending a Seventh-day Adventist church, I was touched by how people seemed to genuinely care about each other. I also was impressed by how both the pastor and laypeople alike imparted the Word. They were so knowledgeable about the Bible and had many portions memorized. This was the case of Brother Quesada and Brother Ballester.* They were pillars of the Central Seventh-day Adventist Church in Madrid, Spain. They were not ministers, but their knowledge of Scripture was solid. I was pleased to listen to them as Sabbath School teachers, sermon preachers, or as presiders at a prayer meeting. I can still remember some bits of their messages and even turns of phrases and expressions. For years, they held various offices and were loved and respected by the congregation.

At some point, Brother Quesada had questions about the local conference administrative procedures. He wanted changes that the conference brethren didn't implement. Brother Ballester agreed with him and so did another member of the church. The three of them, with their families, stopped going to church. They were not badmouthing the conference or the leaders, they were not trying to attract others to their side, they simply were not attending. They said they did not want to abandon the biblical beliefs that the church had taught them; neither did they want to live inconsistently with the doctrines. They just were making a point not to attend a church governed by those leaders who, apparently, did not listen. They began holding their own Sabbath services in one of their homes or out in nature. Offerings were used for charity. They continued to teach the Sabbath School quarterlies to their children, study the Bible, pray together, and read Ellen G. White. With the exception of attending church, they were leading their lives as any other church member.

* Both names are pseudonyms.

But this arrangement didn't last more than a few months. If one of the families was not able to attend, the others would worship at home by themselves. When they had a disagreement or a question about doctrine, they did not have any authority to turn to. Moreover, they did not have the wider context of brothers and sisters to relate to, to help, and to bring aid. Sadly, they did not have the strength or the humility to return to the congregation. What began with good intentions, aimed at continuing to live their faith, became sour without the church congregation. As a result, they little by little put aside their spiritual needs or filled them with alternatives; worse, they ended up blaming the conference leaders for their alienation.

Some may think that because salvation is personal, one can develop one's spirituality in isolation. But the Bible, both in the Old and New Testaments, clearly shows, across the history of the people of Israel and throughout the lives of the first Christians, that God invites everyone to corporate worship. There must be reasons why God wants His children to worship jointly and to deepen their social and emotional ties with each other in church communities. This chapter is about evidence showing that people who attend church tend to yield higher indicators of well-being and health when compared to the unchurched.

The dividends of the church community

The Walla Walla Valley in eastern Washington has an ideal terrain for road cycling. It is a fairly flat area, with a dry climate most of the year and a number of mountain ranges nearby that allow flat rides as well as the possibility of going up mountains and returning downhill at the end of the day. One day I said to myself, *I must get the right equipment and start riding all these options that the map shows me.* But I did nothing at first. Things did not happen until I joined the Warped Wheel Cycle Club of Walla Walla University. Once I had the chance to go with other cyclists, I realized that I could have longer, more frequent, and more enjoyable rides. I learned a lot about my own strength as well as about routes, equipment, outfits, and so on.

I must admit that there were some drawbacks associated with the group. For example, I observed that others used this or that item, and I ended up purchasing things that, after a few uses, proved unnecessary; or that the competition became a little excessive and some of us older folk had to strain in order to keep up with the younger cyclists. But, by and large, the effect of the group was benign, and I would never have accomplished my goals without the presence and support of others.

The principle of group support applies to most areas of life, including spiritual growth. The healthy church community is a place where we see happy people, feeling content and at home. And when someone is unhappy, he or she might find the necessary warmth in the church setting to improve his or her mood. The church is a place where conversation goes beneath the surface and where emotional sharing may take place. True, deep emotional exchange does not happen with everyone, but there are always one or two individuals that become our confidants. In most cases, the church community provides the environment where altruism can be practiced with members as well as with people beyond the church walls. And, of course, corporate worship is to praise God through music, prayer, Bible reading, and the sharing of spiritual insights, experiences that do not reach sufficient highlight when practiced in isolation.

As promised in Matthew 18:20, Jesus will be in the midst of those gathered in His name. The result can be a notable change like those His disciples experienced: their behavior was outstanding and the observers "took note that these men had been with Jesus" (Acts 4:13, NIV). Ellen G. White, commenting about this passage, says that those who have been with Jesus will "manifest the freshness and power and joyousness of perpetual youth. The heart that receives the word of God is not as a pool that evaporates, not like a broken cistern that loses its treasure. It is like the mountain stream fed by unfailing springs, whose cool, sparkling waters leap from rock to rock, refreshing the weary, the thirsty, the heavy laden."[1]

On the floor in the cloisters of Worcester Cathedral in Worcester, United Kingdom, there is the inscription *Miserrimus* ("most miserable")—on a nameless gravestone. William Wordsworth (1770–1850) wrote a poem to this inscription and William Godwin (1756–1836) a novel based on this site. By contrast, down in Rome's catacombs—those vast underground tunnels where early Christians hid from their fierce persecutors—a stone bears this word: *Felicissimus* ("most happy").

How can Christians be sorrowful in times of prosperity and happy in the middle of the most stressful conditions? Is it humanly possible to be most happy when knowing that martyrdom may arrive at any moment? Only the power of the Holy Spirit (Acts 1:8; 2:2–4) could accomplish such seemingly impossible tasks. And one of the channels used by the Spirit is the community support Christians consistently practiced, "continuing daily with one accord in the temple, and breaking bread from house to house, they ate their food with gladness and simplicity of heart, praising God and having favor with all the people" (Acts 2:46, 47, NIV).

Nonspiritual benefits of attending church

The spiritual blessings of church attendance are most valuable: "That I may dwell in the house of the LORD all the days of my life" (Psalm 27:4). But there are also benefits that can be highly desirable even to nonreligious people. They have to do with the quality of child development and family life.

Attending church services facilitates family interaction. This does not only mean that the family can sit and worship in church. It also means making plans to go to church, getting up, getting ready, and leaving at the same time. These activities force families to adapt to each other, help each other, and resolve any possible tension derived from preparedness and lateness. When church attendance is part of the regular family habit, it creates a solid family tradition that brings stability and regularity. It becomes an anchor in family life, causing strong lifelong ties and bonds that may pass on to the next generation.

At the worship place, the music and reverent environment typically offered can provide great blessings to churchgoers. Such context is especially soothing and therapeutic to children, who may not have any other occasion to experience it outside the church walls. Music has been found to relax muscle tension and soothe aggressive thoughts and behaviors. Aside from providing a superb way to develop music appreciation, it can also affect mood positively and diminish negativity.

Messages heard and discussed at church services and activities promote behaviors that are not always "religious" but highly useful for developing character and living in harmony with others: the promotion of moral behaviors, the practice of forgiveness, the development of resilience, a hopeful outlook toward the future, a strong stand for what is right and wrong are all values often learned and embraced in the church context. These principles are powerful antidotes to popular messages such as, "If it feels good, do it!"

The Seventh-day Adventist Church offers one of the best systems of religious education for all ages from shortly after birth to adulthood. A significant proportion of parishioners' offerings go to the Sabbath School divisions so that they are well equipped. In addition, these classes are active and well attended in almost all churches worldwide. Apart from a solid Bible knowledge, children learn to share, to develop patience, to respect others, to interact with them, to be quiet and still during special moments (like prayer), to wait for their turn—in essence, to develop self-control. At the same time, the church discourages adverse emotions (hatred, jealousy, anger) and behaviors (violence, drinking, lying, premarital sex, delinquency, tobacco, and other drugs); these principles can keep churchgoers out of much trouble and contribute to the well-being and harmony of society.

Children's Sabbath School can impact those who do not want anything to do with church. My wife and I have friends of our generation who left the church during their young adult years. Many developed a critical attitude toward religion. Yet, years later, having small children, they felt their offspring needed Sabbath School and church and returned in order to enrich those little ones with the same blessings that they received years back. They concluded that even if not a perfect place, the church is the best value-instilling option in the midst of our troubled times.

There are also opportunities to develop useful skills. For example, children and youth are encouraged to stand up and address a small (sometimes large) group of people, providing the first lessons in public speaking in a safe and real environment. The same principle is often applied to playing an instrument, singing, or reading. A great deal of unchurched parents would appreciate these opportunities in the context of the public schools where they send their children. But, oftentimes, it is not possible due to the high ratio of pupils per teacher and because curricula now come packed with demanding academic standards and preparation for high-stakes tests, leaving no time for these kinds of skills. Besides, the school community is made up of many peers and few adults, whereas the church congregation contains a great diversity of ages.

This fact makes churches the suitable place for everyone to develop social skills in a real and diverse setting. The church resembles a big family where oftentimes members come from several levels of income and a variety of cultures, races, and occupations. This mix provides a superb form of socialization not easily found anywhere else.

The majority of churches invite people of all ages to participate in outreach and mission activities or trips. In this way, service is provided to those in need, thus performing not only Christian duties but also a service of altruism to humanity that is of high value even to nonreligious people. Other opportunities that contribute to character development are summer camps and other recreational events where people sharing common values can gather and interact with each other. Typically, young people need to spend time raising money, planning, preparing, conversing about these trips, and thus they avoid a number of risky activities.

As I attended one of the three yearly meetings we have with the Washington Association of Colleges for Teacher Education (WACTE), one of the faculty members of a public university approached me and said, "I understand that you work for Walla Walla University. Are you a Seventh-day Adventist?" When I responded affirmatively, he continued: "My grandmother was Adventist and when at times I stayed with her, she would take me to church on Saturdays, and I attended Sabbath School." As he briefly described the events, I could see a gentle smile on his face as when recalling fond memories. I don't know the actual effect the experience may have exerted upon this man. In all appearance, going to church must have been at least a happy occasion. What effect it had upon his worldview, his morality, his behavior, or his faith, we may have to wait until the new earth to find out.

Parents who value church attendance very highly will instill the habit of churchgoing from the earliest years of their children's lives. Those who initiate the churchgoing tradition at a later age can yield the benefits even when children resist (they will prefer to stay home playing or watching cartoons). In these cases, parents need to be patient and consistent until children are drawn to church and begin liking it or until a habit is formed.

Church attendance and physical health

The language of Psalm 18 denotes God's answers to David's plea—one heard "from his temple" (verse 6, NIV). The result is an overextended blessing shown through expressions of physical strength: "With your help I can advance against a troop, with my God I can scale a wall" (verse 29, NIV). "He makes my feet like the feet of a deer; he causes me to stand on the heights. He trains my hands for battle; my arms can bend a bow of bronze. . . . My ankles do not give way" (verses 33, 34, 36, NIV). When I was in my twenties, I didn't think of the times when I would not have strength enough to lift up a burden or to climb up a rocky section of a mountain, but, as decades went by, I noticed a decline and realized that aging is a reality that carries deficits in physical strength. This text becomes especially meaningful when strength is known to subside.

God can intervene into the physical processes to transmit health and strength. Sometimes He chooses not to. But it is certain that God does not transmit health and strength to those who reject His blessings. One of the most precious promises to the children of Israel was that of keeping them free from illness: "Worship the LORD your God, and his blessing will be on your food and water. I will take away sickness from among you" (Exodus 23:25).

Epidemiologists George Comstock and Kay Partridge at the Johns Hopkins University School of Hygiene and Public Health were pioneers in the area of the health-church attendance connection.[2] Their remarkable findings became the basis of much of the research over the following fifty years. They collected several waves of data over the 1960s and 1970s from the Washington County, Maryland, census data. Comstock and Partridge found a number of connections between health and attendance to religious services. The data represented about ninety thousand participants—over 98 percent of the entire county population. Along with a large number of health indicators, researchers asked, "Does this person *usually* attend religious services? More than once a week; about once a week; more than once a month; two to twelve times a year; less than twice a year; and never." Results showed a number of health connections:

- Tuberculosis (TB) incidence per one hundred thousand over five years was differential for various levels of attendance: TB diagnosis for those attending church at least once a week was fifty-seven cases; there were eighty-four cases with TB in the group of those attending once a month. Finally, there were 138 TB cases among those attending church only twice a year or less.
- Mortality among men caused by arteriosclerotic heart disease was much higher in men with sporadic church attendance than it was in men attending weekly. The risk for the latter was 60 percent of that of men attending infrequently. This result was after allowing for the effect of tobacco, socioeconomic status, and water hardness.
- In women, death rates from emphysema, cirrhosis, and suicide were significantly higher among infrequent church attenders. Pulmonary emphysema caused eighteen per thousand deaths among women who attended church weekly versus fifty-two per thousand deaths in women attending less than weekly. Cirrhosis of the liver caused five deaths per thousand in the group of women going to church weekly versus twenty-five in their less attendance counterparts. And suicide was the cause of death in eleven per thousand women who attended church regularly every week versus twenty-five suicidal deaths in those with less-than-a-week attendance.

Since those early attempts to examine the links between church participation and health, many studies have succeeded in establishing this relationship. Harold Koenig, professor of psychiatry at Duke University, in his *Handbook of Religion and Health,* second edition, covering the 2001–2011 decade, recorded 1,060 peer-reviewed studies where organized religious attendance was a variable associated with one or more variables of mental and physical health.[3] In addition, the *Handbook* refers to 429 peer-reviewed studies where nonorganized religious attendance, like personal prayer or personal Bible study, meditation, and so on, are found associated with indicators of mental or physical health. Although results are not all conclusive, about 70 percent of them offer good evidence that participation in religious services goes along with good physical health in heart disease, hypertension, cerebrovascular disease, dementia, immune system dysfunction, endocrine dysfunction, cancer, and mortality.

Today we are not dealing with an isolated study here and there, showing that religious people seem to have a higher level of health than nonreligious people. We see an increasingly large bulk of solid research pointing with clarity at the health advantage of religion.

A few examples of recent studies on the religion-physical health connection follow. Eliezer Schnall from Yeshiva University in New York, together with other seven researchers examined health and religion data from 92,395 women.[4] They collected a number of health indicators and a self-rating instrument where participants evaluated their overall health, a measure correlated with actual health and found as a strong predictor of mortality across numerous studies. The researchers controlled for (held constant) the effect of demographic, socioeconomic, and prior health variables in order to observe the association of selected variables with the risk of all-cause mortality. The selected variables were religious affiliation, frequency of religious service attendance, and the level of strength and comfort provided by religion. All three characteristics were found to correlate with a reduced risk of mortality *from all causes*. In other words, those women with a religion affiliation, who attended service frequently, and who perceived religion as a source of strength and comfort, were subject to a significantly lower level of mortality when compared to those who did not find support in religion.

Elva Arredondo's study clarified how the process really happens.[5] This researcher from San Diego State University, together with four other associates, recruited 211 Spanish-speaking Latino women via a random list of phone numbers connected to Spanish surnames. The study, called *Secretos de la Buena Vida* (Secrets of the Good Life), consisted of a phone interview in Spanish about religious practices, as well as a home visit to hold a face-to-face, half-an-hour interview about health behaviors (i.e., details on what people ate and how they exercised). When compared with nonchurchgoers and occasional attendees, regular attendees enjoyed the healthiest indicators of lifestyle behavior: higher intake of dietary fiber, lesser intake of fat, and three times as much vigorous exercise. The advantage remained significant after controlling for socioeconomic indicators, such as education, marital status, employment, and age. In other words, the responsible factor in healthier behavior seemed to be church affiliation and attendance, rather than better education, for example.

Studies like these remind us that churches are good centers of promotion of not only spiritual growth, but also of health behaviors. Many Seventh-day Adventists are champions of this mission, living by the "health message," which has remained robust across so many decades. I have oftentimes asked myself, "What would my state of health be had I not embraced the Adventist message?" With almost 100 percent certainty, and looking at my contemporaries and my family history, I would be drinking alcohol, smoking cigarettes, and eating whatever I wanted with little regard for what is healthy or unhealthy. Probably by now I would have been hit by some of the typical "modern day illnesses," and I would have been warned of serious hazards to my health. As a result, I would be trying to repair my past intemperance, attaining the minimal level of healthy practices to get by. I am so glad that I was given an understanding of the biblical worldview of health, not just because of the benefits obtained but also because of the love for the Lord that the religious element brought to me.

This study also found that women (85 percent of them born and raised in Mexico) who attended church regularly were significantly acculturated to American life when compared with those not attending religious services. Church had not only been crucial in developing a healthy lifestyle, but also instrumental in achieving successful adaptation to the host cultural milieu.

Laura Koenig and George Vaillant investigated the effect of church attendance on health and well-being in men from a group whose first assessment took place at fourteen years of age and the most recent at seventy-nine.[6] This was a major study initiated in 1950, and it focused on alcohol use and physical health. However, multiple pieces of data were also collected over the years, such as church attendance (never, occasionally, monthly, or weekly). Church attendance at forty-seven years was a predictor of health at seventy. Further statistical analysis showed that church attendance was indirectly linked to health—the actual predictors were the use (or abstention) of alcohol and tobacco and the presence or absence of a good mood. However, in the case of well-being, church attendance at forty-seven was a direct predictor (with no mediators) of well-being twenty-three years later, and this is an excellent indication of the weight that religion has upon mental and social health, since well-being meant satisfaction with work, children, friends, and marriage. This fact takes us to the next section of the link between church attendance and mental health.

Church attendance and mental health

Depression and anxiety are, in that order, the top mental disorders worldwide. In common language, they represent severe sadness, hopelessness, restlessness, and fear. The Bible is full of hopeful expressions, such as joy, rejoicing, be still, do not fear, do not fret, be of courage, and so on. Invariably, these messages of reassurance are in the context of God's invitation to accept Him, to love Him, and to obey Him. Recent research is finding, again and again, that attending church is contributing to the prevention and relief of mental disorders.

Let us mention a few examples of research showing the mental health benefits of going to church. Most studies exploring the relationships between these variables are done with a large variety of samples in multiple locations. Yet, they all point in the same direction: *church attendance seems to play a protective role against mental illnesses.* Christopher Lewis and a group of associates conducted a study in the highly religious culture of Northern Ireland.[7] They studied a sample of individuals taken at random from five thousand households. Participants took a measure of psychological well-being (the GH-Q12) and answered questions about affiliation to religious denomination, as well as frequency of attending their place of worship. The principal finding was that higher frequencies of religious service attendance were associated with better psychological health.

The connection between going to church and enjoying a healthy mind seems particularly relevant in the elderly. Jim Mitchell and Dave Wheatherly from East Carolina University School of Medicine conducted research in rural eastern North Carolina about religiosity and mental health.[8] Participants were inquired not only about religious attendance but also about religious belief, prayer, and the role of religion in the process of illness. They were also asked about their mental and emotional health at present, and in comparison with, five years prior to the interview. Consistent with the mainstream studies, women and African American elderly people were more likely to profess and to attend or participate in church than were their counterparts. The bottom line of the study was that reduced physical functionality and reduced mental health went together with limited church attendance. Likewise, fewer symptoms of mental illness in general and specifically fewer depression symptoms were associated with greater church attendance and participation.

Results are similar in locations far from North America. Rita Law and David Sbarra conducted a follow-up study over a period of eight years in Australia.[9] Church attendance had a protective effect against the emergence of mood disorders (curiously, this protection was more pronounced in married than in nonmarried churchgoers). In this study, consistent attendance made the real difference: those who went to religious services regularly over five years enjoyed a lower level of depression when compared with those whose attendance was erratic. Some gender differences were also found: when men were inconsistent in attendance, they developed a higher risk of depression than did the inconsistent women.

Only now, after having realized the centrality of attending church, I sense how critical it was for my family to be committed to providing transportation for a couple of elderly people to come to church every Sabbath. It was encouraging to see them happy and to notice that going to worship was for them the highlight of the week. Although I was not aware of the health implications for the elderly, I now look back with much more satisfaction and a sense of service. We may have been helping postpone early cognitive deterioration of these lovely older people, since we used to pick them up at their homes early Sabbath mornings!

And this principle does not apply only to the aged. Young professionals, teachers in the United Kingdom, also showed that going to church kept them safe from emotional instability. Researchers from Trinity College and the University of Wales administered a personality inventory to 311 elementary teachers working in southwest England in order to assess psychoticism, together with a few measures of spirituality, including church attendance.[10] It was clear that the correlation between these variables was inverse; in other words, the higher the church attendance, the lower the psychotic tendencies of teachers. It is interesting to see studies like this showing the soothing effect of religious life upon one of the most stressful professions: teaching. Teachers are indeed in one of the top five most stressful jobs just behind air traffic controllers, combat soldiers, firefighters, and coal miners.

Students themselves also seem to profit from church attendance in regards to their mental health. Christopher Lewis from the University of Ulster, together with several associates in Norway, collected data from 479 children and adolescents in secondary schools in Norway (ages eleven to eighteen).[11] Using a common European inventory (the Eysenck's Personality Questionnaire), researchers observed the correlation between church attendance, prayer, and indicators of psychoticism. Results showed that those involved in the mentioned religious behaviors enjoyed lower levels of psychoticism in comparison with their counterparts not attending church or attending sporadically.

The study led by Carlos Reyes-Ortiz seems to confirm the assurance transmitted by the psalmist that "a thousand shall fall at thy side, and ten thousand at thy right hand; but it shall not come nigh thee" (Psalm 91:7, KJV).[12] This investigation focused on Mexican Americans only, and investigated the connection between church attendance and fear of falling. A large group of 1,341 men and women aged seventy and older participated. This study found that fear of falling was higher in women than it was in men. In addition, participants with a history of falling, arthritis, hypertension, or urinary incontinence were more fearful than were those without such ailments. Church attendance was a clear predictor of reduced levels of fear of falling: the more frequent attendance, the less afraid they were of falling. This particular relationship remained significant after controlling for relevant socio-demographic data, medical conditions, depressive symptoms, cognitive functions, falls, ability to function in daily tasks, and lower body performance.

An investigation carried out with Mormons and non-Mormons revealed that the highest immunity against mental disorders was for those active, regular churchgoers. Ray Merrill and Richard Salazar from Brigham Young University studied the relationship between church attendance and mental health among 4,287 Mormons and 1,270 non-Mormons.[13] Those more likely to seek professional mental health were the less active Mormons and those with no religion preference. This analysis was done after adjusting for alcohol use, tobacco use, education, income, physical activity, general health status, employment, body mass index, gender, and age.

Acts 2:44–47 gives us good hints on the lifestyle of that first generation of Christians. In a brief and compacted manner, we are reminded of the mental health benefits of living the life of early believers:

- *Sharing (verse 44).* Making one's resources available to others brings about a great sense of well-being. It adds satisfaction to see that others experience joy or relief from pain due to our willingness to share. Jesus calls those "blessed" (Acts 20:35).
- *Worship and praising God (Acts 2:46, 47).* A small sample of the large amount of evidence showing the benefits of corporate worship throughout this chapter.
- *Communion (verse 46).* Remembering the Lord's Supper is a direct way to seek reconciliation, a clear and powerful process to attain mental and physical health.
- *Fellowship (verse 47).* According to the biblical account, this closeness translates into glad and sincere hearts and ease of interpersonal interaction.

The sum of this passage is the wonderful result of bringing more and more people to the pathway to salvation. Notice that the record does not attribute the success to the proselytizing efforts of the believers; rather, it was God who "added to the church daily those who were being saved" (verse 47).

Adolescent problems and issues

Delinquency and substance abuse are among the top problems of adolescence anywhere in the world. This is a time of struggle for these youngsters; in their search for identity and their place in the world, sometimes they end up exploring areas that might place them in trouble. However, children that have enjoyed regular church attendance with their families are very likely to continue within the church during their teenage years and be protected from these problems and issues. Alcohol and substance abuse have attracted the maximum interest in the research community in the last couple of decades. Harold Koenig found over 450 scholarly studies connecting religion and spirituality with substances; about 85 percent of them showed a significant relationship between religion and spirituality and a decreased use of substances.[14] When he examined the best-designed studies (247), there were about 90 percent positive results. The direction is clear: being connected with a church is a safeguard against the use of substances, and this is especially true in adolescents.

Brent Benda, from the University of Arkansas School of Social Work, explored church attendance and religiousness effect on adolescent delinquency and their use of alcohol and other drugs.[15] Benda analyzed data from 3,395 seventh-to ninth-graders from sixty-six school districts in a southern state. They were from both rural (67 percent) and urban (33 percent) areas, and he found that religiousness in these teenagers meant good protection from unlawful acts: alcohol use, other drug use, and delinquency. (Delinquency included fighting, shoplifting, stealing from others, staying out all night without permission, and skipping school.) Religiousness was found to be more important in the behavior of girls than it was in boys. Religion is especially beneficial to adolescents because of their search for meaning and purpose. Religious communities provide reasons and strength to resist temptation and to make good choices. They also offer the courage to relate to the omniscient and omnipotent God—not often popular in this peer group. The strength of the peer group remained solid in this study: the strongest single link found was between friends' use of alcohol and/or drugs and their own use. In other words, the strongest source of protection against the use of substances came from the association with other young people from the church who were making the right choices.

Adolescents are also highly vulnerable to smoking. This age is the time of initiation, as most young people typically start the use of cigarettes at around sixteen. In spite of the knowledge that tobacco is addictive and hazardous to health, 20 percent of American teens smoke. Three thousand teens start the habit every day, and nearly one thousand of those will die because of the tobacco. Smoking is also a gateway to other substances; for example, teenagers who smoke are three times more likely to use alcohol, eight times more likely to use marijuana, and twenty-two times more likely to use cocaine.

The good news for churchgoers is that these risks are considerably reduced, and teens will enjoy protection from the initiation and continuation of the smoking habit. Carla Berg from the University of Minnesota Cancer Center in Minneapolis studied the role of church attendance in a number of areas, including smoking.[16] They found that teens with the highest risk of initiating and maintaining a smoking habit were those older than their peers, low academic achievers, depressives, and those who did not attend church (or go sporadically). Those whose parents smoked were especially at risk. In addition, parental attitude toward smoking emerged as a strong factor in this investigation. It is important to remind parents that as strong as the peer group is at this age, adolescents who perceive that their parents strongly disapprove of smoking are less likely to initiate, and progress to, regular smoking.

This study also found a relationship between having depressive symptoms and the likelihood of being a smoker. I will discuss the religiosity-low depression connection in the next chapter, but suffice it to say that when young people lack the sufficient emotional support offered by church and family, they are more likely to be depressed and to resort to compensatory behaviors, such as smoking and the use of other substances.

The areas of conduct and social functioning are of great concern to parents, teachers, and community members, and rightly so. Being able to have proper social skills and a smooth interaction with others opens up pathways that other abilities and talents will not. But how do we ensure that teenagers are more courteous, respectful, and patient with others? A study found that when mothers attend church, they tend to have better socially functioning teenagers. Stuart Varon, medical director of the Johns Hopkins Children's Mental Health Center, and Anne Riley, associate professor at the Johns Hopkins School of Hygiene and Public Health, conducted a study to examine the link between maternal church attendance and the behavioral and social functioning of their adolescent children ages eleven to thirteen.[17] The research was carefully conducted, not simply administering a questionnaire but holding personal home interviews with the 143 youth and their mothers. With the exception of household income, a mother's church attendance was the strongest predictor of the mental health and social functioning of teenage participants. In fact, a mother's going to church was a better predictor than was a mother's religion, a mother's education, a child's race, a child's gender, or a family structure. The investigation also found out that adolescents whose mothers attended church at least weekly enjoyed a greater degree of life satisfaction, were more involved with their families, and possessed better skills in solving health-related issues; they also felt greater support from their peers than those youths whose mothers had lower levels of church attendance.

Providing sufficient support for teenagers and youth to remain in church is a highly desirable task for everyone. Family is perhaps the number one agent. The role of Christian schools can also be decisive in many cases. Jerome Thayer, from Andrews University, based on data of various Adventist studies, reports a significantly higher percent of young adults remaining in the Adventist Church if they were given an Adventist education.[18]

Conclusion

Through faithful church attendance and participation, God has provided wonderful rewards for His children: a better mental and physical health, optimal relationships, and an endless list of useful advantages for a fuller life. But going to church is not just about those things. Most importantly, religious services provide the opportunity to meet God: "The Lord is in his holy temple; let all the earth be silent before him" (Habakkuk 2:20, NIV).

After several decades, I can still remember the efforts made by a youth pastor to instill in us young people the idea that going to church was about meeting God, not just friends. He used the passage of Acts 20:9—"Seated in a window was a young man named Eutychus, who was sinking into a deep sleep as Paul talked on and on. When he was sound asleep, he fell to the ground from the third story and was picked up dead" (NIV). The minister explained that because Paul "kept on talking until midnight" (verse 7, NIV) and because of the warmth added by "many lamps in the upstairs room" (verse 8, NIV), Eutychus's sleep was easily induced. But an important question remained unanswered: Why was Eutychus sitting on the window to start with? The youth pastor's interpretation was that Eutychus was probably not listening to Paul's sermon; he was on the lookout for pretty girls or other interesting things happening along that street in Troas!

Distractors can be of various guises depending on whether one is motivated or unmotivated, young or old, male or female, poor or wealthy, but we all must keep focused on the uttermost reason to go to church: to meet God. Faithful, active, and pious church attendance is a personal choice to be made. Those who value it highly will be highly committed to it. King David testified about how crucial it was for him to dwell in the house of the Lord: "Better is one day in your courts than a thousand elsewhere; I would rather be a doorkeeper in the house of my God than dwell in the tents of the wicked" (Psalm 84:10, NIV).

God told Solomon to ask whatever he wanted, and he chose wisdom (2 Chronicles 1:7–10). On the other hand, David, his father, opted for a different request: "One thing I ask from the Lord, this only do I seek: that I may dwell in the house of the Lord all the days of my life, to gaze on the beauty of the Lord and to seek him in his temple" (Psalm 27:4, NIV). In the end, God set David, in spite of his imperfections, as an example of integrity and uprightness (1 Kings 9:4) to Solomon and to many generations of kings thereafter.

Study Questions
- Find Bible passages where the reader is admonished to worship together,

such as Hebrews 10:25: "not giving up meeting together" (NIV). In your concordance, use words such as "assembly," "congregation," "house of the Lord," "tabernacle," "convocation," "church," and so on. How do the Old and New Testaments differ? What is the context of each text?

- Using an encyclopedia or searching the Internet, find out the service attendance expectations from various religions. Do you see a difference in the outcome of believers when they are *required* to attend church or when they are *encouraged* (or it is simply left up to them) to attend religious services? What is the right balance for you?
- What is the meaning of God's commands to attend convocations, or sacred assemblies, for the Sabbath day (Leviticus 23:3)?

Application Thoughts

- The chief reason why many people remain in (or abandon) the church has to do with the attitude of fellow worshipers. What can you do to ensure that your brothers and sisters are faithful to the church and love the Lord?
- How do you reconcile the openness of Jesus' statement: "I have not come to call the righteous, but sinners" (Mark 2:17, NIV) and the text where He states: "If they refuse to listen even to the church, treat them as you would a pagan or a tax collector" (Matthew 18:17, NIV)?
- Reflect on the meaning of these words: "Guard your steps when you go to the house of God. Go near to listen rather than to offer the sacrifice of fools, who do not know that they do wrong" (Ecclesiastes 5:1, NIV). List a few things you can do to follow this counsel.
- Ellen White says that Mary and Joseph, albeit in the midst of religious events, lost sight of Jesus and had to agonize searching for Him for three days. She then says, "Many attend religious services, and are refreshed and comforted by the word of God; but through neglect of meditation, watchfulness, and prayer, they lose the blessing."[19] Is it possible to be regular in attending church and yet lose sight of Jesus? What arrangements does your life require to prevent anything like that happening?

---

1. Ellen G. White, *Christ's Object Lessons,* 130.

2. George W. Comstock and Kay B. Partridge, "Church Attendance and Health," *Journal of Chronic Diseases* 25 (1972): 665–672.

3. Harold Koenig, Dana King, and Verna B. Carson, *Handbook of Religion and Health,* 2nd ed. (New York: Oxford University Press, 2012).

4. Eliezer Schnall et al., "The Relationship Between Religion and Cardiovascular Outcomes and All-Cause Mortality in the Women's Health Initiative Observational Study," *Psychology and Health* 25 (2010): 249–263.

5. Elva M. Arredondo and John P. Elder, "Is Church Attendance Associated With Latinas' Health Practices and Self-Reported Health?" *American Journal of Health Behavior* 29 (2005): 502–511.

6. Laura B. Koenig and George E. Vaillant, "A Prospective Study of Church Attendance and Health Over the Lifespan," *Health Psychology* 28 (2009): 117–124.

7. Christopher A. Lewis, "The Association Between Church Attendance and Psychological Health in Northern Ireland: A National Representative Survey Among Adults Allowing for Sex Differences and Denominational Difference," *Journal of Religion and Health* 50 (2011): 986–995. The study included 5,205 participants, 41.5 percent males and 58.5 percent females, 40 percent Catholics and 56 percent Protestants, with the remaining belonging to other religions.

8. Jim Mitchell and Dave Weatherly, "Beyond Church Attendance: Religiosity and Mental Health Among Rural Older Adults," *Journal of Cross-Cultural Gerontology* 15 (2000): 37–54. Two independent random samples were used: one of 2,178 persons aged 60 to 104 (average of 73) and another of 868 participants between 65 and 101 years of age, with an average of 75 years.

9. Rita W. Law and David A. Sbarra, "The Effects of Church Attendance and Marital Status on the Longitudinal Trajectories of Depressed Mood Among Older Adults," *Journal of Aging and Health* 21 (2009): 803–823. They followed up with 791 people with an average age of seventy-six.

10. Leslie J. Francis and Peter Johnson, "Mental Health, Prayer and Church Attendance Among Primary Schoolteachers," *Mental Health, Religion & Culture* 2 (1999): 153–158.

11. Christopher A. Lewis et al., "Personality, Prayer and Church Attendance Among a Sample of 11 to 18 Year Olds in Norway," *Mental Health, Religion & Culture* 3 (2004): 269–274.

12. C. A. Reyes-Ortiz et al., "Higher Church Attendance Predicts Lower Fear of Falling in Older Mexican-Americans," *Aging & Mental Health* 10 (2006): 13–18.

13. Ray M. Merrill and Richard D. Salazar, "Relationship Between Church Attendance and Mental Health Among Mormons and Non-Mormons in Utah," *Mental Health, Religion & Culture* 5 (2002): 17–33.

14. Harold Koenig, *Spirituality and Health Research: Methods, Measurement, Statistics, and Resources* (Conshohocken, PA: Templeton Press, 2011).

15. Brent B. Benda, Sandra K. Pope, and Kelly J. Kelleher, "Church Attendance or Religiousness: Their Relationship to Adolescents' Use of Alcohol, Other Drugs, and Delinquency," *Alcoholism Treatment Quarterly* 24 (2006): 75–87.

16. Carla Berg et al., "The Roles of Parenting, Church Attendance, and Depression in Adolescent Smoking," *Journal of Community Health* 34 (2009): 56–63. Participants were 299 female adolescents from an urban pediatric clinic of the Midwest.

17. Stuart R. Varon and Anne W. Riley, "Relationship Between Maternal Church Attendance and Adolescent Mental Health and Social Functioning," *Psychiatric Services* 50 (1999): 799–805.

18. Jerome Thayer, "The Impact of Adventist Schools on Students," paper presented at the Fourth Symposium on the Bible and Adventist Scholarship, Riviera Maya, Quintana Roo, Mexico, March 16–22, 2008.

19. Ellen G. White, *The Desire of Ages,* 83.

Chapter 7

The Benefits of Joy
and Gratitude

"A cheerful heart is good medicine,
but a crushed spirit dries up the bones." —Proverbs 17:22, NIV

I talked to Bob Stumph for the first time one year after he was informed of having gastroesophageal junction cancer, and two months after he was told that the cancer had metastasized into the liver and lungs and other lymph nodes. The doctor gave him five to thirteen months to live. He had already gone through surgery, radiation, and chemotherapy and was undergoing another round of chemotherapy. We had a good conversation and I noticed he was very animated, explaining his experience in great detail and, above all, in an enviable mood despite the roller coaster of events of the previous twelve months. Bob's words kept referring to his complete trust in the Lord, and, although he recognized not understanding the whys, he put himself in God's hands unconditionally.

Talking about when he first heard the dreaded news of cancer, Bob said, "I had no sense whatsoever of anything going wrong with my health. I was on a good diet, exercising, and doing everything, as a good Seventh-day Adventist. I have been a pastor for a good forty years—I was in pastoral ministry even before I went to school to take theology. One day I noticed unusual symptoms and went to the doctor. An endoscopy was performed and, after I woke up from the anesthesia, the doctor said, 'I don't have good news for you. You've got cancer and you are in an advanced stage already.' Three days later, the cancer was confirmed via a pathology report. My doctors assured me that this was very unusual to happen with my lifestyle. I was puzzled too. From there on, I started the whole planning for treatment in Seattle under the care of an excellent surgeon and an outstanding oncologist, both with the University of Washington, VA, and Cancer Research. Both top specialists in the field. But my real trust was in God. At the beginning, the news of cancer brought questions to me: 'What do I do now? I have always had confidence in God.' A horrific experience that twenty-five years earlier solidified my trust in God came to mind, and I thought that if I didn't doubt then, I was not going to doubt now. Yes, I was shook up, but this made me stronger, more reliant on what the Lord could do. This did not shadow my faith by any means."

One of the first things Bob decided to do was send weekly e-mails to his family and friends who had been praying for him all those months. I read those messages. They are warm and full of hope; they share the mundane news of every week, the development of the illness, and always include a reflection on a Bible text, a story, or incident with spiritual applications. "My faith was never affected—it may have intensified," Bob stated. "What I decided to do was not to keep this thing to myself—my first major decision. I decided to let people know right away in order to have a stronger support through corporate prayer. I knew that the more people prayed, the stronger things would happen. People are praying for me all the time. I hear from people all the time. I feel those prayers; I absolutely do as well as the words of encouragement that they send. I can't go in the dumps with so much support. I am fully lifted up with all the things surrounding me.

"Devotions, study, and prayer have been very comforting," Bob said, when asked about coping with his situation. "I have had this habit for years: at night I begin to say the Lord's Prayer. Then I reflect on the meaning of each sentence, each word. I never get to the end of the prayer because there is so much to meditate about it. I know that it makes my connections strong during this time."

Talking about the moment he learned that the cancer had metastasized after nine months of various forms of treatment, Bob said, "I was paying a courtesy visit to my oncologist and he, right there and then, found out with the CT scan report in hand that the cancer had metastasized. When he informed me, he gave me numbers: five to thirteen months to live. This caused me to say, 'Lord, if You want me to rest, let's be quick about it, so I don't endure a lot of pain.' I was downhill for about a month. Then the oncologist offered a new regimen of doing a cleanup chemo, and he got me on this regimen; and he is pretty confident that this kind of treatment could take me five or six years. But I am willing for the Lord to have His way in my life. Whatever the Lord wants, I am fine. His plan is far better than mine."

Asked about the sources of joy in these uncertain times, he said, "Just about everything has brought me joy. I don't know what it is to be sad. Yes, I have cried with my wife, but I have done much more of anticipating eternity. I think of spending eternity with my family, and sharing salvation—a major thing to do in glory. These things have brought me happiness. I try to imagine what heaven is going to be like in detail after the resurrection and the events following, going into eternity. Also, I contemplate the life of Christ, especially the last hours of His life. My prayer is, 'Lord, You are going to help me the way You have helped me all my life in any hardship I have ever experienced.' "

The same God that brought gladness to the king of Israel has granted Bob Stumph the excitement of eternal salvation, as the psalmist says, "Surely you have granted him unending blessings and made him glad with the joy of your presence" (Psalm 21:6, NIV). Indeed, God has been present in Bob's life over his entire existence and most intimately over the past difficult months. In the same way, the Lord is open to bless and guide anyone else who wants to allow His influence and, thus, experience the joy of salvation, even in this world full of sin and suffering.

This chapter is about the benefits that Christian joy, happiness, and gratefulness can bring to the believer in sickness and in health and under whatever conditions. The Voice saying "Rejoice!" resounds throughout the entire Scriptures, for God wants His children to be joyous and free from the sadness, gloom, and dejection that can easily grow in our lives.

Religion and joy

According to the General Social Surveys of Americans, in the years 1972 and 2008, 48 percent of those attending church services more than weekly rated themselves as "very happy," but only 26 percent of those never attending church services said they were "very happy." That religion brings joy to the faithful is obvious to those who are religious; although this fact is not always so obvious to others, the scientific community is using the tools of medical and social sciences to find the same truth that believers already know by experience. Over the past two decades, Harold Koenig, in his review of religion and health research, found at least 326 quantitative studies on the relationship between religion and spirituality (R/S) and a sense of well-being.[1] Of the 120 studies deemed as most rigorous methodologically, 82 percent found that greater happiness, satisfaction with life, and an overall sense that life is good was found in those with high R/S.

If we look at the area of religion and depression, which would be at the opposite end of joy, Koenig found that 444 quantitative studies had been conducted in the years 1990 to 2010 on the topic. Sixty-one percent of them reported that less depression or faster recovery from depression were attained via religious intervention. In contrast, only 6 percent found greater depression in those who were more religious. The remaining 33 percent found relationships, but they were too small to be statistically significant.[2]

The empirical study of religion and happiness goes back more than half a century. The earliest study I encountered goes back to 1957 when C. T. O'Reilly surveyed a random sample of Roman Catholics from Chicago.[3] He found that happiness was related to religiosity. He classified participants according to the level of religious activity and asked them to rate themselves on a three-point continuum of happiness (very happy—moderately happy—less happy). Within the "very happy" group, he found that 55 percent were "more active," whereas 34 percent were in the "medium" level of religious activity, and only 11 percent in the "less active" group were very happy. This study provided a groundbreaking step indicating that, by and large, religious involvement could be a source of happiness or at least run parallel with happiness. From there on, many valid and reliable measures have been developed and used widely to offer a repeated confirmation that religiosity and happiness run together.

Let us look at a few examples. Kristopher Gauthier and his research team from Wake Forest University, in Winston-Salem, North Carolina, studied women and men recruited from three sources: (1) undergraduate classes at a small midwestern liberal arts college, (2) alumni from the same college, and (3) church members of various congregations from the metro-Detroit area.[4] Researchers were interested not only in the general religiosity to life satisfaction interface but, particularly, how religious doubt fits the equation. Religious doubt was understood as misgivings about traditional religious teachings, the feeling that religion didn't really make people better, or the feeling that overall religious teachings are contradictory or don't make sense. The findings indicated that high levels of religiosity were associated with high levels of life satisfaction and that high levels of religious doubt correlate to low satisfaction in life. Not that doubts are always wrong, but, in the process of resolving them, doubts can cause cognitive dissonance or create shame or guilt capable of interfering with life satisfaction. This study also found that women rated higher than did males in religiosity, which is usually the case. Men scored much higher than did women on religious doubt.

Most of the research on religiosity, spirituality, individual happiness, subjective well-being, and so on, was American. However, I found more than I expected from other countries—some from American researchers using foreign populations, others conducted directly by international investigators. For example, I found one study by Christopher Lewis from the University of Ulster, in Londonderry, Northern Ireland, who studied the connection between religious coping and happiness.[5] They collected data using the widely accepted Happiness Oxford Questionnaire as well as measures of personality, religious orientation, and religious coping. They found intrinsic religious orientation and happiness interrelations and also connections between positive religious coping and happiness. The stronger of the two associations was that of intrinsic religion and happiness. People who spent significant time in private thought and prayer (as opposed to "going to church because it helps me make friends") had the highest levels of reported happiness. Likewise, happiness was attained via religious coping as demonstrated by those adhering to statements such as, "I focus on religion to stop worrying about my problems," or "I know that God does not abandon me." Out of these two findings, the stronger connection, statistically, was the one on intrinsic religion. According to this study, we sometimes focus too much on the social aspect of religion, which does bring joy to the believer, but quiet encounters with the Lord can be even more powerful.

A personal encounter with our God, a one-on-one interaction, is the most meaningful experience in spiritual growth. It reminds me of the value of one-on-one tutoring in the field of education. No matter how many superior instructional methods emerge over others, good-quality individual tutoring is the most efficacious. My department at the university has an ongoing project with the children at the Farm Labor Homes of Walla Walla. The kids living in that compound, being English-language learners, have a difficult time reading. Our education students go there regularly and sit with these children, listening to them read and guiding them in the complex process of developing literacy. We also trust that these children will be able to see Jesus via their tutors. Our encounters with the Lord are really the crucial moments to develop the mysterious and miraculous process of growing in Christ.

Author Emyr Williams from the Warwick Religions and Education Research Unit at the Institute of Education, University of Warwick, United Kingdom, performed a study of a trans-European sample.[6] This group explored happiness and satisfaction with life in participants according to various levels of marital status and religious attendance. Analysis of the collected data revealed overall high levels of satisfaction with life and higher feelings of happiness in subgroups who attended religious services on a regular basis. This fact held true even after controlling for relevant variables (age, sex, and being married) known to affect happiness. Again, we can see the fulfillment of God's promises to His followers: "The LORD has done great things for us, and we are filled with joy" (Psalm 126:3, NIV).

Even in Japan, results are consistent with findings in Western cultures. Michael Roemer from Ball State University in Indiana, sampled some Japanese adults in order to replicate the many studies carried out among Christians in the area of religion and happiness.[7] The purpose of the study was to examine whether religious devotion significantly mitigates the effect of stressful situations and brings about life satisfaction and happiness. Participants were from six major regions in Japan. They came from the Buddhist tradition, the New

Religions (those established in the past 150 years including beliefs and practices from Buddhism, Shintoism, and other traditions), the Christian religions, and "no affiliation." Results were consistent with the idea that religion provides a boost in well-being and a protection against adverse circumstances; religious devotion was found linked to life satisfaction and happiness; furthermore, religious devotion buffered the negative effects of unemployment as well as the disadvantages of low-class status.

Also, to compensate for the overwhelming majority of studies with Christians, a group of researchers from Bowling Green State University in Ohio studied a sample of Jewish participants.[8] The role of the Jewish religiousness on anxiety, depression, and happiness was the target of this research. These people responded to questions such as, "In general, I consider myself 'not a very happy person' to 'a very happy person' " on a seven-point scale. Or, "Some people are generally very happy. They enjoy life regardless of what is going on, getting the most out of everything. To what extent does this characterization describe you?" Respondents would then choose from 1 to 7: "not at all" to "a great deal." Results revealed that higher levels of trust in God by these Jewish believers were associated with greater personal happiness. Also, it was observed that high trust was correlated with less anxiety and less depression, showing again the beneficial touch of faith on happiness and well-being.

How faith promotes joy

The mechanisms whereby religious beliefs and practices make many people feel happier and more satisfied with life are not really known. But there are a number of explanations that are the product of observations as well as logic. I outline them in the next paragraphs.

Religious groups have inherent social networks that are supportive in nature. Parishioners share beliefs and practices and feel comfortable with one another. All religions promote altruism and a willingness to deny oneself in some way to help others. Therefore, churches tend to provide attractive community settings where people enter confidently and remain with a sense of belonging, satisfaction, and joy.

Although with a great deal of variation across denominations and religions, religious groups often promote healthy lifestyles in regards to diet, exercise, modes of entertainment, and so on. These recommendations discourage people from engaging in risky and addictive behaviors. All these prevent health deterioration and make their followers happier, more satisfied individuals.

These behavioral recommendations are not only limited to physical health but also extend to mental health. Religious beliefs promote principles and

virtues such as love, forgiveness, empathy, self-control, honesty, and contentment and dissuade hatred, jealousy, covetousness, selfishness, deceit, and intemperance. These principles work toward a more balanced state of mind and,
consequently, a higher life satisfaction.

In addition, religious people maintain a personal relationship with God.
This makes them experience a sense of being blessed and obtaining repentance
and forgiveness, preventing deleterious states such as guilt and remorse. They
can look at the future with hope rather than despair and sense divine guidance,
bringing solace and peace to their lives. Being near God also produces a sense of
guidance at every step of life. Alliance with God is also a safeguard against the
ravages of trial, loss, sorrow, and suffering because, even when these things are
present, the believer can find meaning and hope through knowing the reality of
God and His love. In Christianity, there is an ultimate gift of salvation through
the mediation of Jesus Christ in spite of human transgression.

Music is also a powerful source of joy. It can not only be enjoyable but also
therapeutic and spiritually uplifting. The tune and lyrics of a hymn or a song
dear to one's heart can transform a depressive mood into a joyful spirit fairly
quickly. As good music is central to worship, religious individuals have additional opportunities to develop and maintain a joyful state of mind.

Finally, persons of faith can see order and sense in the universe. And when
they see evil, they can explain it in terms of sin, which shall pass away because
of God's provisions to save and transform people who accept and follow Him.
Beliefs like these protect people from despair and offer a joyous outlook in the
short and long term.

In sum, the presence of God in people's lives can transform suffering: "You
turned my wailing into dancing; you removed my sackcloth and clothed me
with joy" (Psalm 30:11, NIV).

Health and joy

In her latest New Year message, outlining a few suggestions for change, Surgeon
General Regina Benjamin said, "Healthy behavior should be joyful; I want to put
joy back into health, joy for the individuals, and joy for the professionals. Never
underestimate the power of joy in health!"[9] Ellen G. White lists specific attitudes
(joy and gratitude included) that can protect us from illness: "Gratitude, rejoicing,
benevolence, trust in God's love and care—these are health's greatest safeguard. To
the Israelites they were to be the very keynote of life."[10]

How does joy cause health? For one thing, chronic unhappiness awakens the
stress response, which keeps the person alert, but promotes high-blood pressure
and low-immune response, thus making the organism vulnerable. In contrast,

128

a state of happiness causes a good mood and enhances the immune system, thus reducing the chances of infections and protecting the body from chronic maladies. Besides, happy people tend to be motivated to take care of their own health: to watch their diet and their weight, to exercise, and to use all available resources for a better physical condition. Happy people tend to be optimistic and to process events more positively than negativistic people. This makes joyous people unlikely to harbor catastrophic thoughts, a precursor to depression. Also a joyful person tends to be liked by others and his or her social network (a prominent factor of health) ends up being stable and of quality when compared with the social network of pessimistic people.

One of the best reviews of literature on happiness as a powerful factor on health is Ruut Veenhoven's, a sociologist from Erasmus University in Rotterdam, Netherlands.[11] In this review, happiness emerges as a very strong predictor of longevity in healthy populations. The effect of unhappiness estimated in this study is the same as the effect of consistent smoking on a person. Veenhoven chose the best studies methodologically, all longitudinal, conducted within normal populations. They were done in the United States, Japan, Germany, Sweden, Finland, Canada, England, and the Netherlands. They focused on twenty-four effects, of which sixteen showed a positive effect of happiness on longevity, eight were still positive but not statistically significant, and none were negative. The attitude of overall happiness added 7.5 to 10 years of life—about the same added value as being a vegetarian!

The most significant effect of joy on health and longevity is found in the "Nun Study." Deborah Danner and two other colleagues from the University of Kentucky tracked a collection of six-decade-old documents to study the effects of joy on longevity.[12] A group of 180 nuns who had written their autobiographies in their young adult years were followed up at an advanced age (seventy-five to ninety-five). It all began on September 22, 1930, when the mother superior of the School Sisters of Notre Dame in North America sent a letter to all sisters requesting they each begin a tradition of writing an autobiography. Decades later, this mix of handwritten and typed documents became invaluable research data. The group was made up of women who had joined the congregation between 1931 and 1943, most from Milwaukee, Wisconsin, and from Baltimore, Maryland. Writings were coded into "low positive emotion," "high positive emotion," or "neutral" by two independent coders and verified by a third coder, thus attaining a high degree of consistency. High positive emotions were rich in describing states of joy and happiness; for example, "God started my life off well by bestowing upon me *a grace of inestimable value. . . .* The past year, which I have spent as a candidate studying at Notre Dame College, has been *a very happy one.* Now I look forward *with eager joy* to receiving the Holy Habit of Our Lady and to a life of union with Love Divine."[13] In their semantic analysis, raters were looking for positive emotions, assigning higher values to the top ones in this order: happiness, interest, love, hope, gratefulness, contentment, and so on. Likewise, they searched for negative emotions rating these as most negative in this order: sadness, fear, disinterest, confusion, anxiety, and so on.

Results showed that participants using language with most positive emotions in their early writings displayed the least risk of mortality in late life. In quantitative terms, the group with least positive emotions, in comparison with the group of most positive emotions, had two and a half times more risk of mortality than did the latter. How this process works is still unknown. But just knowing that emotions expressed in early adulthood (ages eighteen to thirty-two) became a predictor of health and longevity decades later should help us arrive at the decision to harbor a lot more joy in our hearts. And I am not suggesting that a person enter a religious order to accomplish this; in fact, some cloistered nuns had a joy-free attitude and died earlier than did the happy ones. I am just bringing this in as an example of how joy can promote health, well-being, and long life; this becomes deeper and more meaningful if such joy is based on an ongoing relationship with Jesus Christ, who can bestow the best joy if we request it: "Ask and you will receive, and *your joy will be complete*" (John 16:24, NIV; emphasis added).

Morgan Green and Marta Elliott from the University of Nevada–Reno also studied the relationship between religion, health, and psychological well-being (happiness).[14] They used data from the University of Chicago–based General Social Survey (GSS) and extracted the cases with responses on physical health, happiness, and religiosity. In the context of health and happiness, the most relevant finding was that people who identified strongly with their religious beliefs reported high levels of health and well-being (happiness). Being religiously affiliated, *per se,* did not bring about any higher-than-average levels of health and well-being. Only those who had a strong sense of belonging to their religion tended to get health and well-being benefits, regardless of what religion, and regardless of their work, family, or social support. The analysis of data also revealed no connection between income and happiness, suggesting, again, that there is no specific level of income that facilitates happiness. There are high-income, medium-income, and low-income people who are happy, and there are also unhappy people at all levels of income.

Joy seems to be a good promoter of health, but sometimes illness takes over anyway, as in Bob's case at the beginning of the chapter. Or accidents happen, as in the study below. But in the midst of those devastating circumstances, God is ready to bring rays of hope, peace, and joy to the victim. The study by Irmo Marini and Noreen Glover-Graf from the University of Texas explored how faith brought happiness to patients with spinal cord injuries, even in the midst of their situation.[15] Researchers contacted former spinal cord injury (SCI) patients of a SCI Model System hospital in the southeastern United States.

In 90 percent of the cases, these people suffered from SCI because of auto accidents, falls, sports, and other injuries. By and large, they claimed to be religious: of the 156 participants, 19 individuals reported no religion. The remainder indicated a specific religious affiliation. The majority of participants expressed overall satisfaction with God and stated that God had helped them cope with their illness and helped them attain happiness. Although 26 percent said that they were angry at one time with God for their injury, 60 percent said that they felt closer to God since they acquired their disability, 64 percent believed that their spirituality had helped them to accept their condition, 57 percent became more spiritual, and 59 percent became better people.

Material possessions and joy

One of my early memories is going with my mother and sister to pay regular visits to a cousin who was a nun living in a cloister convent outside Madrid. Everything was mysterious about those visits. We started by knocking at a huge, dark, wooden door. First, one of the nuns would identify us through a window covered with an iron grille; a key as big as a butcher's knife was dropped so that we could open the door. Once inside, we found our way to a reception room with two sets of bars, each one a yard apart from the other. The nuns were behind one set, and we remained behind the other. We couldn't touch each other, only talk and make expressions with our hands. Although the light was always poor inside those thick walls spotted with just a few small windows, we could still see. If we needed to exchange a gift or a photo, or if they served us their convent-made cookies, a turning, dark, wooden drum served as a port between the grilles; you placed objects inside and turned the drum. We spent one or two hours, which seemed to me like a whole day, and we left, exchanging lots of smiles and loving words.

Out of the many visits we paid my cousin over the years, what impressed me most was the notable happiness of those women upon receiving a visitor or when telling an account of something. Joy was a constant, with no apparent exception. As decades passed, the order relaxed some of the rules and I saw that the turning drum disappeared, the two grilles became one, and it could open up as if it were a window. That was quite a change. Then, one day, the nuns invited us to see their garden and their chapel, and we even went to our cousin's sleeping cell. When I saw such a small place with a desk and a cupboard containing all her possessions, it struck me that certainly joy had nothing to do with possessions. My cousin had letters, papers, pencils, a few books, some small mementos, and a compact wardrobe with plenty of empty spaces between robes. Everything was meticulously clean and in perfect order, and when she held any of her things, she would do it as one holds a little kitten and always keeping a frank smile. As mentioned before, one does not have to be poor to be happy, but there seems to be no relationship between happiness and possessions.

William Swinyard, from Brigham Young University, and two other colleagues, explored the relationship between happiness and materialism and the role of religion on those two variables.[16] For comparison purposes, they studied samples of adults from the United States (425 participants) and Singapore (293 participants). Both samples were asked to rate themselves on life satisfaction from "terrible" to "delighted," with five grades in between. They also evaluated their beliefs in materialism (with questions such as, "How much do you equal possession with success?"). And they gathered their levels of religiosity (with statements to rate such as, "I try to carry my religion over into all my other dealings in life"). Findings showed differences between the countries: adults in Singapore were less happy and more materialistic than those in the United States. Additionally, an inverse relationship between materialism and happiness was found: in both nations, materialistic individuals tended to score low on the measures of life satisfaction, and the opposite was true for low-materialism participants. In the words of the researchers, "happier people seem to have a satisfying inner spiritual world. One has only to look at the intrinsic religiosity scale items to see this: they spend time in religious thought, their beliefs have provided answers to at least some of their spiritual questions, they try to live those beliefs daily, and they are keenly aware of a divine presence."[17]

It is said that when Alexander the Great saw the breadth of his domain, he retreated to his camp and wept, for there were no more worlds to conquer. The image encapsulates the futility of accumulating goods. Much energy is put into acquiring things and when people (the very few who do) reach the top, happiness is not there.

The Bible does not condemn material accumulation. There are Old Testament characters such as Abraham, Jacob, or David who became very wealthy via God's blessings. We see Joseph of Arimathea in the New Testament, a disciple of Jesus, a wealthy man who provided a new tomb in which to lay the Lord's body. We are also told about the results of wisdom:

Long life is in her right hand;
in her left hand are riches and honor.
Her ways are pleasant ways,
and all her paths are peace (Proverbs 3:16, 17, NIV).

At the same time, we are advised: "though your riches increase, do not set your heart on them" (Psalm 62:10, NIV).

The choice of joy

Mihaly Csikszentmihalyi was born on September 29, 1934, in what is now Croatia. As he grew up, he observed that the horrors of the Second World War affected different people very differently, and he always wanted to know the reasons behind these differences. He encountered psychology by chance. He traveled to Zurich, Switzerland, to enjoy skiing, but the snow started to melt, and skiing wasn't an option. He wished he could go to the movie theater, but he had no money. He saw an ad about a free evening psychology lecture in downtown Zurich and decided to go. It was fascinating to him to listen to Carl Jung and his interpretation on how the war had affected Europeans. His desire to know more about psychology and the different ways of dealing with stress and attaining happiness took him to the University of Chicago, where he earned a PhD in psychology. Today, Csikszentmihalyi is the world's leading researcher on happiness and creativity, and, together with Martin Seligman, is the founder of positive psychology. He promotes the idea that joy and happiness are conscious decisions that people either make or don't make. To explain what happiness is, he created the concept of "flow," a state of complete absorption on a task that is of high challenge and high skill and constitutes the maximum level of intrinsic motivation, a situation where one gets fully involved, such as a musician performing, or a religious person studying and praying.

The choice of joy and happiness does not have to entail a big decision that will make a difference for a long time; small decisions about small things may explain joy to its fullest extent. This was the purpose of a study conducted by Daniel Hurley and Paul Kwon in Pullman, Washington.[18] They found that joy, happiness, and the sense of subjective well-being are not magical and out of our control. They are really born of small things and have a lot to do with individual choices. If we know how to savor the moments and how to rate ordinary things as uplifting (rather than neutral), we can attain high life satisfaction and higher levels of happiness.

These researchers from Washington State University followed up on 142 undergraduate psychology students and asked them to report about savoring the moment (generating, prolonging, or intensifying positive emotions while a positive event is occurring), positive affect, and satisfaction with life at the beginning of the experiment. Two weeks later, the same students reported uplifts (everyday positive events during the two previous weeks), positive affect, and satisfaction with life. The two major findings of their study were the following:

1. Those most capable of *savoring the moment* displayed higher levels of positive affect and satisfaction with life.
2. Those most capable of *identifying a greater number of "uplifts"* experienced higher levels of positive affect and satisfaction with life.

These results remind us of how much choice we have in deciding whether or not we are going to enjoy something, albeit simple. Everyone can exercise the art of enjoying things by experiencing anticipation, feeling good by imagining the outcome, learning to enjoy oneself in an ordinary task, practicing the art of storing memories for later recall, finding delight in looking back on happy times, and rekindling joy from happy memories.

What this study considered uplifts were not moments of elation, but finding joy in daily things, such as doing work, receiving and giving support, conversing with someone, or observing ordinary occurrences. This reminds us of the possibility we have to process everyday events as really positive, rewarding, and uplifting. In fact, the same authors in a different study trained participants on how to increase positive outcomes and decrease negative ones.[19] By comparison, they found that the intervention group experienced significant decreases in depressive symptoms and negative affect than did the control group, showing that being joyous is not a matter of luck or entirely due to personality or hereditary factors; rather, it can be taught and learned.

The person of faith can utilize additional and more reliable means, the ones provided by God, for He assures us of His interest in His children, who in turn can use joy against sadness, and happiness over misery. In this way, His followers can hold on to scriptural promises: "You make known to me the path of life; you will fill me with joy in your presence, with eternal pleasures at your right hand" (Psalm 16:11, NIV), or "The LORD has done great things for us, and we are filled with joy" (Psalm 126:3, NIV). And even when things are not going well, God is there to communicate joy: "When anxiety was great within me, your consolation brought me joy" (Psalm 94:19, NIV).

An attitude of gratitude

In preparing this book, I asked a few old friends' permission to tell their stories as introductory vignettes for each chapter. Very spontaneously and sincerely, I shared with one of them how grateful I was for his words given to me decades ago, and how he had made such an impact in my life, especially in my spiritual journey. His reaction was very gracious, and I was reminded of his solid religious foundation. After that morning conversation with my friend, I experienced joy, energy, hope, and a general state of well-being for the rest of the day. I know such positive emotions did not come just because of the fond memories exchanged, for I have talked to old friends and not felt like that. I am sure that my joy came from having expressed sincere gratitude and true appreciation for something precious I received many years ago.

I already mentioned Sonja Lyubomirsky in the chapter on the benefits of service. She is head of the Positive Psychology lab at the University of California–Riverside. Her book *The How of Happiness* is a practical publication on how to increase happiness via a number of activities and behaviors, twelve in number.[20] She chose these activities, not because of conjecture or common sense, but because they have been found to be connected to happiness through scientific studies. The number one activity is to *express gratitude*.

Together with her doctoral students, Dr. Lyubomirsky designed an experiment to find out the effect of a simple gratitude exercise on participants' happiness. They instructed a group of people to write (every Sunday night for several weeks) five things for which they were grateful or thankful in the past week. They also instructed another group to do the same, but more frequently—Tuesday, Thursday, and Sunday; and they had a control group for comparison purposes that received no instruction. All took a measure of happiness before and after the intervention. The results showed that the greatest increases of happiness from before to after the intervention were those who had "counted their blessings" on a weekly basis. Interestingly, those expressing their gratitude every other day were not much better than those in the control group. Why didn't they experience growth? A likely explanation is that an expression of true appreciation needs to be authentic and when something is done too often, it may become a routine, habit, or chore and it may lose effectiveness.

As a regular requirement, Lyubomirsky asks her psychology students to write a gratitude letter to anyone of their choice and to then explain their experience. Nicole, a student, composed a letter to her mother and later on said, "I felt overwhelmed with a sense of happiness. . . . As I was typing, I could feel my heart beating faster and faster. . . . Towards the end of the letter, as I reread what I had already written, I began to get teary eyed and even a little choked up. I think my expressing of gratitude to my mom overwhelmed me to such a point that tears streamed down my face."[21] Days later, while completing school tasks at her computer, Nicole was frustrated because of the great amount of work. She felt compelled to read her appreciation letter again, and in seconds she had a smile. It was amazing how quickly she felt happier and less stressed after reviewing her letter again.

Unlike the previous study, Steven Toepfer devised a design whereby participants had to write letters that would be sent to the recipients.[22] Participants were randomly selected across three campuses at a large midwestern university. They included not only students but also the members of the university community at large. They were instructed to compose letters of appreciation to a real person, expressing their gratitude. Letters must be nontrivial, expressing gratitude, and submitted in a sealed envelope to the researcher for him to mail. In this way, the psychological realism and ownership of the exercise were emphasized. Participants also completed measures of gratitude, life satisfaction, happiness, and depression at the beginning and the end of the experiment. The results showed the following:

1. Significant increases of happiness, life satisfaction, and sense of gratitude over the test-retest period of four weeks.
2. A significant decrease of depressive symptoms over the same period.
3. Significantly higher scores than did the control group (who took the measures, but did not write letters of gratitude) in the well-being variables and lower scores in the ill-being variable.

Chiara Ruini and Francesca Vescovelli, Italian psychologists from the University of Bologna, worked with a sample of sixty-seven women with breast cancer at the Breast Cancer Center of the Santa Croce Hospital in Loreto, Italy.[23] Women who had been practicing gratitude showed a more successful process of post-traumatic growth and higher levels of well-being, relaxation, and contentment than did women with few or no acts of gratitude.

Isaiah 61 is the prophecy that Jesus read the first time we have record of Him preaching at the synagogue in Nazareth (Luke 4:18, 19). Although the New Testament refers to the first two verses only, the same text goes on to present beautiful promises of hope and eternity: "Instead of your shame you will receive a double portion, and instead of disgrace you will rejoice in your inheritance. And so you will inherit a double portion in your land, and everlasting joy will be yours" (Isaiah 61:7, NIV).

Certainly that inheritance of the promise will bring us more than we could ever expect—a double portion; and the result will be "everlasting joy." In real life, inheritances do not bring anything eternal and very frequently they mean trouble, disappointment, and family feuds. A great lesson about true values surrounding an inheritance can be learned from a contemporary parable told by Jim Stovall in his book *The Ultimate Gift.*[24]

The story goes, briefly, like this: Oil tycoon Red Stevens died in his old age. When the law firm read his last will to the heirs, the most surprising statement was that he left his twenty-four-year-old great-nephew, Jason, the ultimate gift. But before receiving his bequest, the young man had to complete twelve monthly assignments within a year. Each assignment was a nonmaterial, precious "gift": work, friends, learning, problems, family, laughter, giving, and so on. Despite being a selfish, bad-tempered young man who had never worked, he agreed to follow the instructions and, throughout his monthly trials and tribulations, he realized that his character was changing.

One of these gifts is gratitude. Red had an old friend in the days of the Depression. He was a hobo, a tramp who was very wise and full of rich experiences. Though homeless, he had never had a bad day. His secret came from his mother. It was called the golden list and consisted of visualizing every day, before getting up, a golden tablet on which there were written ten things he was thankful for. The tramp passed it on to Red and Red practiced it daily for the rest of his life. Now he was passing the legacy down to Jason. Jason started to practice gratitude (as well as the other assigned virtues) and obtained the benefits.

At the end of his "lessons," Jason gave his testimony to the attorney on how marvelous his great-uncle's gifts had been. They changed his life totally, and his vision had been completely renewed. Full of joy and gratitude, Jason was ready to leave the law office, but the lawyer called him back to show him the last video recording from Red Stevens. Red Stevens stated his pride for Jason having come to this point; it was because Jason had relished all twelve gifts. The ultimate gift consisted of Red Stevens's charitable trust fund of over one billion dollars. Jason was given full control of the fund, which was to support the Stevens Home for Boys, the Stevens Library Program, several scholarship programs, hospitals, and any others that Jason deemed significant.

Ellen White has a powerful statement about gratitude, health, and depression that I first discovered on a small piece of laminated paper on a colleague's desk. It says, "Nothing tends more to promote health of body and of soul than does a spirit of gratitude and praise. It is a positive duty to resist melancholy, discontented thoughts and feelings—as much a duty as it is to pray."[25]

Conclusion

A few years ago, a special issue of *National Geographic* was devoted to three groups that were identified as the oldest, healthiest people in the world: the people of Ogimi, Okinawa, Japan; the people of Silanus, Sardinia, Italy; and the

Seventh-day Adventists of Loma Linda, California. Among many other details, the report says that Sardinians live in a mild and pleasant climate, share the work burden with their spouses, and eat omega-3 foods. Of the Okinawans, the article tells that they keep lifelong friends, eat small portions, and find a purpose for their lives. And about the Seventh-day Adventists, it is said that they eat nuts and beans, observe the Sabbath, and have faith. Common to all groups is that they put family first, do not smoke, are active every day, keep socially engaged, and eat fruits, vegetables, and whole grains. The first two were rural, not necessarily spiritual communities, but the third was a distinctive religious group and the element of faith was crucial. This was a great opportunity for the Seventh-day Adventist Church to be displayed as a group blessed by following a healthy lifestyle in connection with their religiosity and communion with God.

Dan Buettner, the author of the report, makes a fair description of the everyday lives of these special people. And he closes with a one-sentence summary of his encounters with these centenarians in a way that underlines the positive emotion that accompanied them to the end of their lives: "After interviewing more than fifty centenarians on three continents, I've found every one likeable; there hasn't been a grump in the bunch."[26]

A believer may experience times of turmoil; that is part of our journey. But contemplating the whole picture and trusting the promises of Jesus Christ will change our outlook completely and will produce joy. The apostle Peter puts it in this supreme way:

> In all this you greatly rejoice, though now for a little while you may have had to suffer grief in all kinds of trials. These have come so that the proven genuineness of your faith—of greater worth than gold, which perishes even though refined by fire—may result in praise, glory and honor when Jesus Christ is revealed. Though you have not seen him, you love him; and even though you do not see him now, you believe in him and are filled with an inexpressible and glorious joy, for you are receiving the end result of your faith, the salvation of your souls (1 Peter 1:6–9, NIV).

Study Questions

- Use the Internet or go to the nearest library to find the basic tenets of "positive psychology." How is positive psychologists' understanding of happiness different from the concept of joy presented in the Bible? How is it similar? How can you avoid being led by worldly concepts, yet benefit from the useful things they can offer a Christian?

- Habakkuk 3:17 presents an extreme scenario of lack of food and income. What would be the way out of such a situation according to verses 18 and 19? What would be your prayer now to prepare you for times of dearth, yet rejoice in the Lord?
- Luke 10:21 talks about Jesus rejoicing (filled with joy and gladness) in the Spirit. What does this mean? How does it compare with human joy?

Application Thoughts

- Choose to be joyful the rest of today! Breathe very deeply and tell the Lord you have decided to be joyful today. Then ask Him to help you to reach that goal.
- Whenever you feel gloomy, recall the thoughts, readings, conversations, or memories you just had. Pray that you may be able to do something about those things that disturb you or ask for the ability to put them aside if nothing can be done.
- Can you remember one or two individuals whose words or actions were a blessing to you? Compose a gratitude letter or e-mail and send it to them. Pray for them, take time to express your appreciation in detail, and listen to your feelings afterwards.

---

1. Harold G. Koenig, *Spirituality and Health Research* (West Conshohocken, PA: Templeton Press, 2011), 15, 16.

2. Ibid., 17.

3. C. T. O'Reilly, "Religious Practice and Personal Adjustment of Older People," *Sociology and Social Research* 42 (1957): 119–121. The study included 108 men and 102 women.

4. Kristopher J. Gauthier et al., "Religiosity, Religious Doubt, and the Need for Cognition: Their Interactive Relationship With Life Satisfaction," *Journal of Happiness Studies* 7 (2006): 139–154. The study included 123 women and 65 men from eighteen to seventy-eight years of age, with an average age of thirty-two.

5. Christopher A. Lewis et al., "Religious Orientation, Religious Coping and Happiness Among UK Adults," *Personality and Individual Differences* 38 (2005): 1193–1202. They recruited 138 UK adults, 55 men and 83 women.

6. Emyr Williams et al., "Marriage, Religion and Human Flourishing: How Sustainable Is the Classic Durkheim Thesis in Contemporary Europe?" *Mental Health, Religion & Culture* 13 (2010): 93–104. The sample group consisted of 20,383 individuals from Great Britain, Italy, the Netherlands, Northern Ireland, Spain, and Sweden. Data were collected in three waves, via a face-to-face interview with participants eighteen and older.

7. Michael K. Roemer, "Religion and Subjective Well-Being in Japan," *Review of Religious*

Research 51 (2010): 411–427. The source of data was the existing Japanese General Social Surveys, which offered a sizable sample of 14,322—45 percent male and 55 percent female with an average age of fifty-two. Data, which helped observe cause-effect relationships, was collected yearly, over four waves.

8. David H. Rosmarin et al., "The Role of Religiousness in Anxiety, Depression, and Happiness in a Jewish Community Sample: A Preliminary Investigation," *Mental Health, Religion & Culture* 12 (2009): 97–113. Authors recruited 565 participants, with a male to female ratio of 42 to 58 percent. The average age was thirty-seven years, ranging from seventeen to seventy-seven.

9. Regina M. Benjamin, "Surgeon General Benjamin: Put the Joy Back Into Health," YouTube video, accessed June 24, 2013, http://www.surgeongeneral.gov/videos/2012/01/joy-back-in-health.html.

10. Ellen G. White, *The Ministry of Healing*, 281.

11. Ruut Veenhoven, "Healthy Happiness: Effects of Happiness on Physical Health and the Consequences for Preventive Health Care," *Journal of Happiness Studies* 9 (2008): 449–469.

12. Deborah D. Danner et al., "Positive Emotions in Early Life and Longevity: Findings From the Nun Study," *Journal of Personality and Social Psychology* 80 (2001): 804–813.

13. Ibid., 806.

14. Morgan Green and Marta Elliott, "Religion, Health, and Psychological Well-Being," *Journal of Religion and Health* 49 (2010): 149–163. Study included 439 men and 561 women, the majority of them Caucasians, but with representation from African-Americans (14 percent) and Hispanics (8 percent).

15. Irmo Marini and Noreen M. Glover-Graf, "Religiosity and Spirituality Among Persons With Spinal Cord Injury: Attitudes, Beliefs, and Practices," *Rehabilitation Counseling Bulletin* 54 (2011): 82–92. One hundred and fifty-six (ninety-four male, sixty-two female) were studied.

16. William R. Swinyard et al., "Happiness, Materialism, and Religious Experience in the US and Singapore," *Journal of Happiness Studies* 2 (2001): 13–32.

17. Ibid., 28.

18. Daniel B. Hurley and Paul Kwon, "Savoring Helps Most When You Have Little: Interaction Between Savoring the Moment and Uplifts on Positive Affect and Satisfaction With Life," *Journal of Happiness Studies* (2012); advance online publication. doi: 10.1007/s10902-012-9377-8.

19. Daniel B. Hurley and Paul Kwon, "Results of a Study to Increase Savoring the Moment: Differential Impact on Positive and Negative Outcomes," *Journal of Happiness Studies* 13 (2012): 579–588.

20. Sonja Lyubomirsky, *The How of Happiness* (New York: Penguin Press, 2008).

21. Ibid., 99, 100.

22. Steven M. Toepfer et al., "Letters of Gratitude: Further Evidence for Author Benefits," *Journal of Happiness Studies* 13 (2012): 187–201. Study included 219 men and women, with a mean age of twenty-six.

23. Chiara Ruini and Francesca Vescovelli, "The Role of Gratitude in Breast Cancer: Its Relationships With Post-Traumatic Growth, Psychological Well-Being and Distress," *Journal of Happiness Studies* (2012); advance online publication. doi: 10.1007/s10902-012-9330-x.

24. Jim Stovall, *The Ultimate Gift* (Colorado Springs, CO: Cook Communications Ministries, 2001).

25. Ellen G. White, *The Ministry of Healing*, 251.

26. Dan Buettner, "The Secrets of Long Life," *National Geographic* 208 (2005): 2–27.

Chapter 8

The Benefits of Interpersonal Relationships

"How good and pleasant it is when God's people live together in unity!"
—Psalm 133:1, NIV

*J*eremy Reavis, thirty-two, goes to the same church as my wife and I. A few months ago, as he was close to his release from jail, his mother, who also attended our church, asked for prayers and support for Jeremy, that he might have a successful transition after a ten-month term associated with methamphetamine addiction. As a result, Pastor Mark Etchell and church member Ron Cate visited Jeremy in prison and helped him with his transition to normal life.

I talked to Jeremy and was impressed at how well he was doing. "It is Jesus Christ in my life," he said. "Without Him, I would not be able to survive." He also told me how the church helped him in the process: "As soon as I left the prison, I went to live at the Christian Aid Center and just last week I moved into my apartment. The church people have been amazing. Some came every week and even twice a week, people I had never met before. They have not judged me for my past life. They have been caring and have accepted me in spite of my past. When the time came for me to move out of the Christian Aid Center, the church helped me move into my apartment, they brought me all I needed. They loved me and surrounded me and they helped me with whatever I needed. On my birthday, they gave me a party—just because they wanted to. It has been amazing!"

He told me that whether with a one-on-one interaction or in a large group, the church had been supportive and caring. Jeremy was thrilled when talking about it. The warm welcome (and subsequent emotional and spiritual support) he experienced at the church made a big impact. When asked further about what he gained from his interaction with church people, he said, "I have gained courage from one-on-one interactions with Pastor Mark and with Ron Cate, who is now my mentor. He is amazing; he sits and listens and he understands. I have also been supported by the church as a group. They have been very uplifting. I have felt like part of a family, and that is what it should be. Before my bad life, I was a giving person, and the experience with the church now is home for me. Love and giving of yourself as a servant—that's what it's all about."

Jeremy is still struggling to keep away from anything related to his past addiction. His current job as a janitor at McDonald's is helping him to keep busy and to veer his mind off the drug culture. When I asked how he is coping, he said, "I need to be careful with everyday stuff, stress, and keep in mind that I am recovering from addiction. I need to keep away from the wrong, not to isolate myself, but seek the presence of other Christians. Addiction is always there. But the most important thing is Jesus. It's Christ in my life. I find Jesus through prayer, and reading my Bible on a daily basis to keep the right path. He is in my mind and keeps my mind out of drugs. Every day I ask Him, 'Keep me clean through the day; keep me on the right!' Jesus is awesome; it is all Jesus Christ and I glorify Him."[1]

Much of the happiness (as well as the misery) of people's lives is caused by others. People took Jeremy to the drug culture, and people helped him come out of it. He knows the folks whom he needs to seek, and the company he must avoid. Jesus also works through people, and Satan does too. Friends, spouses, relatives, parents, siblings, children, coworkers, neighbors, and brothers and sisters in church may be a clear source of satisfaction; but they can be a source of conflict as well.

Research shows that a solid and supportive social network, both one-on-one and larger groups, is a font of health and well-being. In the same way, toxic relationships may cause serious emotional disturbances and contribute to physical and mental illness. When relationships are imbued in biblical principles and the people involved follow the steps that Christ took, the derived benefits are at their best. This chapter reviews the professional literature on interpersonal relationships and their proven advantages. It also shows how Christians can benefit from those relationships, obtaining a sense of well-being, better mental and physical health, and an improved service to God and fellow man.

How do relationships work?

The discipline of social psychology provides answers to the question of how relationships work. Social psychology is a required course in all departments of psychology. In fact, it is a very popular requirement among students and also a desirable course for faculty to teach (they never seem to frown upon teaching

"Social"). After all, we are people, we relate to people, and we can easily identify with the themes of this subject. It is indeed very interesting to learn about behaviors, feelings, thoughts, and so on, that result from people being together instead of isolated.

One feature that always arises in groups is norms. Whether in an association of two, three, or more, norms will emerge—many times unwritten, but at least broadly understood by everyone. Norms reflect the shared values of people involved and help everyone to go through the right steps to accomplish tasks. Couples have norms (for example, who cooks, who does the laundry, who bathes the baby), workplaces have norms (for example, a time to arrive or leave or the expected quality of a product), school classrooms have norms (for example, who talks when or how homework should look), sports have norms (for example, how long the game lasts or how many players are on each team), and so on. Norms are good in many ways: they prevent conflicts or misunderstandings, promote harmonious functioning, provide insight in understanding the behaviors of others, and help identify those who do not respect them. But they can be a source of conflict, such as when someone breaks a rule that is widely accepted by members and a sanction has to be imposed. This creates tensions in the whole relationship.

Another characteristic present in groups is power. There are always members with more power than others and, depending on how they exercise authority and on the attitude of the people, there may be difficulties. Power may have been legitimately granted or taken arbitrarily. Sometimes power arises because it is inherent to some types of personalities or because someone has the ability to inspire or to show knowledge and wisdom. Leadership styles vary considerably, and the well-being and success of the group will also vary depending on the leader.

Beliefs and attitudes of group members are additional important features. People are different and think differently. There are members that are heavily involved, have strong opinions, and are vocal; on the other hand, there are others whose opinions are not so strong and prefer to acquiesce to avoid conflict. Some people are always ready to advance; others are more cautious in the next steps; others yet, wish to remain unchanged, to stagnate. When viewpoints are substantially different, the chance of conflict increases and, as a result, some will fight, while others withdraw.

Communication is a crucial component of relationships. Problems many times arise simply because of difficulties communicating. Communication problems are a source of much irritation and serious conflicts. Too many times the message one sends is decoded by recipients differently from what is meant. In order to avoid all the bad side effects of poor communication, messages—verbal and nonverbal—need to be carefully chosen and sent with the right emotional tone.

All of the above can be fascinating to study, especially with a real-life case in hand. At the same time, when things go wrong in the midst of a group, things can get extremely complicated. There is a concept that many reject because they consider it nonscientific—that of love; that is Jesus' humble and profound solution to the complexity: "Love one another; as I have loved you" (John 13:34, NIV). His summary of the entire law system is the following: "In everything, do to others what you would have them do to you, for this sums up the Law and the Prophets" (Matthew 7:12, NIV). And the essence of universal duty is to love the Lord completely and love your neighbor as yourself (Matthew 22:37–39). Differences in norms, power, attitude, communication, or other things can be repaired with love. Any relationship based on love will reap the multiple benefits of relationships; at the same time, interpersonal interactions, deprived of love, are bound to fail and to yield undesirable consequences.

Relationships and health

Relationships affect both physical and mental health. I will always remember the evangelist in my hometown, Madrid, who came from far away to offer a series of meetings that began with a stress-management seminar. He surveyed the audience with a written question: "What are your three foremost sources of stress?" Even before the deacons had finished counting, he already had the transparency showing the number one source of stress: *relationships*. Someone asked him after the meeting how he knew the result. He replied, "It is always the same: spouse, children, parents, neighbors, bosses, colleagues. They are the main cause of concern but also the best source of happiness—it depends on how healthy the relationship is!" When relationships are unhealthy, stress and psychosomatic illness may follow. This explains the correlation between the quality of human interactions and health, both physical and mental.

Professor Masoud Bahrami of Isfahan University of Medical Sciences in Iran conducted a qualitative study with ten nurses in Adelaide, South Australia.[2] These nurses cared for cancer patients, both inpatient and outpatient. Some of the informants were interviewed more than once, searching for what made a difference in the quality of life of their patients. Findings revealed a number of significant themes: physical, psychological, spiritual, environmental, and, as special interest to us in this chapter, the social interaction aspects.

Relationships were seen as crucial. The faithful support of the family made the whole difference. A nurse referred to those who were dying: "Dying is a very lonely experience . . . when a person has gone through a long trajectory of illness and the family has already buried him. They've decided that he's outlived his prognosis. Sometimes the family has already separated. . . . I see patients realizing they are a burden on their own remaining family members because they didn't die in the timeframe that the doctors had told them."

However, the experience is radically different with truly supportive families. Nurses stated that the quality of life of the patient went up considerably in the presence of a very supportive family who interacted with the patient. If the same person in the same situation lacks the family support, then the quality of life goes down. The interaction with people, especially those who loved them, is a critical issue in the quality of life of these individuals.

Another study, with Seventh-day Adventists as participants, shed light on the effect that early family relationships have on health and later quality of social interaction. A team of Loma Linda University researchers led by Kelly Morton studied data from a large group (6,753) of adults from multiple races, members of the Adventist Church between the ages of 35 and 106.[3] Through extensive surveying that included measures of mental and physical health, and present and past quality of relationships, participants provided data to perform multiple analyses. Results showed that those coming from risky families (family environments characterized by conflict, aggression, chaos, and neglectful or abusive parenting) tended at the time of the study to engage poorly in religion and in social interaction, and that early family environment had caused intrusive, insensitive, rejecting, and helpless social interactions at an adult age. It also caused negative emotionality, which had a direct effect on perceived physical health. The study concluded that risky family environment appears to be enduring and negatively affects one's adult religious life, emotionality, social interactions, and perceived health, with more reported symptoms of depression, neuroticism, and negative effect.

Neal Krause and Elena Bastida, from the University of Michigan and Florida International University, respectively, focused their study on a group of elderly Mexican Americans who provided information on how church-based emotional support influenced their health.[4] Participants were residents of Texas, Colorado, New Mexico, Arizona, and California. Data were gathered via face-to-face interviews in the homes of the participants using Spanish when necessary (84 percent of the interviews were in Spanish).

Participants provided information about church attendance, emotional support from their church, sense of belonging to their congregations, feelings of personal control, and self-rated health. The statistical analysis showed that those going to church more frequently received more emotional support from fellow church members than were those going only occasionally. Also, those who received more support from other church members enjoyed a more advanced feeling of belongingness to their congregation. And those with such a strong sense of belongingness had a stronger sense of personal control. Finally, those with a stronger sense of personal control were more likely to enjoy better health. As we see, variables under study were all social and religious in nature and provided a chain of benign effects ending up in better health.

Another study conducted in England explored an interesting area: the benefits of the social interaction of older adults singing. Ann Skingley and Hilary Bungay, senior researchers at Canterbury Christ Church University in Kent, United Kingdom, gathered data from seventeen individuals who were taking part in community-based singing groups.[5] They collected data via observations of the practice and performance sessions, extensive one-to-one interviews with the participants, and focus-group discussions with volunteers from the singing clubs. The benefits of participation in singing clubs were enjoyment, better mental health and well-being, an increased portion of social interaction, improvements in physical health, cognitive stimulation and learning, and improved memory and recall.

Although this area of social interaction through singing activities has not been studied widely, it is a promising area. If we think of church activities, there is always, in every church, a singing group (or several) that gather together to practice, discuss performances, socialize, and even travel to other locations to perform, spending, in the process, abundant time in quality social interaction.

One-on-one interpersonal interactions

Interactions between two persons can go from a quick commercial exchange to the deep sharing of personal communication at the level of inner feelings experienced by two friends. The benefits of friendships are notable and additional gains are obtained from Christian friendships.

A friendship is an intentional association that provides satisfaction between two individuals. Examples of satisfaction obtained from friendships include companionship, emotional security, practical help, and self and mutual affirmation. Friends can enjoy time together, thus avoiding loneliness, rumination, low moods, or unwanted behaviors that may result from loneliness. Friends also get practice in the complex task of communication, which requires skill, especially if messages go beyond the exchange of facts into feelings, emotions, and perplexities with a load of nonverbal components greater than the verbal content. Friends may also discuss topics from the news, politics, ideas, and opinions, testing them in a secure environment without the fear of censure. Friends must be highly accountable, keeping strict confidentiality, and this requires a commitment of time and effort in the relationship. Friendships also provide an ideal setting for emotional support, which is impossible to obtain at casual encounters with no background knowledge or mutual understanding. Friendships are also places to share things that have gone wrong or fears toward the future, things that cannot be shared without becoming vulnerable, and this takes only best friends. And friendships are places to learn about oneself, about the other, about similar and different perspectives and styles of thinking and acting, about character traits that are worth imitating and those that are better avoided.

Studies over the past two decades have been showing a connection between health and happiness and the quality of friendship—the higher the friendship quality, the higher the levels of health and happiness. The study conducted by Alan King and Cheryl Terrance shows strong mental health benefits coming from friendships.[6] These researchers from the University of North Dakota gathered the mental health characteristics of 398 college students, asking them about their most significant friendship status via an acquaintance questionnaire of seventy items, such as "I feel free to reveal private or personal information about myself to my best friend," or "My best friend is willing to spend time and energy to help me succeed at my own personal tasks and projects, even if he is not directly involved," or "Because I regard my relationship with my best friend to be very exclusive, I would consider it wrong to carry on the same type of relationship with anyone else," and so on. Participants also took a respected clinical test (Minnesota Multiphasic Personality Inventory—MMPI). The results showed a tight connection between friendships and several scales of the MMPI.

For instance, those with troubled friendships tended to have personality characteristics toward the pathological end: social anxiety, social withdrawal, behavioral eccentricities, illogical thinking, low self-affirmation, tendency to complain, feelings of insecurity, and the tendency to magnify the challenges of relationships. On the contrary, those holding healthy and vibrant relationships revealed a balanced and pleasant personality. Connections like these indicate that good relationships may facilitate healthy and adaptive personality characteristics—the therapeutic function of a good relationship. It also means that favorable characteristics, to start with, may help build a stronger and more mutually supportive friendship.

There are plenty of studies done with married couples and the ample social support that marriage provides. I have chosen the following one because it belongs to an increasing sector of the population—old age, and participants reflect the blessing of having lived together for a long time. It is a research project by Robert Waldinger and Marc Schulz from Brigham and Women's Hospital and Harvard Medical School.[7] They focused on forty-seven older adult couples and followed up on them during an eight-day period in order to explore marital satisfaction and social time spent with others. They were given measures of marital satisfaction and happiness. In addition, researchers held a daily evening phone interview during eight consecutive days to collect data about the social interaction during the past waking hours. The biggest portion of social time was spent with their spouses followed by time with friends, children, and grandchildren. The data analysis revealed that the more time was spent with others, the greater level of happiness. When happiness decreased, so did the perceived health. However, marital satisfaction buffered decreased levels of happiness. It is therefore concluded that marital satisfaction overall works as a support against the daily fluctuations of perceived health, and it constitutes a solid factor to promote happiness.

By means of one-to-one matching community volunteers for weekly social activities, Brian McCorkle and his colleagues explored the benefits and drawbacks of developing new social relationships for people with serious mental illnesses.[8] This was a qualitative study consisting of twenty individual interviews with eleven volunteers and nine clients, one hour each, to ask them about their one-to-one friendships. Of particular interest were the statements from the clients that described the experience as "genuine friendship," "sisterhood," and similar terms. One said, "I like it that she's been there even for me, when I needed someone to lean on, that I could talk to her." Several clients kept saying how helpful it was that their volunteer friend knew about their mental illness, so they could relax about how he or she would react when they found out. The relationships improved with time until they could adjust and become more comfortable with each other. They began to reveal increasingly personal, intimate items in their lives. They moved from a helper-helpee relationship to true friendship. The result was that these patients, through natural interaction with their friends, gained insights, felt accepted, improved their interpersonal communication, and learned new things to do. These clients became more socially active, more assertive and more verbal; they also showed more attentiveness to others and more flexibility in being accommodating to people.

But the gains were obtained not only by the clients; volunteers also showed satisfaction with their function and became more sensitive to power and equality in the relationship. In addition, they said that after the experience, they were able to advocate for their clients, felt involved in a deep friendship, and felt free to talk openly and honestly in ways they could not in their other social circles. These results show that intentional friendships can be a cost-effective and powerful method to provide support to mentally ill people, helping them develop social skills, expand their social networks, and improve their quality of life. Experiences like these remind us of the power of friendship and they communicate much hope in seeing that solutions were attained by simple human interactions between individuals with serious mental disorders and volunteers who had received only three to five hours of training.

Many studies have been done on people with schizophrenia in order to observe a variety of characteristics, behaviors, and abilities, but rarely do these studies involve friendships. Ellen Harley from a community mental health team of the National Health System in the United Kingdom, together with colleagues, designed a study to investigate friendships in 137 adults with established schizophrenia living in southeast England.[9]

As expected in a sample of people with schizophrenia, friendship networks were small but of relatively high quality and highly valued. Females showed higher emotional commitment than males did. The group was divided into about three equal parts in terms of commitment: (1) no emotional commitment to friendship, (2) some emotional commitment, and (3) marked emotional commitment. No one in group 1 had friends, 58 percent in group 2 had friends, and 100 percent in group 3 had friends. Most of the participants without friends were not concerned about it. Those avoiding friendships said that it was hard work to make and maintain friends, that they were afraid of being let down or afraid of having arguments.

Some answers were instrumental and typical for someone with psychotic symptoms: "I have three friends: my drug pusher, he gives me speed; my Case Manager sees me every week; and the shopkeeper, he gives me cigarettes on credit sometimes. I also have spirits coming to me, they visit at night and we talk. They are good friends, three of them." The most central finding of this study was that those patients reporting quality friendships (a little over half of the sample) referred to a predominantly positive interaction and a relationship that was warm, enjoyable, relaxing, and rewarding. The friendship experience constituted a great support for their illness.

A Northern Arizona University study led by Meliksah Demir examined the personal sense of uniqueness that keeps friendships alive.[10] Authors limited the scope of the study to same-sex friendship quality in three samples, each employing a different measure of happiness. The process of using three different methods to assess happiness served as a triangulation procedure, which ensured the reliability of the results. The sense of uniqueness each one in the dyad experienced made the friendship solid, enjoyable, and durable.

What did uniqueness mean in this context? Uniqueness was understood as seeking help and advice from each other, affirming each other's goals, spending time on numerous different activities, sharing secrets, and celebrating

149

accomplishments. The other main finding was that one-on-one friendship is a mediator of happiness. This held true for every one of the three groups and for males and females.

Julianne Holt-Lundstad from Brigham Young University did another study with same-gender friends to see whether hostility influenced cardiovascular reactivity at the time when participants were discussing experiences with their friends.[11] They recruited healthy male and female college students and their same-sex friends of 6.5 years of acquaintance on average. The sample was randomly divided into two types of assignment: one was assigned a *positive,* one-on-one discussion about a past personal experience; the other was assigned a *negative* (stressful), one-on-one discussion about a past personal experience. In each pair, one was assigned the role of support provider and the other support recipient.

Cardiovascular measures were recorded during their conversations. Results revealed that the greatest systolic blood pressure and diastolic blood pressure reactivity was in young men and women discussing stressful past experiences. These results suggest that hostility may pose barriers to the natural benefits of interpersonal interactions. Furthermore, this association between hostility and reactivity was present in both support recipients and support providers, suggesting that hostility could undermine the health benefits of both aspects of support transactions. This reminds us of the fact that social interactions can be either highly satisfying or quite harmful.

Christian friendship has something to add. The Bible holds very high standards for friendship (see John 15:13) and describes exemplary friendships such as Ruth and Naomi; David and Jonathan; King Hiram and David; Job and his friends; Elijah and Elisha; Daniel and his friends; Jesus, Mary, Martha, and Lazarus; Paul and Timothy. They portray loving behaviors, attitudes, and excellent character traits that have been an inspiration to many throughout history. A friendship with a fellow believer brings a number of advantages:

- *Input from a Christian friend will incorporate corresponding principles.* For example, in expressing opinions about a serious difficulty with your marital relationship, the believer friend will encourage the couple to work issues out or seek counseling rather than opting for divorce.
- *A Christian friend will be willing to sacrifice in order to help you.* This is the case of Jonathan risking his own relationship with his father in order to help David (1 Samuel 20).
- *A Christian friend will extend forgiveness.* As commanded by Jesus

Christ (Mark 11:25), a true friend will extend forgiveness and will do it generously and not condescendingly, just as Paul admonishes, "value others above yourselves" (Philippians 2:3, NIV).

- *The spiritual discernment of a Christian friend will enrich the friendship.* Abiding by God's commandments, mutual, regular prayer, and the presence of Jesus in their lives are examples of spiritual discernment that are foolishness to the nonbeliever (1 Corinthians 2:14) but they bring great blessings to Christian friends.
- *Christian friends will appeal to the authority of the Scriptures.* In case of conflict, honest Christian friends will be sensitive to what the Bible has to say about critical matters and will humbly accept responsibility for any wrong and return to the ways of the Word of God.
- *Christian friends will encourage one another in the Lord.* Coping with loss or difficulty can be understood in the context of the struggle of good and evil and with the hope of salvation and Jesus' return, which is only possible in the context of biblical faith.
- *A Christian friend does not expect anything in return.* Christian relationships are based on altruism. Exchanges happen naturally, but there are no ulterior expectations for favors given.
- *A Christian friend will open up his or her heart if necessary.* There might be times when a deep emotional burden, such as a wrong choice, sin, or trespass is shared with a true fellow believer friend to seek comfort. This does not substitute confession to God, and sequels may remain even after divine forgiveness, hence the need to talk to someone.

When I authored a Sabbath School quarterly for the first quarter of 2011, one lesson was about relationships, and one of the parts was based on James 5:16. I entitled it "Confess Your Sins to Each Other," which are the words rendered by the NIV translation ("Confess your faults one to another" in the KJV). I received quite a number of letters and e-mails about this part of the lesson; some from people disapproving the use of the NIV version because such expressions—they argued—would condone the doctrine of confession from Catholic theology. Others condemned my comment that disclosure of committed sins to a close friend may help alleviate the burden of sin, even when I concluded by saying that the most important thing is confessing to God, who is the only One able to forgive.

I replied to each apologizing for giving an impression that I certainly did not mean in regards to the auricular confession. After growing up with such a background, I understood that confessing to a priest or to anyone with the expectation to be forgiven has nothing to do with God's will for us as revealed in the Bible. In fact, confessing my sins to God (1 John 1:9) was for me one of the most refreshing doctrines that I welcomed when I joined the Adventist Church. In regards to opening one's heart to a friend, I never said that one must do that, or that it is a way to be forgiven (except when one has offended that person), but it was merely a way to open up and share, to unburden oneself, to experience some catharsis, not forgiveness, which can only be granted by God.

At a later time, I found a quote from Ellen G. White where she wrote to Brother P., who had erred in some way:

> It is not required of you to confess to those who know not your sin and errors. It is not your duty to publish a confession which will lead unbelievers to triumph; but to those to whom it is proper, who will take no advantage of your wrong, confess according to the word of God, and let them pray for you, and God will accept your work, and will heal you. For your soul's sake, be entreated to make thorough work for eternity. Lay aside your pride, your vanity, and make straight work. Come back again to the fold. The Shepherd is waiting to receive you. Repent, and do your first works, and again come into favor with God.[12]

I believe that there is a place for the professional counselor to skillfully help with difficult situations connected to mental health and behavior problems, but I am sure that much primary care can be provided by good friends, loving families, and caring godly people associated with church circles. When Paul wrote, "Carry each other's burdens" (Galatians 6:2, NIV), I am sure he meant not only the boxes to be loaded onto the U-Haul truck (which is one part) but also to help others to lighten the load of suffering, oftentimes the result of mistakes and sins.

The blessings of social interaction

A few years ago the book *All I Really Need to Know I Learned in Kindergarten* became very popular for its simple yet profound wisdom.[13] Much of the advice offered in this outstanding self-help publication had to do with the right interaction with others: share everything, play fair, don't hit people, clean up your mess, don't take things that aren't yours, say you're sorry when you hurt somebody, hold hands and stick together. They are simple rules, simple enough for little ones to learn and, at the same time, able to facilitate harmony and even yield additional benefits of health and well-being.

It seems clear that when social interactions are satisfactory, things go well. The professional literature has found that those who are well connected have fewer colds, lower blood pressure, and lower heart rates. Also, married people live longer, and the rates of substance abuse and mental illness are lower in people that have a sense of belonging. Older adults are especially at risk as they lose their spouses and close friends. That is why mental health practitioners recommend to them tasks such as searching for groups of people their age or with their interests and establishing links, making new friends, following group activities, traveling or going to new places, participating in church congregational activities, or volunteering for a good cause.

Relational problems affect young and old and may complicate matters years later. We see it in a study that followed up on adolescents until their young adulthood. A team of researchers led by Emma Adam, professor of education and social policy at Northwestern University in Evanston, Illinois, conducted a longitudinal study collecting data at three waves.[14] First, when the participants were eleven to twenty years of age; then, one year later; and when they were between eighteen to twenty-seven years of age. The purpose was to determine whether social interaction deficiencies earlier in life were associated with poor health during young adulthood. She found out that the best predictors of poor mental and physical health were precisely of a social nature: subjects reporting poor parental support, loneliness, romantic relation instability, and intimate partner violence had the poorest mental and physical health levels at the time of the third wave.

Another family study from the University of Arizona, led by Chris Segrin, was designed to determine whether loneliness in families with only adults in the household was associated with poor health.[15] All participants belonged to three age categories: young adults, their parents, and their grandparents. They were given a loneliness scale, a measure of self-reported health, and a survey of self-reported physical symptoms. Results indicated that high levels of loneliness were associated with high numbers of physical complaints and low levels of health. This was true for parents and grandparents, although not so for young adults with an average age of twenty-one.

A different research design was applied to compare people living with family members and people living by themselves. This investigation was conducted in China by researchers Li-Juan Liu and Qiang Guo from the Second Military Medical University in Shanghai.[16] Results show that those who lived by themselves not only experienced higher levels of loneliness, but they also had low levels of health, both physical and mental. This was so notable that each of the scores of the loneliness scale correlated negatively with each of the sections of the health survey. In other words, the tendency to find poor health in lonely people was not just due to certain aspects, but it was for all aspects. In conclusion, if people living alone (who scored high on loneliness) could reduce their loneliness levels, health and quality of life could be increased as a result.

Also in China, a study was conducted to see how taxi drivers in the city of Beijing coped with the high stress of their occupation. Ingrid Nielsen, from Monash University in Melbourne, Australia, and a team conducted the study.[17] They gathered the data from taxi drivers outside the Beijing railway station where hundreds of cabs congregate. Research assistants approached taxi drivers, and 512 drivers agreed to participate in an interview conducted right there and then. The results showed that for these individuals the support of personal relationships as well as community connectedness served as moderators for the high levels of stress they had to constantly face.

The support of the faith community

English Baptist pastor John Fawcett (1739–1817) was sent in 1765 to a small congregation at Hebden Bridge, England. During seven years, he and his wife worked intensely to minister to this church, one that was like a family. Back in those days, churches would pay their pastors according to their means, and these parishioners had very little. As a result, when Dr. Fawcett received a call from a much larger church in London, he accepted the invitation after having pastored the Wainsgate Baptist Church for seven years. As his few possessions were being placed in the wagon, many came to say goodbye. Once more they begged him to reconsider. Touched by this great outpouring of love, he and his wife began to weep. Finally, Mrs. Fawcett exclaimed, "O John, I just can't bear this. They need us so badly here."

"God has spoken to my heart too!" he said. "Tell them to unload the wagon! We cannot break these wonderful ties of fellowship."

This experience gave Fawcett the inspiration to write the hymn "Blest Be the Tie That Binds."[18]

We already saw in chapter 6 in some detail the benefits of churchgoing on a regular basis. There are additional studies that underline the advantages of positive social interaction on religious commitment. Pamela King and James Furrow from Fuller Theological Seminary explored how social interaction, trust, and shared vision in religious communities enable religiousness and moral behavior among public high school students.[19] They were asked about their religious participation, the importance of religion in their lives, and their social connections with family and friends. Researchers also collected data on empathy (questions about their ability to fully understand the thoughts, feelings, and experiences of others) and altruism (questions on whether or not they are involved in a list of acts of kindness and/or sharing). Researchers found that adolescents who had experienced a trusting interaction with significant people in their lives such as parents, friends, and adults that shared their worldview, took their religion more seriously and participated more extensively in moral outcomes. Furthermore, the context of support and trust presented by those personal associations also caused the tendency to increase altruistic and empathetic acts.

Richard Rymarz, from the University of Alberta in Edmonton, Canada, based on a historical and sociological analysis, concluded that the most prominent factor to foster religious commitment is the social network and the sense of community offered by congregations and denominational settings, such as schools.[20] These are some of the reasons presented:

- When everyone believes except the village atheist, doubting becomes virtually impossible; when few believe, doubting becomes spontaneous and belief more difficult. The social and religious support of the community constitutes a pillar of faith and this is especially weighty in children and adolescents.
- A solid community of faith offers the most appealing context for others to join, more than literature about doctrines, because the group provides the best practical and plausible applications of religious beliefs, over publications that present the truth but no real representation in the lives of people.
- The group provides the context where individuals can ask the difficult questions and participate in safe debates about matters of religion and faith.
- The community of faith has mentors available who can both explain and exemplify the beliefs and practices of the church.
- In the context of other believers, people can develop an identity, a sense of belonging to a common faith evidenced by lifestyle. Such identity is portable and represents an anchor to preserve faith. Young Irish laborers working in London during the Industrial Revolution would fast on Fridays, thus remembering their religious tradition. Seventh-day Adventists can observe the Sabbath and their dietary restrictions wherever they go and, as such, be reminded daily and weekly of their religious identity.
- The church can grow and develop more adequately when it is divided up

into congregations, companies, or other forms of group arrangement.

Social media

Over the last few years, millions of people of all ages worldwide have been using various forms of social media blogs (e.g., Blogger), networking sites (e.g., Facebook or Twitter), or video exchange platforms (e.g., YouTube). Numbers have increased even more as mobile devices created new opportunities to be socially active at any time and anywhere. These are powerful tools, unthinkable just one generation ago. As with any other new technology, Christians wish to be faithful to lifestyles according to the principles of Jesus. So they ask themselves, "Is it appropriate for a Christian to enter into these activities?" Answers vary from those who condemn social media because of the hidden dangers behind an apparently innocent exchange of data to those who claim that they are great avenues to interact with people they would not reach otherwise, and that they can help people and share their faith in a fresh way.

There are advantages to social media. Information can be shared very quickly to homogeneous groups who can offer immediate input with graphic possibilities in real time. Since there are no barriers of distance, believers can be, say, praying for the same emergent situation from distant locations and keep the communication with others going. Social media is also an excellent way to keep in touch with family and friends when separated by distance or incompatible schedules. Photos, news, sounds, and videos can be posted, and thus the gap of distance can be eliminated. It can serve as a handy tool to pose open questions, practical problems, or job opportunities to trusted people. In just a few hours, one can obtain a large number of ideas and answers. And, provided that one has Internet access and a computer or device, its use is at no extra cost. This is some incredible deal compared with what exchanging all these modes of information would have cost thirty years ago!

But this powerful tool comes with risks. One is safety. The systems are too transparent and the ease of posting too much detail soon makes available an excess of information accessible to anyone (if the user has not set their preferences well) or, even when restricted, there is some risk that malicious people gain access to use information to their benefit and at the detriment of the user. As a result, fraud, identity theft, robbery, or assault may happen; of course, this is true of many other online activities. Another risk is that of focusing too much on online connections at the expense of necessary face-to-face encounters. This is particularly risky for children and adolescents who can grow up without learning good skills of meeting and holding face-to-face conversations. Another issue that has brought people to the counseling room is that of addiction to social media, becoming compulsive about posting and reading what others post every moment, and they seem unable to stop. Even when the use does not reach the proportion of addiction, it may become absorbing enough to take too much time every day.

Social media should always be used with caution; following a few simple recommendations may reduce the risks significantly. It is safer to have a reduced number of friends than too large of a group that has access to the information posted. It is also necessary to keep face-to-face encounters alive and regular, especially with those near us. In addition, we need to remind ourselves that what we say is in many ways public. Finally, we must keep in mind the nature of the medium: what we say is often not understood in the way we mean, and it is necessary to take a second (and third) look at what we key in before posting it, and still be prepared for misunderstandings.

Christian users need to go an extra step; after all, our code of conduct and principles should be at a higher bar than that of others. For example, teenagers from very wealthy families recently posted impressive photos of their dining tables perfectly set with exotic food beautifully arranged and an impressive landscape view through a huge window. It was obvious that they were showing off their means to kids in the world who couldn't ever experience such everyday treatment. There is no rule of etiquette that prohibits this display of vanity. But this ostentation is very distant from the Christian standards of humility. Another example is language, jokes, tone of the conversations, or sarcastic messages meant to be cute but causing pain or confusion in others. Instead, well-chosen, affirming, positive messages of encouragement and hope can bring relief to some perplexed soul and give glory to God.

Let's remember the words of the apostle, saying, "whether you eat or drink, or whatever you do, do all to the glory of God" (1 Corinthians 10:31). This applies to social media as well. Finally, we are asked to not neglect meeting together (Hebrews 10:25), which should lead to a moderate use of social media without forgetting personal encounters.

Interpersonal interactions in the epistles

There is an amazing resemblance between the early church as presented in the epistles and the contemporary Christian church in terms of relationships. It is no wonder because the most basic human nature and tendencies remain similar across times. Recommendations are therefore very current, and putting them into practice would do away with most existing interpersonal problems, leaving just the benefits to be enjoyed.

Husbands are told to love their wives just as Christ loved the church (Ephesians

5:25). This truly is a profound mystery (verse 32), a counter-cultural advice that, if practiced, would bring the end of emotional, verbal, and physical abuse of wives.

Christians are asked to never take revenge, but let God do it (Romans 12:19). The waste of mental health, as well as the time and energy expended in paying evil with evil, would be channeled to much more productive accomplishments.

Parishioners are asked to help, support, and encourage others in their church communities (1 Thessalonians 5:11). Much of the sadness, hopelessness, and per-plexities in churches today would be alleviated if those not suffering at the time would provide such support to those who are.

Church members are asked to pay the greatest respect and love to church leaders (1 Thessalonians 5:12, 13). Criticizing the church leaders has become a great obstacle to accomplish the mission of the church. Although, at times leaders are at fault, solutions would arrive much quicker with the respect and love that the apostle recommends.

Christians are admonished to listen more, speak less, and cool down from anger (James 1:19). This is the solution to many of the misunderstandings we en-counter everywhere, and practicing this advice would bring much harmony to church communities.

Believers are advised to remain united in thoughts, love, soul, and mind (Philip-pians 2:2; 1 Peter 3:8). Practicing this would make people forget about the entan-gling details that separate us and would naturally strengthen the body of Christ in its task to take the gospel message to those who lack it and need it so much.

People are to keep up the habit of meeting together and encourage one another all the more (Hebrews 10:25). Participating more in church services, praying more in groups, and gathering additionally as brothers and sisters would com-pensate tremendously for the overspread spiritual lethargy of many Christian communities.

People are urged to be hospitable without complaining (1 Peter 4:9). Practicing this, not just with friends, family, and neighbors (Luke 14:12), but also with those in need, willingly and lovingly, would bring improved health and well-being to both host and guest.

Church members are advised to be tender-hearted and forgiving to one another, just as God has forgiven through Christ (Ephesians 4:32). Although a human be-ing could never forgive the way God does, imperfect forgiveness perfected by the grace of God would heal even deep wounds that keep people separated and prevent them from proceeding on the Christian path.

Conclusion

The two-ox rule can illustrate in some way the power of joining forces.

Teamwork adds everybody's efforts and then throws an extra bonus. If one ox is able to pull one thousand pounds and another ox can pull one thousand pounds, how much weight will the two oxen yoked together pull? The answer is that as a team those same cattle will pull four thousand pounds. Physics, physiology, and psychology together may not be able to explain this phenomenon, but it is true.

In the realm of humans, we have reviewed the benefits that can be obtained by being together and working together. Proverbs says, "As iron sharpens iron, so one person sharpens another" (Proverbs 27:17, NIV). I like this text because it does not place one person above the other; in the process of sharpening, both pieces of iron lose particles but gain sharpness. When I help and encourage someone, my role is not higher or lower. When someone else is comforting or supporting me, he or she is not above or below me. We are both iron sharpening iron.

No matter what role you play today in connection with others, you are needed for mutual edification, and the best quality of fellowship is guaranteed if we follow Jesus: "If we walk in the light, as he is in the light, we have fellowship with one another" (1 John 1:7, NIV).

Study Questions

- Read 1 Samuel 25. What people skills can you learn from Abigail? What is her communication style, verbal and nonverbal? By contrast, what are Nabal's interpersonal skills? What are the consequences of each of these behaviors?

- Romans 12 is packed with good advice for a Christian to relate successfully to other people. For example, verse 10 tells me to give others more honor than I give myself. List in your own words all the pieces of relational advice you can find in this chapter.

- The book of Proverbs contains dozens of tips to interact with people in a godly manner. Read the entire book (it will take about an hour and a half) and write in a notebook those tips that you consider useful to improve your connections. Begin with Proverbs 1:8: "Listen, my son, to your father's instruction and do not forsake your mother's teaching" (NIV).

Application Thoughts

- Paul said, "Do not be misled: 'Bad company corrupts good character' "

(1 Corinthians 15:33, NIV). However, we cross our paths with all sorts of people. What can you do when you encounter a person who fits the label of "bad company"? Think of how Jesus acted with the outcasts of His day. Think also that Jesus called peacemakers "blessed" and "children of God" (Matthew 5:9, NIV).

• We don't know the nature of the issues between Euodia and Syntyche mentioned in Philippians 4:2, 3. But it is sad that such pillars of the early church were mutually estranged. Do you know of people in your church congregation that are in this kind of situation? What could you do to help them work things out?

• Think over your life. What can you do to improve your one-on-one relationships? What about small group connections? And what about your large group interactions?

---

1. J. Reavis, personal communication, December 2, 2012.

2. Masoud Bahrami, "Meanings and Aspects of Quality of Life for Cancer Patients: A Descriptive Exploratory Qualitative Study," *Contemporary Nurse* 39 (2011): 75–84.

3. Kelly R. Morton, "Religious Engagement in a Risky Family Model Predicting Health on Older Black and White Seventh-day Adventists," *Psychology of Religion and Spirituality* 4 (2012): 298–311.

4. Neal Krause and Elena Bastida, "Church-Based Social Relationships, Belonging, and Health Among Older Mexican Americans," *Journal for the Scientific Study of Religion* 50 (2011): 397–409. The sample was made up of 663 retired persons, ages sixty-six and older (average of seventy-three), 39 percent male and 61 percent female, 77 percent Catholic and 23 percent Protestant with an average of six years of schooling.

5. Ann Skingley and Hilary Bungay, "The Silver Song Club Project: Singing to Promote the Health of Older People," *British Journal of Community Nursing* 15 (2010): 135–140. Study included five males and twelve females, of an average age of seventy-seven.

6. Alan R. King and Cheryl Terrance, "Best Friendship Qualities and Mental Health Symptomatology Among Young Adults," *Journal of Adult Development* 15 (2009): 25–34. Study included 398 young adult men and women, junior and senior college students, 26 percent men and 74 percent women, average age of twenty-three with an overwhelming (94 percent) majority of Caucasians.

7. Robert J. Waldinger and Marc S. Schulz, "What's Love Got to Do With It? Social Functioning, Perceived Health, and Daily Happiness in Married Octogenarians," *Psychology and Aging* 25 (2010): 422–431. These were survivors of the longitudinal study that began at the Harvard University Health Service in 1939, when participants were eighteen or nineteen. At the time of the latter study, men were 82.9 years of age on average, and women 78.8.

8. Brian H. McCorkle et al., "Compeer Friends: A Qualitative Study of a Volunteer Friendship Programme for People With Serious Mental Illness," *International Journal of Social Psychiatry* 55 (2009): 291–305.

9. Ellen W. Y. Harley et al., "Friendship in People With Schizophrenia: A Survey," *Social*

Psychiatry and Psychiatric Epidemiology 47 (2012): 1291–1299. The average history of their disorder was 20.4 years. Patients took several scales connected to their social situation, friendships, and perceived stigma. They also participated in individual interviews to discuss their friendships.

10. Meliksah Demir et al., "I Am So Happy 'Cause My Best Friend Makes Me Feel Unique: Friendship, Personal Sense of Uniqueness and Happiness," *Journal of Happiness Studies* 13 (2012), doi: 10.1007/s10902-012-9376-9. There were 2,429 individuals, 27 percent male, 73 percent female.

11. Julianne Holt-Lunstad et al., "Can Hostility Interfere With the Health Benefits of Giving and Receiving Social Support? The Impact of Cynical Hostility on Cardiovascular Reactivity During Social Support Interactions Among Friends," *Annals of Behavioral Medicine* 35 (2008): 319–330. The total number was 214, 56 female dyads and 51 male dyads.

12. Ellen G. White, *Testimonies for the Church*, 2:296.

13. Robert Fulghum, *All I Really Need to Know I Learned in Kindergarten* (New York: Ballantine-Random House, 1989).

143. Emma K. Adam et al., "Adverse Adolescent Relationship Histories and Young Adult Health: Cumulative Effects of Loneliness, Low Parental Support, Relationship Instability, Intimate Partner Violence, and Loss," *Journal of Adolescent Health* 49 (2011): 278–286.

15. Chris Segrin et al., "Loneliness and Poor Health Within Families," *Journal of Social and Personal Relationships* 29 (2012): 597–611. Participants were 456 adults from 169 family units.

16. Li-Juan Liu and Qiang Guo, "Loneliness and Health-Related Quality of Life for the Empty Nest Elderly in the Rural Area of a Mountainous County in China," *Quality of Life Research* 16 (2007): 1275–1280. This included 275 elderly individuals living alone and 315 living in company (315 participants), all in a rural mountainous area. The average age of each group was seventy years; and those with physical or mental disabilities were excluded.

17. Ingrid Nielsen et al., "Subjective Well-Being of Beijing Taxi Drivers," *Journal of Happiness Studies* 11 (2010): 721–733. Most (95.8 percent) were males and reported an average number of 12.57 hours of work per day and worked for 6.5 days a week.

18. Paul Lee Tan, *Encyclopedia of 15,000 Illustrations,* entry 1672.

19. Pamela E. King and James L. Furrow, "Religion as a Resource for Positive Youth Development: Religion, Social Capital, and Moral Outcomes," *Psychology of Religion and Spirituality* 5 (2008): 34–49. A total of 735 public high school students (ages thirteen to nineteen) in Los Angeles made up the sample under study. Gender was well balanced (47–53, male to female) and ages ranged from thirteen to nineteen.

20. Richard Rymarz, "Nurturing Well-Being Through Religious Commitment: Challenges for Mainstream Christian Churches," *International Journal of Children Spirituality* 14 (2009): 249–260.

Chapter 9

The Benefits of Religious Coping

"Be of good courage, and He shall strengthen your heart." —Psalm 31:24

D r. Edelweiss Ramal, a professor of nursing at Loma Linda University, told me her story while we were working together at an accreditation visit at Montemorelos University, Nuevo León, Mexico. She truly experienced the apostle Paul's advice to "not be anxious about anything, but in every situation, by prayer and petition, with thanksgiving, present your requests to God. And the peace of God, which transcends all understanding, will guard your hearts and your minds in Christ Jesus" (Philippians 4:6, 7, NIV).

She said, "I had memorized Philippians 4:6, 7 a few months before I received the diagnosis of breast cancer." It was a good habit she had to memorize key passages from Scripture, but this one would be very relevant. "Never had I realized how much this particular promise would impact my physical, emotional, social, and spiritual life."

After the diagnosis was certain, Edelweiss had to deal with hard questions and emotional turmoil: "As I began to experience the emotions, thoughts, and feelings that result from being a cancer victim, such as doubts (How can this be if I have lived a healthy lifestyle and do not have any of the risk factors?); fears (What will happen to me? To my family?); anxiety regarding treatment (Shall I choose conventional or alternative treatment? What if my family does not agree with the treatment I prefer?), Philippians 4: 6, 7 started taking on a very special and personal meaning."

She found solace in Bible reading and prayer; she felt as if God were speaking to her through Philippians 4: *Don't be anxious, even in the face of cancer. Yes, pray, and plead with Me, but always find something to be thankful for; in fact, find many things to be thankful for. My daughter, if you fulfill the condition of the promise, you will have so much peace that you will surprise everyone. What's more, you yourself will not even begin to understand how you can be so peaceful while experiencing one of the most dreaded diseases.* The verse did not say that her prayer was going to be answered with healing, but it assured her that she would be blessed with a peace beyond understanding. And so He did. Peace became a reality.

For her, it was beyond human comprehension that on the day she went to the hospital for surgery, the peace of God was guarding her heart and mind in Jesus Christ. Her husband took a few pictures of her as she went to the hospital and on to the operating room. Months later, already recovered, as she reviewed those pictures and looked at her radiant face, she kept saying, "I don't understand how I could have been so peaceful before my surgery! This kind of peace truly transcends all understanding!"

Six years later, she praises the Lord, not only for having healed her but also for His leading in her life with such peace and joy. She recently wrote to me: "Every time I was tempted to dwell on negative thoughts, or felt anxious about a decision that had to be made, I would repeat the text in my mind and claim God's promise. He was truly faithful in guarding my heart and my mind through Christ Jesus. It has been six years since I was diagnosed, and life has offered me other anxiety provoking experiences. Nonetheless, I continue experiencing God's wonderful peace, and He continues protecting my heart (feelings and emotions) and my mind (thoughts and decision-making process). And I continue surprising myself and others. This can be your experience as well."[1]

Stressful situations like living with mental or physical illness, losing a dear one, or facing financial struggles pose great challenges to believer and nonbeliever. A number of studies show that many turn to their faith and religion in search of comfort, meaning, and hope. If there is strength to face the ordeals, it comes from God; therefore, we need to hold onto that power and help those suffering to do the same.

This chapter deals with religious coping as one effective way God has provided for people to go through adversity. It is another benefit of faith available to us while we pass by this earthly stage. There are a large number of studies conducted over the past twenty years showing that, in moments of difficulty, the majority of people resort to religious coping to ameliorate pain and suffering. Furthermore, research shows that positive religious coping provides comfort, support, and hope in times of physical and mental illness, trauma, and stressful situations. Indeed, negative religious coping (expressing anger at God, having religious doubt as a result of adversity) tends to destabilize psychological well-being, although in some cases this has brought some relief, possibly as a temporary mechanism to release frustration.

This chapter reviews recent studies about how people cope under various difficult conditions. In addition, the Bible shows individuals that experienced loss, fear, anxiety, loneliness, pain, and discouragement. A few of these Bible characters will be referred to in order to provide ideas on how to proceed when faced with trials and adversities.

Coping

Coping is a psychological term that goes back to the beginnings of the discipline as a modern science; that is, it goes back to Sigmund Freud. Freud saw in coping the way defense mechanisms work. In this way, coping would be an unconscious process. For example, people moving to a new country—where everything is disconnected from their past experience—end up seeking the company of their fellow countrymen, using the food they grew up with, and watching the news and sports from their country. This is done to compensate for the stressful situation, but without giving any thought or planning to their behavior—it is unconscious. This is called regression, and there are another dozen or so defense mechanisms that Freud discovered and that his daughter, Anna, further explained. Still today, defense mechanism interpretations of coping are valid but applicable to a small proportion of situations only, mostly those causing extreme anxiety.

The current concept of coping is such that the "coper" interacts with the environment willingly and purposefully, via mental processes or behaviors. This is done strategically, utilizing a variety of resources that depend on how the circumstances present themselves and on one's individual background. The goal is to understand, tolerate, reduce, or eliminate the stressful situation.

People might cope with confronting the issue, distancing themselves from it, seeking social support (either looking for practical help or emotional support), trying to escape or to avoid the problem. Others resort to actively disengaging, focusing their thoughts on something very different, or even using methods like alcohol or drugs, thus opening the door to further problems. Still others cope using a search for meaning, seeking growth out of adversity, accepting the reality of the difficulty, and turning to God and to religion, while actively searching for solutions. When we include God and religion centrally in the equation, we are coping religiously.

Many in the general population use religion to cope. A self-rating religious coping survey asked the question, "To what extent do you use religion to cope?" Forty percent identified religious coping as the most important factor, 27.3 percent as a large extent or more, 22.7 percent as a moderate to large extent, 5 percent as a small to moderate, and 5 percent as none.[2] This is a powerful evidence for the need that human beings have of God!

How does religious coping work?

By and large, research shows that religious coping enhances well-being in the midst of difficulties, but it is not clear how it works. We can, however, speculate. Harold G. Koenig comes up with reasonable explanations that I outline below.[3] Religion offers a positive worldview, a set of beliefs that are hopeful, a focus on redemption, and it presents God as loving and merciful. Religion also provides meaning and purpose to existence (not just chance), which helps explain temporary pain fitting God's ultimate plan. Religion favors psychological integration that permits the believer to understand the tension between good and evil, thus preventing the dissonance that world events create. Religions also present their followers with the visions of hope that motivate them to live and work, without despair, in the understanding that things will become better according to God's plan. Religion empowers the faithful even when they are poor, victimized, or disadvantaged. It transmits the strength to act and to transform the environment rather than to be left a hopeless victim. Religion attributes the control of things to God, doing away with fear and anxiety. In addition, religion provides role models for suffering; for example, the Bible tells stories of individuals whose lives were blessed by God in spite of their tribulations. Religion also offers guidance for decision making and standards of behavior that protect people from much trouble. Religion offers satisfactory answers to ultimate questions, such as "Where did I come from?" "What is my destiny?" "Why is there good and evil?" "How will the end of things be?" Religious organizations provide consistent social support and a place where people can get help and gain motivation to trust in God as a Provider of solutions. Finally, religion offers durability; religiosity endures under all circumstances. It offers a place where prayer, meditation, and the sense of God's presence transcend time and space.

How do people cope religiously? Most frequently, those finding support in religion to face difficulties enjoy a sense of God's presence in their lives; they have the certainty that God is very near, watching, listening, and offering encouragement and support. They keep mental interaction with the Creator through prayer and conversation. They perceive God as loving them and guiding them, both in routine activities and in transcendental steps. They also find strength and comfort in the study of and reflection on Bible promises, doctrines, and beliefs. In addition to the above intrinsic experiences, the religious people find connection with God as well as spiritual strength via corporate worship. And it is comforting to know that current research is finding that those active in these practices may not prevent adversity, but they at least cope much more successfully.

One of the most tragic experiences is to be told that your child has a chronic, debilitating disease that will reduce his or her life span significantly. Daniel Grossoehme and Judy Ragsdale, pastoral personnel at the Cincinnati Children's Hospital Medical Center in Cincinnati, Ohio, studied the way parents of children with cystic fibrosis (CF) coped.[4] This disease is associated with the malfunction of the respiratory system. It requires daily chest physiotherapy to clear mucous secretion; it may cause complications such as malabsorption of nutrients, diabetes, or infertility in males and pancreatic insufficiency. The most feared symptom of CF is pulmonary failure, as it may cause death; hence, the life expectancy of these patients is only thirty-seven years. To conduct this study, researchers extensively interviewed fifteen of these parents. Up to sixteen different religious coping styles were observed, these being the most common:

1. *Pleading.* Parents of children with CF reported that they pleaded with God for their child to heal or feel comfortable. It was the most common form of religious coping. One parent said, "There have been moments of begging and pleading, especially when she's in pain, you know, and I feel so helpless. . . . So, when I feel hopeless, and when I pray for strength . . . I think He grants it in His own way."

2. *Collaboration.* Working together with God to bring healing or improvement of symptoms. "I feel like we're working together because we can pray and all that, but if we don't do her treatments, there's only so much that He can do," said a parent. Others, perhaps exhausted from the daily treatment and the pressure of stress, talked in terms of "I just can't take it anymore," or "You just have to take it one day at a time and let God finish it up."

3. *Benevolent religious reappraisals.* This includes the understanding that God may or may not intervene in a total solution but lead the process in a way that is adequate at the time, according to His omniscience. One parent said, "He's given us this task . . . the doctors are going to tell us what we need to do to be preventive. It's our job to follow through and let God control the outcome of that."

4. *Seeking spiritual support.* Also, they often found the parents approached their clergy or fellow believers to seek help. Some reported their going to their pastor or priest; others gave specific detail on how their fellow believers had prepared food for them, brought them posters with Scripture quotations for comfort, and prayed for them.

Other ways to cope were maintaining hope above all (knowing that this is not the end), turning to God for comfort, praying for others, practicing religious rituals as a distraction from the stressor, and understanding that suffering brings religious purification (spiritual cleansing). There were also negative religious coping, such as being angry at God and believing that the disease has come as a divine punishment.

Religious coping and health

The use of religious coping in dealing with the burden of mental and physical illness is a widely studied area. In my review of research on this topic, the return was so high that I had to narrow my selection to studies published over the last three years. This shows how, at a time when medical science is at the maximum height of development, people understand that, yes, they must seek human intervention, but that they need to reconnect with God, who is above and beyond health and healing, and that He is the only One that can make man truly whole.

Thomas Carpenter, along with other colleagues from Seattle Pacific University, studied the possible connections between religious coping, stress, and depressive symptoms of adolescents from grades nine through twelve, attending Catholic and Protestant schools in the Pacific Northwest.[5] For eight weeks, these young people periodically reported on their stressors and depressive symptoms. Because it is a well-known factor that stressors tend to cause depressive symptoms, the goal was to see whether religious coping would moderate or prevent this connection.

The results showed that negative religious coping made the stress-depression link even stronger; it made things worse. On the other hand, those teenagers who resorted to positive religious coping experienced the effects of stress in a much gentler manner than did the rest. Consistent results have been found with adult populations. An example is a study with 336 adult Protestant church members by Jeffrey Bjorck and John Thurman, who found a benign effect of positive religious coping on stressful situations.[6] Participants reporting using positive religious coping methods (praying, feeling God's presence, finding meaning in pain, etc.) were able to buffer the deleterious effects of negative events when compared with others not using those methods.

Facing the loss of a dear one is devastating. To compensate for the grief caused, many people use religious coping strategies. Searching for meaning is a key factor in dealing with grief. A recent study was designed to determine if meaning attached to God would bring better outcomes than did other approaches void of meaning. Melissa Kelley and Keith Chan, from Boston College in Massachusetts, obtained data from women who had experienced a significant death over the previous year.[7] Most deaths were that of a parent or a husband. About half (48 percent) of these deaths were expected, and the remaining half (52 percent) were unexpected. On average, the entire group displayed symptoms of depression associated with grief.

But they had different frequency and intensity of symptoms depending on certain variables. First, those who were securely attached to God experienced lower depression and grief and an increased stress-related growth (resilience). Second, those using positive religious coping also enjoyed stress-related growth. Third, when there was a strong attachment to others, there was also stress-related growth. And fourth, a secure attachment to God provided the best quality of meaning, which in turn brought about the most mental health benefits.

Student missions are a popular option for college-age young people in the United States. However, there has not been much study about how these men and women cope with the missionary task. One exception is the study conducted by Jeffrey Bjorck and Jean-Woo Kim from Fuller Theological Seminary and the Metropolitan State Hospital in Norwalk, California, respectively.[8] They set several goals, but the most relevant, for the purpose of this book, was to investigate how short-term missionaries' religious coping while on assignment was related to their psychological functioning. The young men and women were going on a two-month mission trip to various destinations, both national and international, eleven countries in all. They provided data during their pre-journey training period and upon return from their service. Data gathered included religious coping, religious support (how much support participants perceived they got from God, their congregation, and the church leadership), and psychological functioning. The findings show that those using negative religious coping had more inclination to anger. But those using high positive religious coping perceived a high support coming from God; thus, they experienced a clear rise in their life satisfaction.

Divorce is a highly stressful process that oftentimes causes depressive symptoms. A study led by Amy Webb from the University of Texas at Austin was designed to find out how religious coping may help with depression associated with divorce.[9] She was assisted by colleagues from her university as well as from Loma Linda University. The main research question was, "What is the role of religion in coping with depression among divorcees?" Participants were members of the Seventh-day Adventist Church from the Adventist Health Study–2. Researchers studied a subset of this very large database of ninety-six thousand—a sample of 10,988 participants in a religion and health study. They provided data on depressive symptoms, divorce, and religious coping style. This subset contained 4 percent of respondents who had experienced a divorce within the five years prior to the survey. These were the specific focus of analysis.

As all participants were believers, the tendency was to rely heavily on religious coping. However, some did more than others, and these differences made the analysis possible. Findings clearly showed that religious coping helped soften the effects of depression. The most powerful form of coping was seeking support from God; this provided the greatest effect against depression, followed by collaborative coping, the position that I should do as much as it is in my hand to fight my difficulty and let God do the rest. And the third was reframing troubling events; that is, seeing the largest picture of past, present, future, and eternity. One interesting analysis was to compare the sample of divorced with the nondivorced participants. Everyone (whether divorced or not) experienced less depressive symptoms when coping religiously, but positive religious coping paid significantly greater anti-depression benefits to those who had gone through a divorce.

Authors recognized that divorce is a social stressor, and especially so among religious people, like the Seventh-day Adventists, where marriage is seen as a divine institution established by God Himself, with the understanding that individual marriages should endure forever. This makes help and support even more necessary to those affected. It is imperative to adopt a spiritually caring attitude in church settings toward divorce, where religious coping may be most appropriate. Prayer, Scripture reading, worship, and so on, can be excellent ways of providing much needed support to recently divorced sisters and brothers in our churches.

The mental health of those caring for a close family member with a chronic disease or disability is of great concern. Sooner or later, signs of disorders (especially depression) may appear in the person providing care. Angelica Herrera, from the University of Texas MD Anderson Cancer Center in Houston, Texas, and her team asked themselves whether religious coping could prevent or soothe depressive symptoms in people under such circumstances.[10] The study was focused on Mexican-American caregivers, interviewed during two hours each, using Spanish as the medium of communication when necessary. They provided care to a relative (e.g., spouse, sibling, in-law) aged fifty or older. They were given measures of religiosity, religious coping, well-being, assessment of the care recipient, and a number of socioeconomic demographics.

When the data was examined, it was observed that those finding support in religious coping displayed less depressive symptoms and perceived the caring burden more positively than did their nonreligious coping counterparts. In addition, high levels of religious coping ran parallel to improved physical and emotional health. Those having a high sense of burden (tending to use no religious coping) were more likely to be depressed and less likely to enjoy mental health. An interesting finding emphasizes the weight of the church community; participants in organized religion were less likely to perceive their caregiving role as burdensome. On the contrary, those with high levels of nonorganizational religiosity (e.g., private prayers, such as the Rosary in these participants), with little or no worship attendance, endured worse mental health. This is one more example of the indirect benefits of belonging to a church community where camaraderie and emotional and instrumental support are a source of health to participants.

Religious coping in people with serious health problems

A group of researchers led by Kelly Trevino of Bowling Green State University in Ohio, focused on a group of HIV/AIDS outpatients in order to observe the effects of their religious coping on various physical as well as mental outcomes.[11] They provided data on two occasions separated by twelve to eighteen months, allowing researchers to observe variations over time and see the effect of religious coping on the changes. Findings revealed that positive religious coping was a predictor of both greater self-esteem and higher levels of spirituality. Additionally, those attaining relatively high levels of positive religious coping reported improvements in well-being over time. In terms of physical health, a count of CD4 cells—those protecting the organism from disease and indicators of improvement in HIV/AIDS patients—were taken at the beginning and at the end of the study. Those reporting spiritual struggle were read a low count of CD4 cells, indicating a loss of defenses after having struggled religiously. These results suggest that psycho-spiritual interventions geared to promote the use of positive religious coping—communion with God, prayer, coming to terms with the place of illness in the large framework of life and beyond—may improve psychological, physiological, and spiritual well-being in individuals with HIV/AIDS.

A team of researchers from Indiana University, led by Kevin Rand, studied a group of men with advanced cancer to see how they appraised their illness and how religious coping favored psychological responses.[12] Results showed that those who appraised their disease with some meaning (e.g., they admitted that because of the illness they got to know themselves better, they took care of things they otherwise would have not, they set new goals, etc.) experienced very low levels of psychological distress and high levels of positive mental adjustment. In addition, cancer patients with frequent and intense use of positive religious coping experienced post-traumatic growth, a positive trauma aftermath, and something good out of so much evil: resilience.

Although most of the research published on religious coping has been conducted in the United States, there is a growing number of studies from other countries. A Brazilian research project led by Susana Ramirez, from the University of Ceará–Fortaleza, explored the relationship between religious coping, psychological distress, and the quality of life of 170 hemodialysis outpatients, all with end-stage renal disease.[13] Researchers obtained clinical data, indicators of anxiety and depression symptoms, and information about seven types of positive religious coping and seven types of negative religious coping. Participants also reported on their perceived quality of life in the physical, mental, social relations, and environmental areas.

Results showed that most of these hemodialysis patients more or less relied on religion to cope. Higher levels of positive religious coping were associated with a better quality of life, especially in the areas of mental well-being and social relations. It was also observed that the higher the religious struggle, the more depression and anxiety symptoms and the more psychological distress they experienced.

Religious coping and trauma

Torture, rape, and *abuse* are abominable words that depict situations of extreme perverse, willful, and aggressive acts. The natural result is trauma. Trauma is characterized by stress, depression, anxiety, and post-traumatic stress disorder (PTSD). How do traumatized people cope? Is there an advantage to religious coping? Is there any growth out of these terrible experiences?

Various studies show that religious coping is one of the best coping mechanisms. Viktor Frankl, the well-known Austrian neurologist, psychiatrist, and Holocaust survivor, went through three concentration camps during 1944 and 1945. Based on his observations and experience, Frankl stated that any experience, no matter how distressing, can be survived if one manages to find meaning and purpose in the process.

And only through faith in God can this be possible. So religious coping is a way to survive ordeals. In fact, resilience has been given attention in the recent years to indicate that something stronger may come out of it all.

Victims of torture provide rich data on how religious coping can help these people survive physically and psychologically. The study housed at George Washington University, and conducted by Professor Christina Gee and graduate student, Suzanne Leaman, focused on a group of African torture survivors living in the United States.[14] Types of torture reported were multiple and were classified under one of the following: physical torture, psychological manipulations, sexual torture, sensory discomfort, forced stress positions, humiliating treatment, and deprivation of basic needs.

Gender, age, and education were controlled in the analysis because it is known that women, older people, and educated individuals are more likely to suffer from depression and PTSD after torture than do others. In this way, the results would show the exclusive effect of religious coping. Findings revealed that sexual torture was the type with the largest PTSD symptoms. Additionally,

171

religious coping strategies were a protective factor of psychological distress and negative religious coping predicted PTSD symptoms. Lastly, those who had been submitted to more physical torture or forced stress positions (e.g., forced standing, forced sitting, forced kneeling) and engaged in more private religious practices reported fewer symptoms of PTSD and depression than did nonreligious "copers."

Another cause of trauma is victimization from a sexual assault. Not many studies focus on this matter, as it is extremely sensitive, but Courtney Ahrens from California State University–Long Beach, was able to explore the experience of 103 female rape survivors.[15] (She used posters in churches, Laundromats, and coffee shops to find people in the area.) Data were collected via one-on-one interviews lasting an average of 2.6 hours each. Topics covered involved religious coping, depression, PTSD, psychological well-being, and post-traumatic growth. Many mentioned that they did not receive much support from the clergy and other members of the church, but that they became engaged in church activities as a way to avoid dealing with the assault directly. They said that they "focused on the world to come rather than the problems of this world," or "prayed or read the Bible to keep my mind off my problem." This study showed significant differences between African-American survivors and their white counterparts. The first group of women relied more intensely on all kinds of religious coping.

Like in other studies, as negative religious coping increased, depressive symptoms grew, and as positive religious coping increased, depressive symptoms decreased. Additionally, women who practiced positive religious coping tended to experience much more post-traumatic growth and well-being than the rest.

Monica Gerber, together with two other colleagues from the University of North Texas, did another study with a more general sample also reporting some degree of traumatic experience.[16] They focused on the concept of posttraumatic growth and asked the question, "Will religious coping contribute to posttraumatic growth?" At least twelve kinds of traumatic events were reported by participants. The top ones were receiving news of serious injury and death; being involved in a car accident, fire, or explosion; having suffered child physical or sexual abuse; and having experienced a natural disaster. Results of this study showed gender differences in the frequency of traumatic events. Women had experienced a significantly higher number of traumatic occurrences than did men, but they also experienced a much higher level of post-traumatic growth. It was also found that positive religious coping was a predictor of positive growth, while negative religious coping predicted the symptoms of PTSD.

It seems as if the Christian needs to endure pain before good things take place. Women in the above study endured more trauma but experienced significantly higher growth because they coped religiously in a positive way. Robert Murray M'Cheyne said, "The way to Zion is through the valley of Boca. You must go through the wilderness of Jordan if you are to come to the Land of Promise."

Negative coping

Negative coping consists of reacting negatively towards God when misfortune hits; it includes things such as showing anger towards God, or blaming Him for all the pain and suffering being endured. It may also include passive religious deferral (not doing anything to palliate the situation and expecting God to solve the problems), falling into religious doubts, and rejection of people who are associated with religion. Researchers have found that negative religious "copers" adhere to sentences such as, "I feel that my disease is God's way of punishing me for my sins," "I've been questioning God's love for me," or "I've been questioning the power of God."

Although negative coping is not an exemplary way to cope, especially for a Christian, it is a natural human reaction under tragic circumstances. Sometimes people have to face very perplexing misfortunes: contracting a serious illness when they have been consistently careful to practice healthy habits, dealing with the loss of a family member due to homicide, or a serious accident where one had no fault. These traumatic experiences shake all personal foundations. However, it is possible to go through this stage and soon surpass it after the initial shock. Being attached to God before the problem arises seems to be crucial. In fact, research recognizes that the role of attachment to God is very important in determining how successful religious coping will be.[17]

Although a small group of studies finds some positive outcomes with the use of negative coping, by and large, studies find it associated with poor physical and psychological outcomes. For example, Yaron Rabinowitz and his team found out that when female caregivers of elder relatives with dementia used negative religious strategies to cope, they were at increased cumulative health risk and also more prone to gain weight.[18] Laurie Burke was able to interact with forty-six African-American homicide survivors.[19] Those using negative religious coping were more likely to have a complicated grief process and were subject to spiritual struggle six months later when compared to those not using negative religious coping. Steven Pirutinsky studied longitudinally a sample of Orthodox Jews.[20] Persons using negative religious coping were much more likely to show symptoms of depression than were those not using negative religious coping; and this study, being longitudinal, indicates a cause-effect relationship between negative religious coping and depression.

Randy Hebert studied religious coping in women with breast cancer.[21] He observed that most women of his sample used positive religious coping, but the small group (15 percent) using negative religious coping had worse overall mental health, depressive symptoms, and lower life satisfaction. This was a follow-up study and when women introduced positive changes in their negative coping, their mental health and satisfaction improved.

Coping in the Bible

There are many occasions when the Bible refers to individuals having to cope with difficult situations. How do these people cope? Are there lessons we can learn from them? I have chosen four of these individuals from the Old Testament and will take a look at how Jesus faced some of the pressures He encountered.

Job is the first in chronology. Briefly but categorically, the Bible states that Job was "blameless and upright; he feared God and shunned evil"; he was wealthy as evidenced by his thousands of farm animals and many servants. He had a wife, seven sons, and three daughters. He must have enjoyed not only material things but also a great deal of respect, for Job is referred to as "the greatest man among all the people of the East" (Job 1:1–3, NIV). However, in a very limited period of time, this righteous man lost all his possessions, his children, and, although his wife survived, she rejected him and told him to "Curse God and die!" (Job 2:9, NIV). Then Satan attacked him with painful sores from head to toe. He was left without any loved ones, no property, and no reputation: "People listened to me expectantly, waiting in silence for my counsel" (29:21, NIV), "but now they mock me" (30:1, NIV). How does this man cope with facing a situation of complete loss?

First, he puts himself in perspective, sees the whole trajectory of his life, and praises God:

> "Naked I came from my mother's womb,
>   and naked I will depart.
> The LORD gave and the LORD has taken away;
>   may the name of the LORD be praised" (1:21, NIV).

Secondly, he continues to trust the Lord in spite of all his suffering: "Though he slay me, yet will I hope in him" (13:15, NIV).

Third, he does express his doubts and keeps asking God "Why?" displaying a realistically human reaction: "Why did I not perish at birth?" (3:11, NIV);

174

"Why was I not hidden away?" (verse 16, NIV); "Why do the wicked live on?" (21:7, NIV). He also manifests his suffering: "I have no peace, no quietness; I have no rest, but only turmoil" (3:26, NIV).

Fourth, in spite of his perplexity, and, even though his friends are of no help to him ("You are miserable comforters," 16:2, NIV), Job sees the end of the tunnel because he is aware of God's ultimate plan, and he affirms, "For I know that my redeemer liveth, and that he shall stand at the latter day upon the earth" (19:25, KJV).

The case is resolved at the end of the book: God reproves Job's friends, restores his possessions doubly, gives him a new family, and keeps him alive to 140. But, during his trial, we see that Job keeps his earthly items separate from his vision. He had his fundamental questions of origin and destiny very clear, he continued to recognize God's supremacy, and he trusted in God despite having a few questions unanswered.

Job's case is crucial to remind us that not everything bad that happens to us is a direct result of our sin. Contracting a terminal disease is no proof of judgment upon the victim. However, it is quite common to find people feeling the burden of guilt, in addition to the illness upon him or her or a dear one. We need to assure these people that although we are all sinners, specific events do not always happen because of specific sins committed, and that total forgiveness is available when we sin, regardless of the transgression.

When the disciples asked Jesus, "Rabbi, who sinned, this man or his parents, that he was born blind?" Jesus answered, "Neither this man nor his parents sinned, . . . but this happened so that the works of God might be displayed in him" (John 9:2, 3).

In the cosmic battle between good and evil, there is no use in looking for a single one to blame, especially when there is a tendency to blame the victim. While staying in a hotel in a foreign country for a speaking appointment, I turned on the radio and began to listen to a program where people called and asked for advice on everyday problems. One noticeably humble woman called to ask what to do about her husband hitting her on a regular basis. It broke my heart to hear her talking and sobbing, but the radio announcer kept asking, "Can you think of anything you are doing to upset him? Are you provoking in any way?" It was clear that the broadcaster could not think of anyone responsible outside the woman. What a contrast with Jesus' attitude of accepting and providing hope to the suffering!

We also encounter the case of Joseph, who was treated unfairly by his brothers and put in a series of highly stressful situations. First, he had to endure hatred and jealousy from them (Genesis 37:5, 8, 11). Then they harassed him, threw

175

him into a cistern, and sold him to Midianite merchants (verses 23, 24, 28) who, in turn, sold him to Potiphar in Egypt (verse 36). How did he cope? Ellen White tells us he knew he was unprepared to cope with the difficulties before him. He had become self-sufficient and exacting. But now, as Joseph was lonely and distant from home, all the sacred stories told to him in his childhood came to his mind with clarity. In the midst of the adversity, Joseph's experience led him to his conversion. He prayed, gave himself fully to God, and resolved to prove himself true to his Lord.[22] He was subjected to fierce temptation and sent unjustly to jail. But he remained faithful and gave God the credit for his success (see Genesis 40:8; 41:16). His coping mechanisms were to remain close to his heavenly Father, to pray, and to wait even when it took years for freedom and vindication to come (Genesis 41).

Naomi also had to face a great deal of adversity. This woman, who had to go through a number of losses in her life, can be an inspiration. The first few verses of Ruth 1 give us a compact view of her misfortunes: to avoid famine, her family was forced to immigrate to Moab, a nation of idolatry and incompatible lifestyle to the Jews. Elimelech, Naomi's husband, died, leaving her and her two boys; thus, she was widowed and they orphaned in a foreign land. Then her sons, Mahlon and Killion, married local women, a fact that no doubt brought family tensions as this was against God's will (see Deuteronomy 23:3; Ezra 9:1, 2). Later on, these young men died.

This devastating situation exemplifies the extremity of human suffering. How did Naomi cope? Most likely, guided by God's influence, she set herself for the land of Judah, where she would worship in freedom and find relatives to support her. She was also willing to accept the sweet and determined support of her daughter-in-law Ruth (Ruth 1:18), who would be the avenue of her healing. In addition, she took special care to encourage and support Ruth in her adaptation to their new location (2:2) and her relationship with Boaz (2:19–22; 3). Accepting help and helping others are part of God's plan to deal with difficulties, and this seems to be the mechanism that, at least partly, helped Naomi's coping.

Lastly, Elijah was one of the prophets subjected to the highest and lowest of emotional experiences. First Kings 17 and 18 describe a series of exhilarating events full of the manifestation of God's power: the prophet fed by ravens, the widow of Zarephath using an endless oil container, her son being resurrected, God sending fire on Mount Carmel, 450 false prophets punished, rain miraculously falling after three and a half years of drought. Then, in chapter 19, we see the protagonist frightened, anxious, and depressed after Jezebel pronounced a sentence to kill him within twenty-four hours. Next, we see Elijah afraid, running for his life, walking a day's journey into the wilderness, and asking God to take his life (1 Kings 19:3, 4).

How did Elijah cope? For one thing, he prayed. And that was a huge positive step. It doesn't matter if one prays for God to take his life; the important thing is to remain open to God's intervention, and He will always do the right thing. Elijah also performed a number of behaviors (some induced by divine agents) that helped him cope: Sleep. Eat bread baked by an angel. Sleep again. Eat again. And then engage in massive physical exercise—forty days and forty nights to cover a distance of four hundred miles from Mount Carmel to Mount Horeb (verses 5–9). The plan worked, for Elijah was restored to mental and spiritual health and had an encounter with God at Mount Horeb, where he received his last commission before departing for heaven (verses 12–18).

Looking at the life of Christ will also help us find inspiration and follow His steps as He asks us to "learn from Me" (Matthew 11:29). At the beginning of His ministry, "The enticements which Christ resisted were those that we find it so difficult to withstand. They were urged upon Him in a much greater degree as His character is superior to ours. With the terrible weight of the sins of the world upon Him, Christ withstood the test upon appetite, upon the love of the world, and upon that love of display which leads to presumption."[23] Also, "He was left to battle with temptation. It was pressing upon Him every moment."[24] Scriptures provided help and support to Jesus and, above all, victory over temptation. Meditation on scriptures, repetition of verses, and memorization of key passages, are the Master's coping mechanisms for us to deal with temptation and other sources of stress.

In addition, Gospel writers mentioned in various locations that Jesus went to a solitary place to have communion with His Father. This was Jesus' way to cope with the demands of people, His disciples' lack of understanding, the harassment of His enemies, and the burden of His mission in favor of humanity. Prayer and Scripture were His two coping pillars. These are also available to us. It seems that in times of trial and difficulty, we may not have motivation to study the Bible in depth with concordance and theological resources in hand. But the repetition of memorized, brief portions of Scripture can be the key to improve our mood, and to leave behind an afflicted moment. The chart on the next page contains a number of brief texts that can be committed to memory and used accordingly.

Memory Verses to Cope

Adversity	"Blessed be the God and Father of our Lord Jesus Christ, the Father of mercies and God of all comfort, who comforts us in all our tribulation, that we may be able to comfort those who are in any trouble, with the comfort with which we ourselves are comforted by God" (2 Corinthians 1:3, 4).
Anxiety	"Be anxious for nothing, but in everything by prayer and supplication, with thanksgiving, let your requests be made known to God; and the peace of God, which surpasses all understanding, will guard your hearts and minds through Christ Jesus" (Philippians 4:6, 7).
Challenges about resources	"I know how to be abased, and I know how to abound. Everywhere and in all things I have learned both to be full and to be hungry, both to abound and to suffer need" (Philippians 4:12).
Depression	"And the ransomed of the Lord shall return, and come to Zion with singing, with everlasting joy on their heads. They shall obtain joy and gladness, and sorrow and sighing shall flee away" (Isaiah 35:10).
Difficulties	"It is God who avenges me, and subdues the peoples under me; He delivers me from my enemies. You also lift me up above those who rise against me; You have delivered me from the violent man" (2 Samuel 22:48, 49).
Fear	" 'Fear not, for I am with you; be not dismayed, for I am your God. I will strengthen you, yes, I will help you, I will uphold you with My righteous right hand' " (Isaiah 41:10).
Fear and apprehension	"You shall not be afraid of the terror by night, nor of the arrow that flies by day, nor of the pestilence that walks in darkness, nor of the destruction that lays waste at noonday. A thousand may fall at your side, and ten thousand at your right hand; but it shall not come near you" (Psalm 91:5–7).
Fear of death	"I will ransom them from the power of the grave; I will redeem them from death" (Hosea 13:14).
Grief and affliction	"For the Lord will not cast off forever. Though He causes grief, yet He will show compassion according to the multitude of His mercies. For He does not afflict willingly, nor grieve the children of men" (Lamentations 3:31–33).
Illness	"My flesh and my heart fail; but God is the strength of my heart and my portion forever" (Psalm 73:26).
Pain and suffering	"And God will wipe away every tear from their eyes; there shall be no more death, nor sorrow, nor crying. There shall be no more pain, for the former things have passed away" (Revelation 21:4).
Sadness	"Delight yourself also in the Lord, and He shall give you the desires of your heart" (Psalm 37:4)
Trials	"My brethren, count it all joy when you fall into various trials, knowing that the testing of your faith produces patience" (James 1:2, 3).
Trouble	"These things I have spoken to you, that in Me you may have peace. In the world you will have tribulation; but be of good cheer, I have overcome the world" (John 16:33).

Unwanted thoughts	"Your mercy, O LORD, will hold me up. In the multitude of my anxieties within me, your comforts delight my soul" (Psalm 94:18, 19).
Weakness	"The LORD is my rock and my fortress and my deliverer; my God, my strength, in whom I will trust; my shield and the horn of my salvation, my stronghold" (Psalm 18:2).

Conclusion

When the late bishop of Madras visited Travancore as part of his pastoral rounds of the South Asian region, he was introduced to a little girl locals caringly called "the Child Apostle." The nickname was given to her because she had suffered fierce persecution in her conditions as a slave and a Christian. She was also able to win converts to Christ by her quiet, steady persistence. As the bishop looked at her face, neck, and arms, scarred by stripes and blows, he was deeply moved, and said, "My child, how could you bear this?" In a sweet voice and to the gentleman's surprise, she replied, "Don't you like to suffer for Christ, sir?"[25]

Not every follower of Jesus will be called to suffer in the same way, but everyone will face difficulties. God cares when we must go through suffering experiences and asks us to do something about them: "Cast all your anxiety on him because he cares for you" (1 Peter 5:7, NIV). If you are going through difficult times or want to be ready for when those times come, remember that bedrock of coping is to remain in Jesus and in His love (John 15).

Study Questions

- Read 2 Samuel 12:1–25. How does King David react to the prophet's rebuke? How does he cope with the enormous burden of guilt? Where does he go as soon as he finds out that his little boy is dead? Why? What coping lessons can you learn from this story?
- Read 2 Chronicles 20. What are the reactions of King Jehoshaphat when he finds out the terrible news? How does he cope? What can you learn out of his prayer to God? How is the problem solved? If confronted with a serious issue of health, family, work, or finances, how would you apply principles and ideas from 2 Chronicles 20? What if God's help does not come as miraculously as it came in Jehoshaphat's story?
- Read 2 Corinthians 12:6–10. How does the apostle Paul cope with the thorn in his flesh? What is his conclusion after having pleaded with the Lord to take it away and He said No?

Application Thoughts

- Memorize the following text: "With men it is impossible, but not with God; for with God all things are possible" (Mark 10:27). Have it ready in your head for the time when something, big or small, becomes difficult.
- Second Corinthians 4:17, 18 talks about "momentary affliction" and a distinct classification of all things between what we see and what we don't see, between the transient and the eternal. How can you keep these two separate in your life? What belongs to the transient and what to the eternal? If affliction comes, how can this idea help you?
- Ellen G. White says that God is "well pleased when we urge past mercies and blessings as a reason why He should bestow on us greater blessings."[26] What can you do to not forget those past mercies?

1. E. Ramal, personal communication, November 9, 2012.

2. Harold G. Koenig et al., *2012 Summer Research Workshops on Spirituality and Health* (Durham, NC: Duke Center for Spirituality, Theology and Health, 2012), 61.

3. Harold G. Koenig et al., *Handbook of Religion and Health*, 2nd ed. (New York: Oxford University Press, 2012), 91–93.

4. Daniel H. Grossoehme et al., "Parents' Religious Coping Styles in the First Year After Their Child's Cystic Fibrosis Diagnosis," *Journal of Health Care Chaplaincy* 16 (2010): 109–122.

5. Thomas P. Carpenter et al., "Religious Coping, Stress, and Depressive Symptoms Among Adolescents: A Prospective Study," *Psychology of Religion and Spirituality* 4 (2012): 19–30. Study included 111 adolescents (28 percent male and 72 percent female).

6. Jeffrey P. Bjorck and John W. Thurman, "Negative Life Events, Patterns of Positive and Negative Religious Coping, and Psychological Functioning," *Journal for the Scientific Study of Religion* 46 (2007): 159–167.

7. Melissa M. Kelley and Keith T. Chan, "Assessing the Role of Attachment to God, Meaning, and Religious Coping as Mediators in the Grief Experience," *Death Studies* 36 (2012): 199–227. Study included ninety-three participants, with a mean age of forty-six, 23 percent men and 77 percent women.

8. Jeffrey P. Bjorck et al., "Religious Coping, Religious Support, and Psychological Functioning Among Short-Term Missionaries," *Mental Health, Religion & Culture* 12 (2009): 611–626. A sample of ninety-eight students was obtained from Nazarene colleges including men (thirty-two) and women (seventy-six).

9. Amy P. Webb et al., "Divorce, Religious Coping, and Depressive Symptoms in a Conservative Protestant Religious Group," *Family Relations* 59 (2010): 544–557. Women were overrepresented, making up 67 percent of the respondents. The average age was sixty-one, and the ethnic background was 60 percent white, 33 percent black, with the remaining 7 percent being mainly Hispanic and Asian.

10. Angelica P. Herrera et al., "Religious Coping and Caregiver Well-Being in Mexican-American

Families," *Aging & Mental Health* 13 (2009): 84–91. They were sixty-six family caregivers working in San Diego County, California, mostly women (89.4 percent), with a median age of 48.5 and mostly Roman Catholic (70 percent) .

11. Kelly M. Trevino et al., "Religious Coping and Physiological, Psychological, Social, and Spiritual Outcomes in Patients With HIV/AIDS: Cross-sectional and Longitudinal Findings," *AIDS Behavior* 17 (2010): 379–389. Participants were 429 (85 percent male and 15 percent female) recruited from medical centers in Pittsburgh, Cincinnati, and Washington, D.C. As far a sexual orientation, 50.3 percent saw themselves as gay or lesbian, 33.3 percent heterosexual, and 11.4 percent said to be bisexual.

12. Kevin L. Rand et al., "Illness Appraisal, Religious Coping, and Psychological Responses in Men With Advanced Cancer," *Support Care Cancer* 20 (2012): 1719–1728. The sample was made up of eighty-six men, with advanced cancer (most commonly gastrointestinal and sarcoma types) and 63 percent of them were receiving chemotherapy at the time of the study. Researchers recruited participants from the Indiana University Simon Cancer Center, and included men older than eighteen, receiving advanced-stage cancer treatment, fluent in English, able to give informed consent, with an anticipated life expectancy of at least three months, and with no cognitive impairment in completing the surveys.

13. Susana P. Ramirez et al., "The Relationship Between Religious Coping, Psychological Distress and Quality of Life in Hemodialysis Patients," *Journal of Psychosomatic Research* 72 (2012): 129–135. They were 64 percent men and 36 percent women with an average age of forty-eight. The large majority were Christian (98 percent, two-thirds Catholic, one-third Protestant).

14. Suzanne C. Leaman and Christina B. Gee, "Religious Coping and Risk Factors for Psychological Distress Among African Torture Survivors," *Psychological Trauma: Theory, Research, Practice, and Policy* 4 (2012): 457–465. Of the 131 subjects (seventy-five women and fifty-six men), about 70 percent were from Ethiopia and Cameroon; the remainder was from Kenya, Sierra Leone, Togo, Burundi, and Mali. Practically all (99.2 percent) were seeking political asylum in the U.S., and were separated from their immediate families, who remained at home in Africa. Data was collected in English, French, and Amharic.

15. Courtney E. Ahrens et al., "Spirituality and Well-Being: The Relationship Between Religious Coping and Recovery From Sexual Assault," *Journal of Interpersonal Violence* 25 (2010): 1242–1263.

16. Monica M. Gerber et al., "The Unique Contributions of Positive and Negative Religious Coping to Posttraumatic Growth and PTSD," *Psychology of Religion and Spirituality* 3 (2011): 298–307. They drew a sample of 1,016 undergraduate students from a large public university in the southwestern United States, 33 percent men and 67 percent women with an average age of twenty. They were given measures of general coping strategies, religious coping, a traumatic events questionnaire, a post-traumatic growth inventory, and a PTSD checklist.

17. I. Ungureanu and J. G. Sandberg, "Broken Together: Spirituality and Religion as Coping Strategies for Couples Dealing With the Death of a Child: A Literature Review With Clinical Implications," *Contemporary Family Therapy* 32 (2010): 202–319.

18. Yaron G. Rabinowitz et al., "Is Religious Coping Associated With Cumulative Health Risk? An Examination of Religious Coping Styles and Health Behavior Patterns in Alzheimer's Dementia Caregivers," *Journal of Religion and Health* 49 (2010): 498–512.

19. Laurie A. Burke et al., "Faith in the Wake of Homicide: Religious Coping and Bereavement Distress in an African American Sample," *International Journal for the Psychology of Religion* 21 (2011): 289–307.

20. Steven Pirutinsky et al., "Does Negative Religious Coping Accompany, Precede, or Follow Depression Among Orthodox Jews?" *Journal of Affective Disorders* 132 (2011): 401–405.

21. Randy Hebert et al., "Positive and Negative Religious Coping and Well-Being in Women With Breast Cancer," *Journal of Palliative Medicine* 12 (2009): 537–545.

22. Ellen G. White, *Patriarch and Prophets,* 213, 214.

23. Ellen G. White, *The Desire of Ages,* 116.

24. Ibid., 118.

25. Paul Lee Tan, *Encyclopedia of 15,000 Illustrations,* entry 12443.

26. Ellen G. White, *The Ministry of Healing,* 513.

Chapter 10

Physical and Mental Health Wholeness

"Yes, my soul, find rest in God; my hope comes from him." —Psalm 62:5, NIV

E lena* is about fifty and had a bout of depression when she was twenty. She experienced a persistent sadness that remained even in the presence of whatever excited her most. She distanced herself from friends, from any kind of socializing, and retreated to her dorm room, where she cried, feeling worthless and negative and pessimistic. She even had serious suicidal thoughts, although she never attempted it. She was lucky to get treatment, both medical and psychological, and she took a few months to recover.

The doctor told her that it was stress related because of the heavy demands from her college degree. She fully recovered, married, had a family, and enjoyed life thoroughly. Unfortunately, after both her children left home, she began to feel depressed again and to harbor those same feelings of thirty years before. Her knowing what to expect, based on her previous experience, did not help; in fact, it was worse because she anticipated the symptoms and dreaded the impending experience. To complicate matters further, Elena was recently diagnosed with heart disease, and this brought additional disruption to her life.

However, there was something new and better this time. Unlike when she was a college girl, now she decided that she would go through these problems of mental and physical health together with her heavenly Father. Elena put these heavy burdens in God's hands and trusted His will for her life. She still went to the doctor and had counseling, but her relationship with the Lord grew deeper and tighter, and this made a huge difference. She prayed often with her husband and continued to help at church with some tasks. Above all, she made the habit of prayer and Bible reading.

Elena says that certain Bible verses were of huge help. She personalized them

* A pseudonym.

(i.e., substituted "us" with "I"), printed them out, glued them onto small cards, and carried them along with her. In between tasks, on public transportation, when she woke up, before going to sleep, and at any time she felt a little discouraged, she pulled out her cards and went over these gems. These are a few of those verses:

- "Why, my soul, are you downcast? Why so disturbed within me? Put your hope in God, for I will yet praise him, my Savior and my God" (Psalm 42:11, NIV).
- "I praise you because I am fearfully and wonderfully made; your works are wonderful, I know that full well" (Psalm 139:14, NIV).
- "Since [I] have been justified through faith, [I] have peace with God through [my] Lord Jesus Christ, through whom [I] have gained access by faith into this grace in which [I] now stand. And [I] boast in the hope of the glory of God. Not only so, but [I] also glory in [my] sufferings, because [I] know that suffering produces perseverance; perseverance, character; and character, hope. And hope does not put [me] to shame, because God's love has been poured out into [my heart] through the Holy Spirit, who has been given to [me]" (Romans 5:1–5, NIV).
- "I waited patiently for the LORD; he turned to me and heard my cry. He lifted me out of the slimy pit, out of the mud and mire; he set my feet on a rock and gave me a firm place to stand" (Psalm 40:1–3, NIV).

Something Elena found very helpful was to pray throughout the day—very frequent, brief prayers. When she was at the computer, the little clock in the corner of the monitor reminded her to pray for just half a minute each half hour, on the hour, and half past. Also, she made a point to briefly pray every time thoughts of low self-worth assaulted her. Then she repeated Psalm 139:14.

Recovery took its time, but she tells that the process was much more bearable compared with her bout of depression in college. She was symptom free a year after the appearance of the first signs. Elena's depression was acute rather than chronic, which is better than the depression that stays with people indefinitely. In her case, the Lord—not performing a spectacular miracle of instant healing—worked patiently with Elena until the depression was gone. What did the experience bring? Elena was left with a better understanding of herself, of others and their struggles, a better relationship with her husband, and above all, a closer and more robust connection with her Lord.

Psalms and Proverbs

Psalms and Proverbs are a rich source of encouragement and guidance on mental, physical, and spiritual health. I recommend them to people who suffer from depression or are anxious, or simply are going through times of struggle. Reading them in a quiet atmosphere, in prayer and humility, puts several physiological mechanisms at work, which in turn communicate mood enhancement and eventually protect people from physical maladies.

Going over the book of Psalms for one hour reverently, and without the pressure of time or disrupting worries, communicates a sizable blessing to mind, body, and spirit. The following are just a small sample of the soothing messages from Psalms.

Interpersonal interaction with the wrong kind of people must be avoided but society with those who follow God's direction brings rich fruits (Psalm 1:1–3). Being near God makes people be joyful, vanquish their fears, and sleep well (3: 4–6; 4:8; 5:11). The Lord likes to answer the pleas of the sorrowful, teary, faint, person in need (6:6–9). Happiness comes because God rescues us (9:14). When the poor and the homeless are with God, they gain hope (9:18). Those mistreated, helpless, and suffering will be rescued (12:5). The Lord supplies our physical needs—plenty of food (17:14), and He is a Source of trust (20:7). God listens to those with all kinds of bodily pains and does not turn away (22:14, 15, 24). We can be free of fear in the midst of danger, even near death (23:4). The Lord cares if we are lonely and troubled (25:16). Certain psalms have a main theme and this makes them appropriate for specific needs:

- Psalm 18 is a song of praise from David exalting God as a bedrock, castle, buckler, and high tower. It describes David's perils using nature's metaphors to the point that anyone going through trouble and difficulty can identify with the magnitude of human suffering and trust in the infinite power of God. The solution to the faithful psalmist comes from God, and this can happen to anyone experiencing turmoil in his or her life.
- Psalm 23 presents Jehovah as a shepherd. Perhaps the most widely known of all psalms, it reveals the humble, loving, and caring character of God as He watches over us. It communicates soothing calm to anyone experiencing fear, doubt, restlessness, irritation, hostility, weakness, or lack of basic needs.
- Psalm 34 is for the consolation of the brokenhearted. It talks about the

Lord's power and love and His availability to assist when His children go through grief, tribulation, or fatigue. It closes with the assurance that no one who runs to Him loses out.

- Psalm 55 is one of several psalms assuring protection against enemies. David is experiencing extreme anguish because of his enemies. Reading this psalm in different versions helps us see the wealth of expressions depicting David's emotions. God comes to his rescue because David comes to the Lord "evening, morning and noon" (NIV) and God hears his voice. Based on his experience, the writer recommends we all "cast your burden on the LORD, and He shall sustain you."

- Psalm 32 is the anti-guilt psalm. The text outlines what happens when one does not confess—groaning and bone wasting. The burden is really unbearable, but the psalmist's counsel is confession. It brings forgiveness, freedom, rejoicing, and protection.

- Psalm 46 is the chief anti-anxiety message from the book of Psalms. God is presented as our Refuge and Strength because He is mighty and impenetrable. When His children are on His side, they have nothing to fear, no matter the threat. In contemporary terms, an "army" of financial, health, relational, safety, or professional difficulties surrounding us is nothing because the Lord of hosts is with us.

- Psalm 68 brings hope to the outcast. Those in humble situations— orphan, widow, lonely, desolate, or prisoner—can confidently approach the all-powerful God. He makes nature resound and mighty nations fall. Anyone feeling small, inadequate, or worthless can feel the strength of God being on his or her side, and sense the honor and power of being a child of God.

- Psalm 103 offers a portrait of God's character. Many qualities of the Creator are mentioned: righteous, gracious, merciful, loving, slow to anger. The text provides an inviting message to remember that no matter how difficult our issues are, having such an amazing God on our side will make problems vanish.

- Psalm 118 is for the distressed. Even from the most extreme emotional pain, one can call upon God and be full of strength and have the ability to overcome all kinds of difficulties. Triumph, prosperity, and salvation are the result of God's goodness and mercy.

- Psalm 121 is the psalm of God's presence. It reminds us that God is constantly and permanently keeping guard over His children's lives. It communicates a total sense of protection. Going through moments of anxiety and uncertainty can be very disconcerting; so, repeating words from this psalm may help us feel God's presence in a very real way.

- Psalm 130 is a song of declaration of God's forgiveness to Israel for her transgressions. God is merciful and, in the same way He forgives His people, He also forgives particular individuals who approach Him with a load of sin and ask to be freed.
- Psalm 139 shows the personalized care from God. God knows everything about us, even our most intimate thoughts, wherever we are, and at all hours of the day. This can provide a sense of great peace, knowing that God can guide at any crossroad of our lives and eventually lead us to eternity.
- Psalm 143 shows the deplorable condition of the psalmist. He is crushed down to the ground, spirit overwhelmed, fainting, and with his heart growing numb. Then he calls upon the Lord and searches for His mercy and loving-kindness to be freed from the distress, just like anyone from the depths of depression can do today.

The book of Proverbs contains another pack of survival resources; it's a very helpful guide in the habits of good character and interpersonal interactions as current today as they were three thousand years ago. These bits of wisdom make good common sense and are being proven through scientific studies. Proverbs teaches us that our hearts (the seat of thoughts and emotions in the biblical context—the mind) are the wellsprings of life (Proverbs 4:23), and that attitudes work for better or for worst, depending on whether they are positive and act as medicine or negative and make us ill (17:22). It also teaches us that anxiety lowers our mood, but just a good word can lift it up (12:25). It points at a direct link between the mind and the physical body—if there is peace inside it, there is health; but when someone is jealous, his bones corrode (14:30). We are also told that if we are joyful, our face is cheerful, but the opposite will make it hard to go through the day (15:13). It even gives some advice on food, drink, and exercise. They will make a difference in our health and behavior: eating too much is like putting a knife to our throat (23:2, 3), the use of alcoholic beverages is followed by very nasty physical and psychological consequences (verses 29–35) and its use is not advisable to leaders lest they make fools of themselves (31:4–7). Lastly, vigorous physical exercise is recommendable to gain strength (verse 4).

Evidence of the benefits of faith

Just a few days ago, a friend was asking me whether I was involved in any writing projects. This opened the conversation about this book. I said, "The point of *The Benefits of Belief* is to show that religious people have plenty of rewards related to health and well-being just for being religious." He replied, "Well, I knew that already!" Of course, from experience, people who enjoy a personal connection with God already know it. However, there are an increasing number of individuals who want to see evidence. And we have plenty now.

Throughout the pages of this book, the reader has had the opportunity to examine a number of rewards for being religious. We have seen that prayer produces lower levels of anxiety, soothes symptoms of depression, and prevents serious mental illness; even intercessory prayer helps groups of cardiac patients recover faster than non-prayed-for patients. Scripture has been found to be a powerful tool for better mental and physical health for people of all ages. Many use scriptures successfully as a coping method to face times of stress and struggle, and to feel less pain when they go through illness. Bible reading has repeatedly shown itself as a facilitator of better relationships and a protection against the use of alcohol, tobacco, and illicit drugs. Forgiveness (both giving and receiving) is a healing agent that nourishes relationships, improves the quality of sleep, enhances a sense of well-being and satisfaction, makes the cardiac function stronger, and makes people gain physical strength; it prevents revenge and the use of addictive substances; it soothes the pains of fibromyalgia, reduces the number of symptoms of illness, and decreases the amount of medication taken.

Being committed to one's principles and beliefs brings about a number of benefits: better academic achievement in youth, avoidance of risky behaviors (delinquency, drugs), better interpersonal interactions, including marital and parent-child relationships, and even better religious leader-follower relationships. It also notably increases health and longevity. Service to others also carries blessings. People who follow this practice enjoy much higher levels of perceived well-being than do those who don't; they also have less likelihood of depression, better health, and longer lives. Regular church attendance also earns dividends: less incidence of heart disease, hypertension, cerebrovascular disease, dementia, immune dysfunction, endocrine dysfunction, cancer, and mortality. Churchgoing helps people to adapt to new locations, facilitates social satisfaction within the family and outside it, and adds a number of mental health advantages: low occurrence of depression, less psychoticism, higher personal satisfaction and sense of service, less fear of disease and ailments, less fear of falling (in the elderly), less substance abuse, and better overall relationships.

The joy and gratitude to God observed in the religious person has also been proved beneficial: both joy and gratitude are powerful agents for good overall health and well-being; joy promotes healthy practices such as weight control, exercise, and diet. It protects from negativistic, catastrophic thoughts, which are precursors of depression; and it helps depressive symptoms decrease. The area of interpersonal interactions, especially from healthy religious communities, is decisive in helping parishioners to anchor their beliefs, to enjoy better physical and mental health, and to perform altruistic and empathetic acts. Religiosity also serves as a successful coping resource in times of severe difficulty; those using positive religious coping can face stressors much better than can those using other strategies; they can handle losses (death of a dear one, unemployment, divorce) better and are able to find meaning in the midst of adversity. Religious coping softens the effects of depression, and those using this method are able to process troubling events with a meaningful perspective. Religious coping helps caregivers to provide care to relatives with a better attitude and disposition than their nonreligious counterparts. Religious people can also deal with chronic illness and trauma (from torture, assault, abuse, accidents) better than nonreligious "copers."

The reason why religious strategies work is because God is all-loving and all-powerful. A colleague once explained that she was helping a child in counseling to deal with fears. This boy was afraid of the dark, of monsters, of witches, and a slew of other characters from TV cartoons. His fear was so horrible that his parents, after trying multiple methods, finally had to take him to a clinical psychologist. The family had a Christian background and chose a Christian psychotherapist. As they held their play therapies and counseling sessions, she and the boy ended up talking about Superman, Batman, and other powerful characters well known to the little fellow. She reminded him of Bible stories showing how Jesus was so powerful that He could send all those monsters and witches away. She taught how to think of Jesus and His mighty force to protect him and to help him to sleep. It worked well; and he left the treatment with the precious skill of practical faith.

But God is not only love and power, He is also wise and knows the end from the beginning. We cannot forget that the relationship between religious faith and illness and/or trouble is not always consistent, even with God on our side. It is a reality of human existence that faithful people also get seriously ill and sometimes suffer from terminal diseases and die young. And at times this happens even when they have done everything to prevent it and have no family history.

But here is where faith can find meaning in pain and assist the victim in looking even further into God's plan of eternal salvation. Suffering has a place in the lives of God's children. We can learn from Bible characters. Take the apostle Paul, for example. He outlines the torture, trouble, persecution, adversity, and tribulation he had to face after accepting Christ (2 Corinthians 11:16–33)! Many adverse situations are unfair or cannot be understood even in the context of good and evil and *overall* sin. Elena, from the beginning of the chapter, grew up and found a deeper relationship with Jesus out of her mental and physical pain. Some going through adversity arrive at an incredible togetherness in family relations. Others develop fortitude and godly characters. Others inadvertently help people around to gain perspective and to be inspired in the experience of the victim. Still others will gain nothing, in all appearance. However, it is always comforting to know that we only see the present, and God sees eternally.

The opposite case has also shaken human logic since the inception of sin: Why do the wicked seem to prosper in all areas? Why does the repeated transgressor of health principles enjoy health and die at a very old age? Psalm 73 offers some light: the first half talks about the questions observers often ask about the blessings of the wicked. The second half describes the triumph of faith in God, the assurance that even though we don't know why certain things happen, God's justice will prevail. The Gospel of Luke also adds perspective; even though the wicked may prosper, it is limited to this life, not an eternal prosperity (Luke 12:16–21).

Conclusion

Late in the morning, when kindergarteners could not handle arduous tasks, the teacher put them to drawing artwork of their choice. She kept walking around the worktables to see how different colors and designs were falling together. She observed a little girl who was working very intensely with her multiple crayons, and she asked what she was drawing. The child replied, "I'm drawing God." The teacher was taken by surprise and simply said, "But no one knows what God looks like." Without hesitation and keeping on task, the little girl said, "They will in just a minute." What a sense of confidence! Something presumptuous in a grownup can be an inspiration in a child.

It is our privilege to know God through Jesus Christ, and to know Him so well that we could readily draw Him, so to speak. This is what having perfect health is about—it is about knowing Him, talking to Him, listening to Him, hoping in Him, and loving Him. This is the way we can get life abundant (John 20:31) and everlasting life (John 10:28).

Study Questions

- Which book of the Old Testament does Jesus quote in Matthew 27:35, 46; Luke 23:46; and John 13:18? What are the circumstances? What can you learn from Jesus referring to scriptures in those circumstances?
- If you have an electronic Bible, search for the phrase "Do not fear." (Or the word *fear* in a concordance.) What is the context where the words are used? What are some of the ways to avoid fear, apprehension, anxiety, and uncertainty according to those texts?
- Using a digital or online Bible or a concordance to search for the word *comfort* in Psalms. Develop a list of at least a dozen verses that may provide good support next time you feel disheartened.

Application Thoughts

- Memorize a text of encouragement, such as, "The LORD is my strength and my shield; my heart trusted in him, and I am helped: therefore my heart greatly rejoiceth; and with my song will I praise him" (Psalm 28:7, KJV). Have it in mind for a whole day and reflect on its meaning as often as you can. Pray to God for your chosen verse to become a reality in your life.
- What would you say to a neighbor who, knowing you are a Christian, asks, "Why is your faith so important to you?"
- Imagine that a friend comes to you and says, "I don't have a desire to pray, I have lost interest in the Bible. I know it is not good, but I just am losing my faith." What would you say? What would you do to help your friend not to lose his or her faith and salvation?